IMAGES
of America

SANFORD

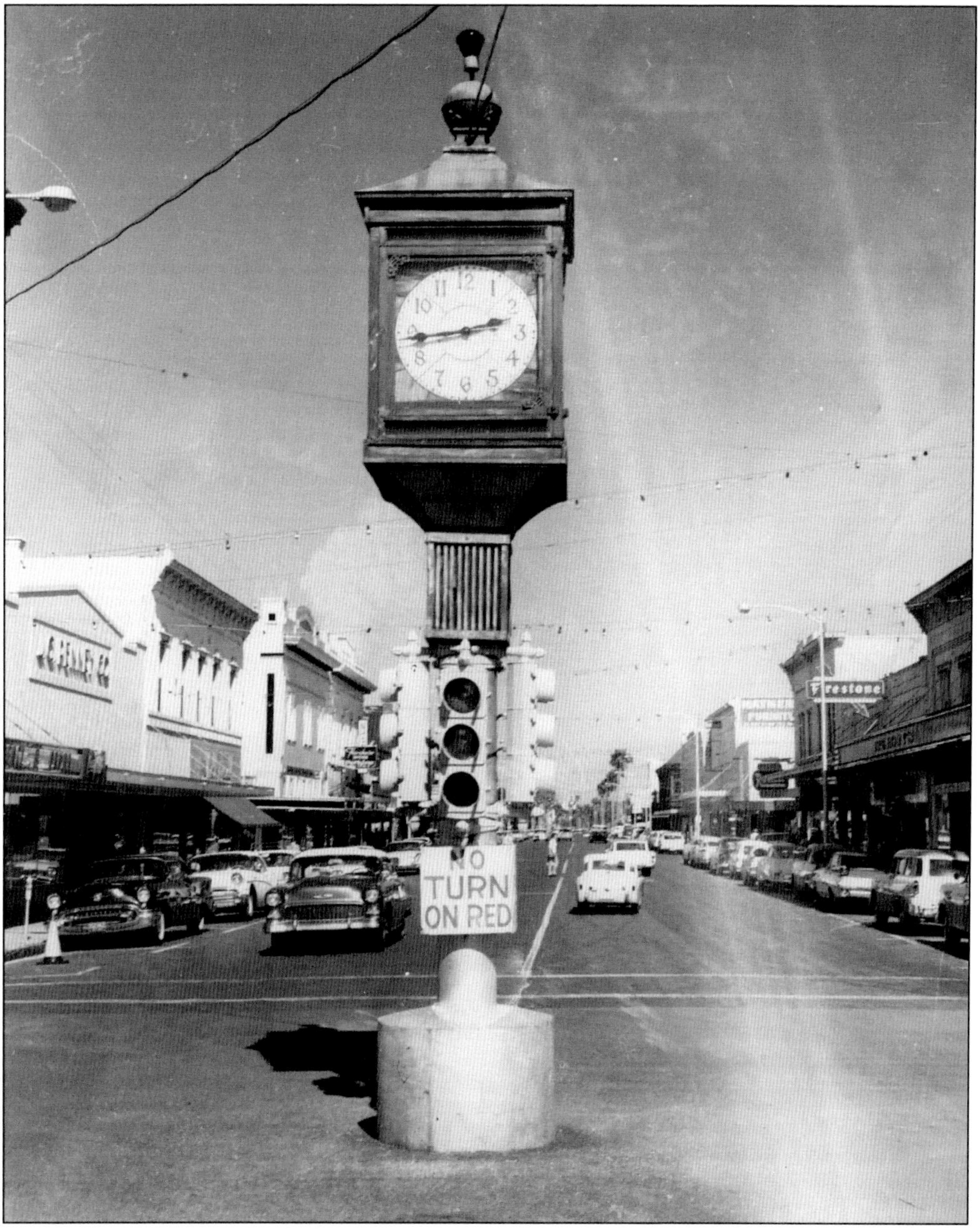

For many generations, Sanford's time has been kept by the big clock that once stood in the intersection of Park Avenue and First Street. The clock was originally attached to the First National Bank in 1908. In 1930, A.H. Moses acquired the huge time piece and convinced the city to place it in the middle of the intersection. There it remained, ticking away its hours as a Sanford landmark until 1961, when the city declared it a traffic hazard. At that time, the clock was removed and placed in storage. The Sanford Elks Club rescued the clock and mounted it on a pole in front of their lodge on Second Street. In July 1985, through the generosity of Stella Oritt, who is the granddaughter of A.H. Moses, and her husband Joe, the old clock was restored to its original condition and has since stood in its own place of honor at Magnolia Square.

IMAGES
of America

SANFORD

Sanford Historical Society, Inc.

ARCADIA
PUBLISHING

ISBN 978-0-7385-1542-7

Published by Arcadia Publishing
Charleston, South Carolina

Printed in the United States of America

Library of Congress Catalog Card Number: 2003106427

For all general information contact Arcadia Publishing at:
Telephone 843-853-2070
Fax 843-853-0044
E-mail sales@arcadiapublishing.com
For customer service and orders:
Toll-Free 1-888-313-2665

Visit us on the Internet at www.arcadiapublishing.com

Contents

ACKNOWLEDGMENTS

This book is dedicated to the memory of Don Vincent who understood the value of historic photographs as windows into Sanford's past. Don inherited a love of photography from his father, William R. Vincent, the owner of a fish market, which, for many years, served as Sanford's archives. The photographic collection at the Sanford Museum was established when William Vincent's sons Don, Bill, and Tom donated the collection. Don's wish for the collection was that the photographs could be shared and made accessible to the people of Sanford. We hope this book serves that purpose.

The Sanford Historical Society, Inc. would like to thank Alicia Clarke, Christine Kinlaw Best, Charlie Carlson, and the staff of the Sanford Museum for their work on this book. A special thanks goes to all those individuals and families who have so generously donated materials, time, and funds to the Society and to the Sanford Museum over the years.

The images found in this book are from the collection of the Sanford Museum, a division of the City of Sanford, unless otherwise noted. The scope of this volume has been limited by the available material.

INTRODUCTION

Sanford is located on Lake Monroe, one of Central Florida's largest lakes and the head of navigation on the St. John's River. It is a city with a multi-faceted history that was pioneered and settled by a diverse collection of personalities. Today, Sanford is the seat of Seminole County, but yesterday, it was the birthplace of Central Florida's history.

The area's history probably began with wandering bands of Paleo-Indians that hunted now extinct animals around Lake Monroe. Two thousand years ago, Timucuan speaking people lived along the banks of the St. Johns River and were still present when the Spanish arrived in Florida. With the Europeans came diseases that, by the middle 1700s, had reduced these first inhabitants to a few remnant bands. The small numbers of Timucua that remained eventually died out or were absorbed into a new composite tribe blended from expatriate Creeks and escaped African slaves. The Spanish called these newcomers "Cimmarone." We know them today as Florida's Seminoles. In 1824, this territory was part of Mosquito County.

In the early 1800s, the First Seminole War in north Florida forced the Seminoles into the area around Lake Monroe. In December 1836, during the Second Seminole War, Col. A.C. Fanning established Camp Monroe just east of present downtown Sanford. In the early morning hours of February 8, 1837, the garrison of this post was attacked by 400 Seminole warriors led by Chief Coacoochee and King Phillip. Capt. Charles Mellon was killed in this engagement and the post was renamed Fort Mellon. By the 1840s, the first pioneers had arrived and established, around the old fort, an end-of-the-line river village called Mellonville. In 1845, Mellonville served as the seat of the newly formed Orange County and rapidly became a distribution point for supplies and material that began the growth of Central Florida. In 1856, the county seat was moved several miles south to a small scrub town called "Jernigan," now Orlando.

In 1870, Henry Shelton Sanford, former United States Minister to Belgium, bought 12,548 acres, originally a Spanish grant, from Confederate general Joseph Finegan. He envisioned a planned city on the shore of Lake Monroe which he thought would one day be a major harbor. One mile west of Mellonville, he began building a city he visualized as "The Gate City of South Florida." In 1877, this new town was incorporated as the City of Sanford. Mellonville was annexed into the city six years later. Henry S. Sanford imported several groups of laborers from Sweden to help establish his St. Gertrude and Belair citrus groves. At his groves he introduced 140 varieties of citrus to Florida.

In 1880, Henry Sanford formed the Florida Land and Colonization Company in London to attract investors to his new city. In the same year, construction began on the South Florida Railroad and Sanford became a railroad and steamboat terminus.

In the 1870s, Henry Sanford set aside land along Sanford Avenue for the African-American community of Georgetown. A black-owned commercial district flourished there for many years. In 1891, the African-American community of Goldsboro was incorporated on the west side of town. Goldsboro was annexed by the City of Sanford in 1911.

In the early hours of September 22, 1887, the east section of Sanford burned down when a fire started in a First Street bakery. This section was rebuilt with buildings of brick. Many of these still stand in the historic district today.

Sanford's economic base was its thriving citrus groves, but in the winter of 1894 and 1895, severe back-to-back freezes wiped out most of the trees. Many growers were faced with ruin, as well as local businesses that depended on citrus money. But Sanford was rescued by its fertile soil and artesian wells that made it an ideal place for growing vegetable crops. One plant that seemed to thrive in local soil was celery. By the first decade of the 20th century, Sanford had become the nation's Celery Capital and one of the premiere agricultural regions of the South. The town was popularly known as the "Celery City." In April 1913, Seminole County was split off from Orange County and Sanford became the county seat. In the 1920s, a building boom followed that brought new high rise structures to the city and a bulkhead to its lakefront.

In 1942, during World War II, the government built the Sanford Naval Air Station which contributed to a transition away from a farming economy and drew more people to the area. The closing of the station in 1968 was a severe blow to the local economy. In 1970, Sanford became the southern terminal for the Autotrain, which brings thousands of tourists to Central Florida's world of theme parks. The Orlando-Sanford International Airport, built on the site of the old Navy station welcomes thousands of visitors each day.

In 1976 and 1986 two historic districts were created downtown and placed on the National Register of Historic Places. Visitors to Sanford are charmed by this downtown historic area of quaint shops, museums, and its beautiful lakefront. In 2003, a major redevelopment of the waterfront is underway. It would seem that Sanford today is truly fulfilling its founder's dreams for "The Gate City."

One

Fort Mellon and Mellonville

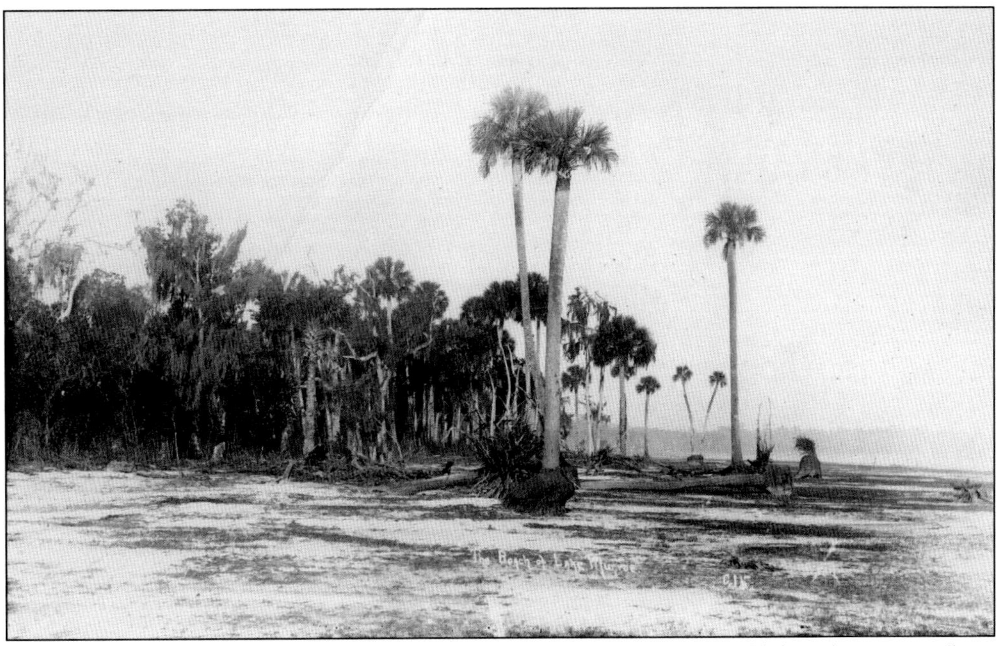

The Seminoles called the St. Johns River "Welaka" meaning "river of lakes" because it flows slowly, spreading out in a chain of lakes on its journey north to the ocean. The St. Johns River flows through the heart of central Florida and the riverboats that plied its waters opened up new land for settlement.

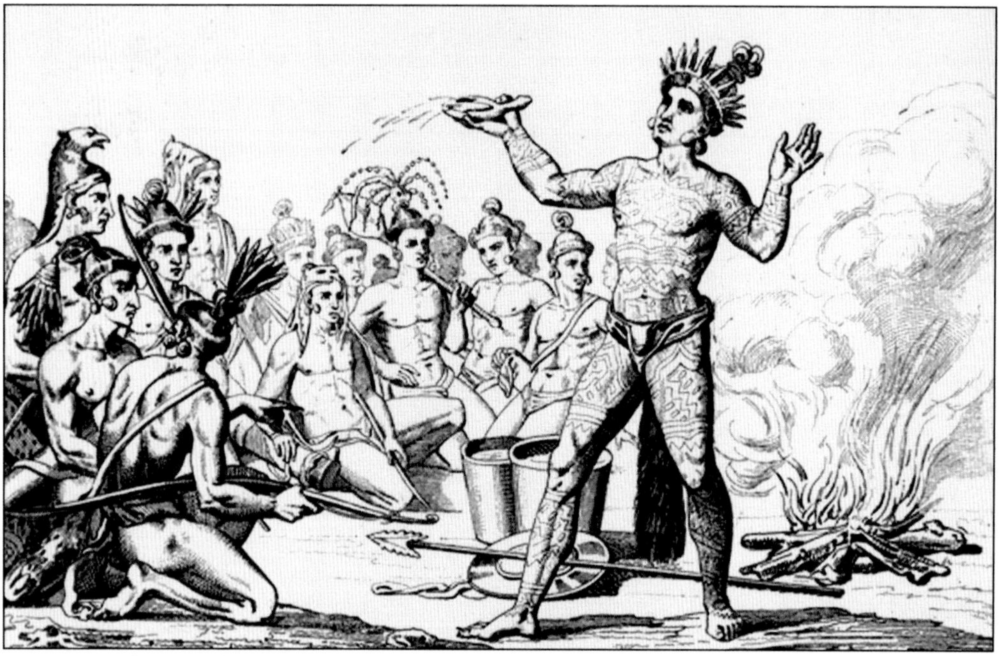

Engravings from 16th century drawings by French artist and cartographer Jacques Le Moyne give us the only visual account of the Timucuan people that lived along the St. Johns River for over a thousand years. The Timucua were several groups that shared a common language and culture and were the indigenous inhabitants encountered by the first Spanish explorers. These people lived in well organized societies and survived mainly by hunting, gathering, and fishing, although agriculture was practiced to a small degree. It is believed that the elaborate tattooing of their bodies signified their position on the social scale. The St. Johns River was the lifeline between Timucuan settlements. The remains of their living sites are marked by shell middens and mounds, many of which have been destroyed by modern development. One of the finest examples in Florida of a burial mound is preserved just east of Sanford on the St. Johns River. (Florida State Archives.)

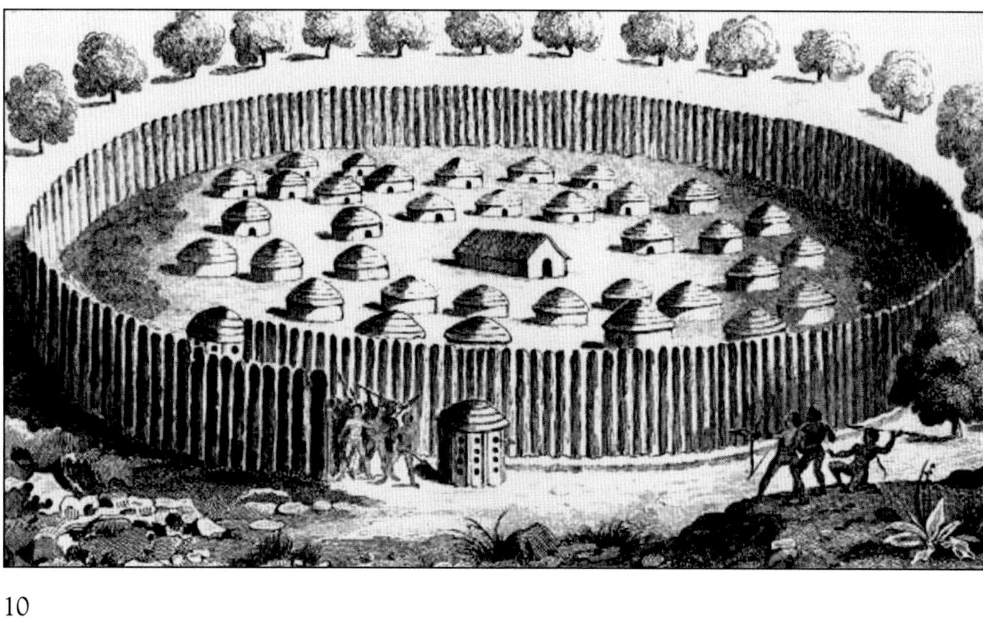

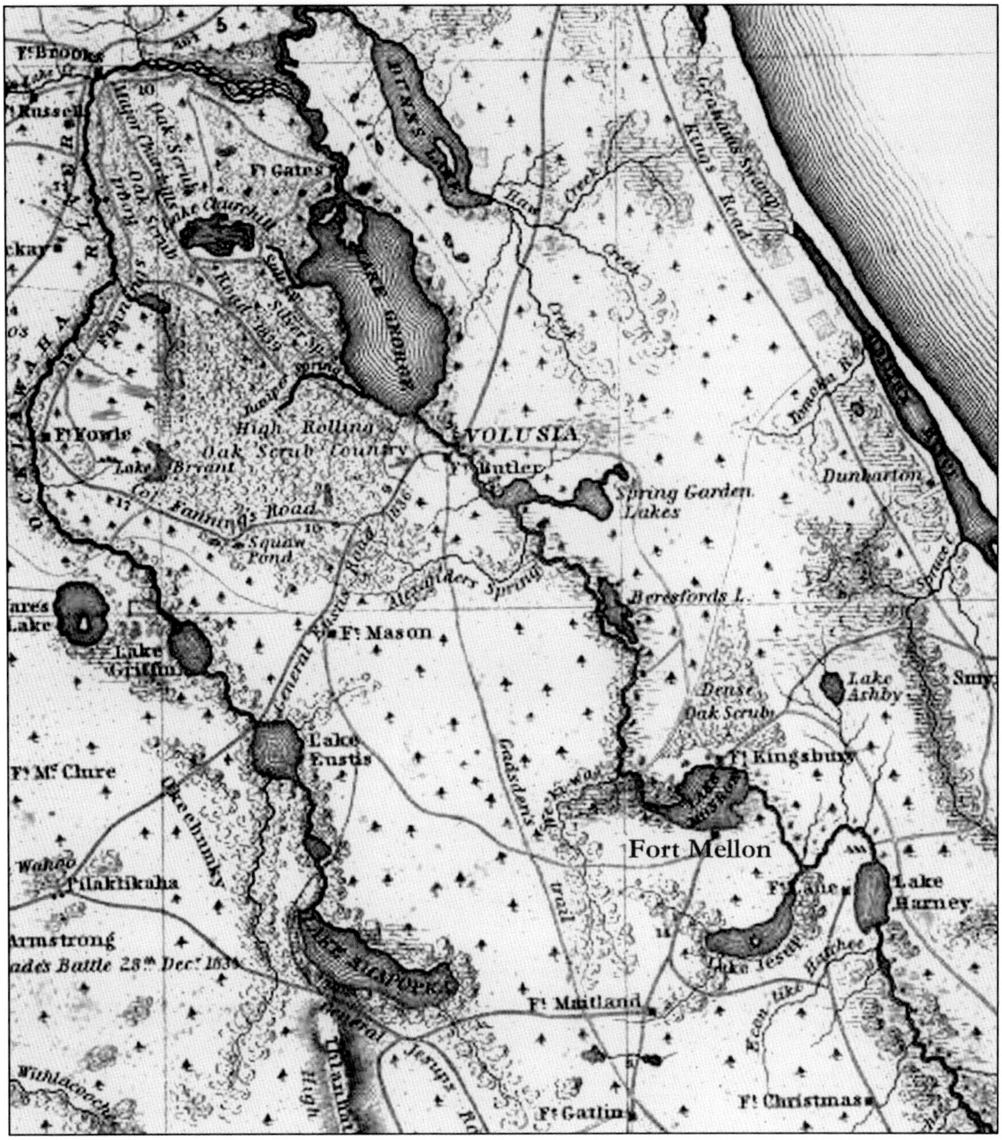

The *Map of the Seat of War in Florida* was drawn by John Mackay and J.E. Blake on orders from Zachary Taylor in 1839. The map shows the United States Army posts established in central Florida. The Second Seminole War was the longest and most expensive of all Indian wars. The conflict was carried to the shores of Lake Monroe when the U.S. Army under Col. A.C. Fanning established Camp Monroe. In the early hours of February 8, 1837, a force of 400 Seminole warriors attacked the small outpost and a young officer named Capt. Charles Mellon was killed. In his honor the post was renamed Fort Mellon. The fort became the main staging and logistical base for the army as it pushed the Seminoles farther south. (Library of Congress, Geography and Map Division, Washington D.C.)

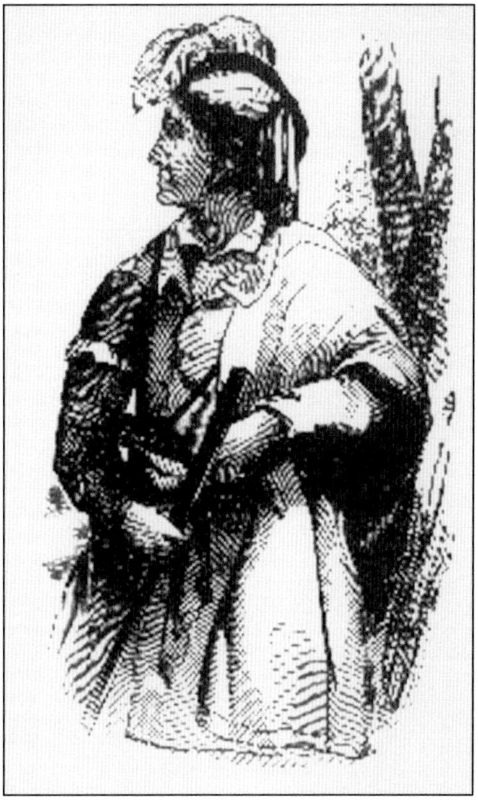

Coacoochee, shown in this lithograph by N. Orr, was also known as "Wildcat." He was born in 1810 to a sister of Micanopy (Chief of the Seminole Nation) and King Philip (Emathla, Chief of the Miccosukee tribe) in Mosquito County, Florida. During the Second Seminole War he led the fight against the Indian Removal Act which called for the relocation of his tribe to land west of the Mississippi River. He was captured under a white flag of truce in October 1837 and was taken to Fort Marion at St. Augustine, but escaped. In October 1841, Coacoochee was recaptured and sent to the reservation in Arkansas Territory (now Oklahoma). In 1845 he moved to Texas and spent many years organizing the resistance against the United States government. He died of smallpox in Mexico in 1857. (Florida State Archives.)

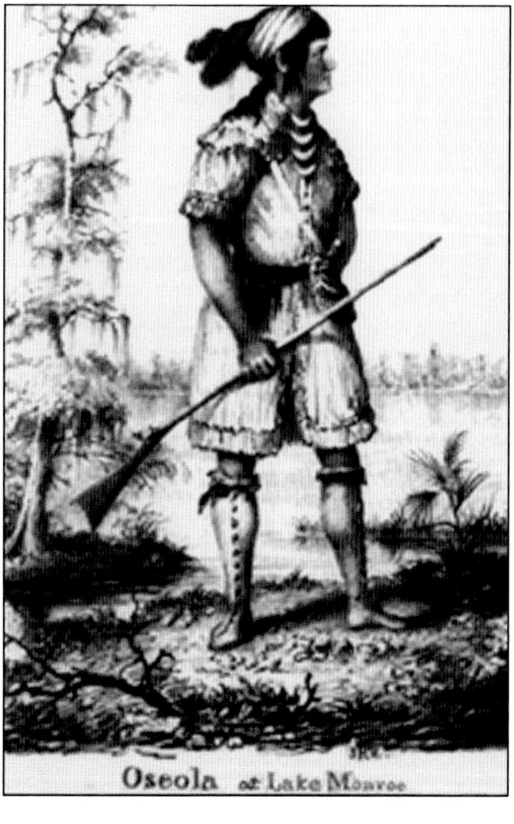

This pencil sketch of Osceola was drawn at Fort Mellon by Capt. J.R. Vinton in March 1837 during an armistice in the Second Seminole War. Osceola (1804–1838) was born in Alabama and came to Florida at an early age. Although never a chief of the Seminoles, he was a fierce leader and led a valiant attempt to resist the government's efforts to remove the Seminoles from Florida. After many battles, Osceola was captured with Coacoochee in October 1837. He was brought to Fort Mellon to board the steamer Santee and was taken to Fort Marion. From there he was taken to Fort Moultrie in South Carolina where he died in January 1838. (Florida State Archives.)

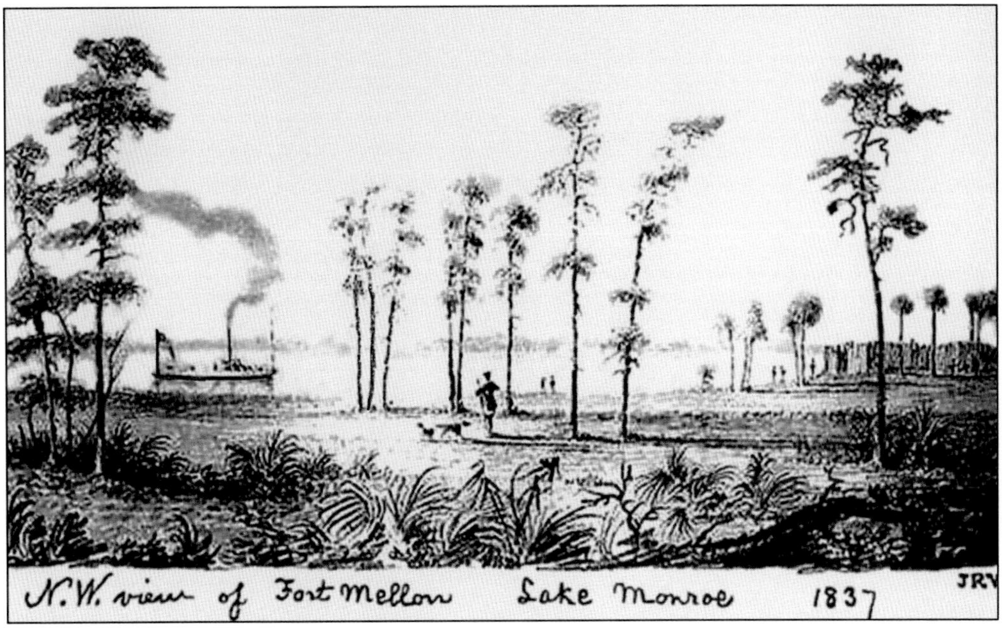

This sketch of Fort Mellon was drawn by John Rogers Vinton in 1837. Vinton served as a captain of the Third Artillery at Fort Mellon. (Florida State Archives.)

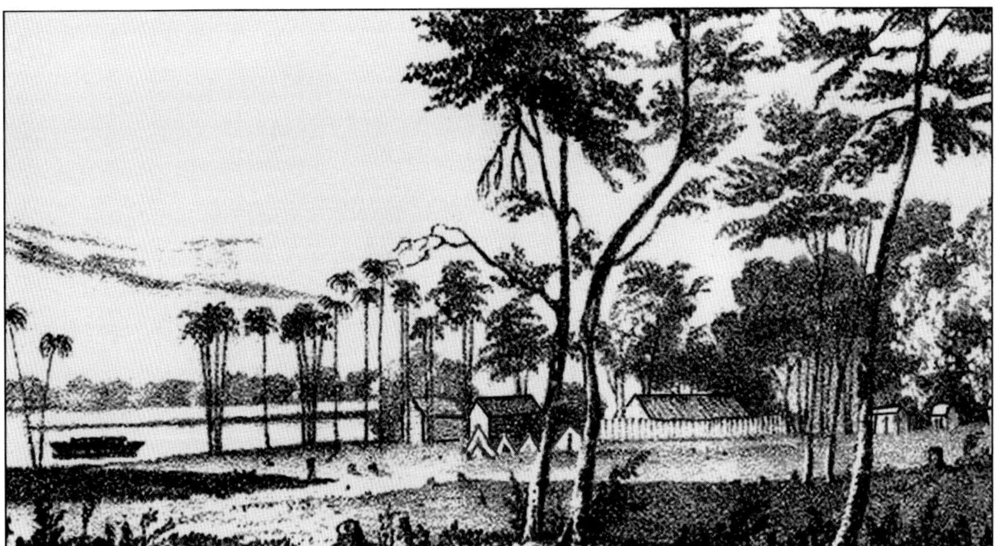

This sketch of Fort Mellon shows picketing, buildings, and tents. The drawing for this lithograph by Greene and McGowan was done by N. Orr in 1837. The lithograph was published in *The Territory of Florida* by John Lee Williams. (Florida State Archives.)

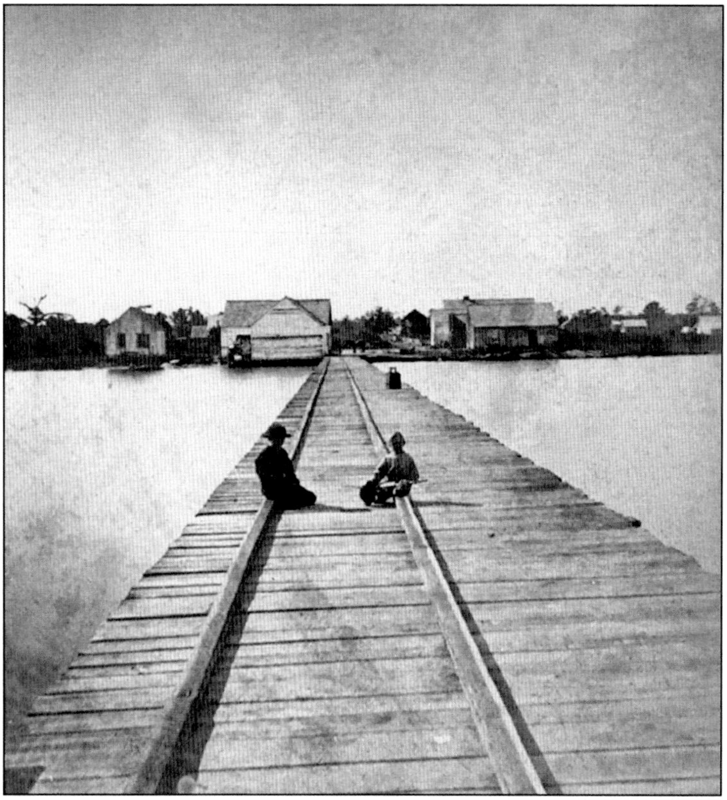

The first steamboat landing on the southern shore of Lake Monroe was the dock at Mellonville at the head of navigation on the St. Johns River. The dock extended from Mellonville Avenue, originally a military road laid out by Gen. Zachary Taylor that went from Fort Mellon to Fort Brooke on Tampa Bay. In the 1840s settlers began to move into the area from Georgia and the Carolinas. Some brought slaves who became the first permanent African-American residents of the region.

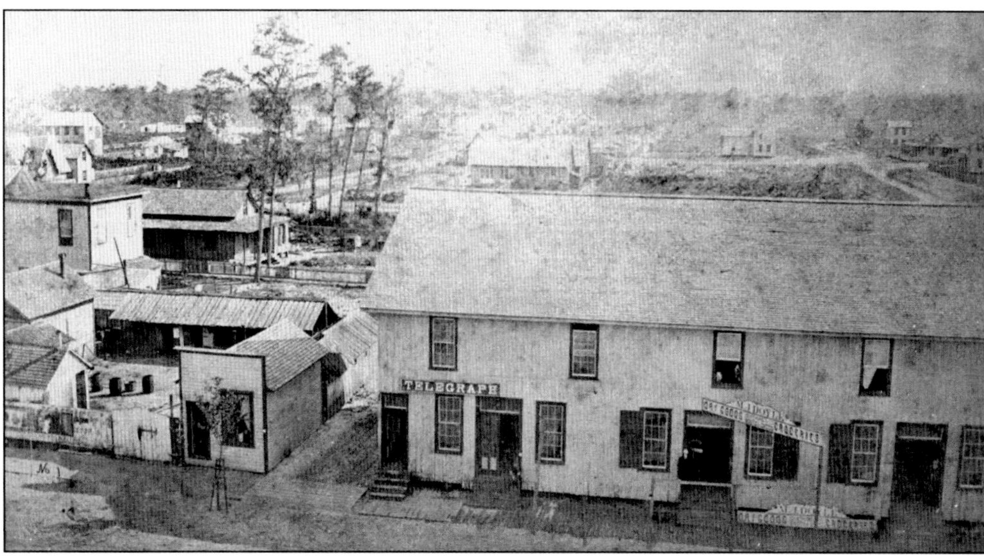

The general store of Michael J. Doyle, as seen in this 1880s photograph, was the center of activity in the river port of Mellonville. It was located at the foot of Mellonville Avenue near the dock. Mellonville grew up around the site of Fort Mellon. When Orange County was formed in 1845, the town was named the county seat and became the river port for settlers in south Florida. The town was linked to Sanford in the 1870s by Union Avenue (Second Street). Mellonville was incorporated in 1875 and annexed into the city of Sanford in 1883.

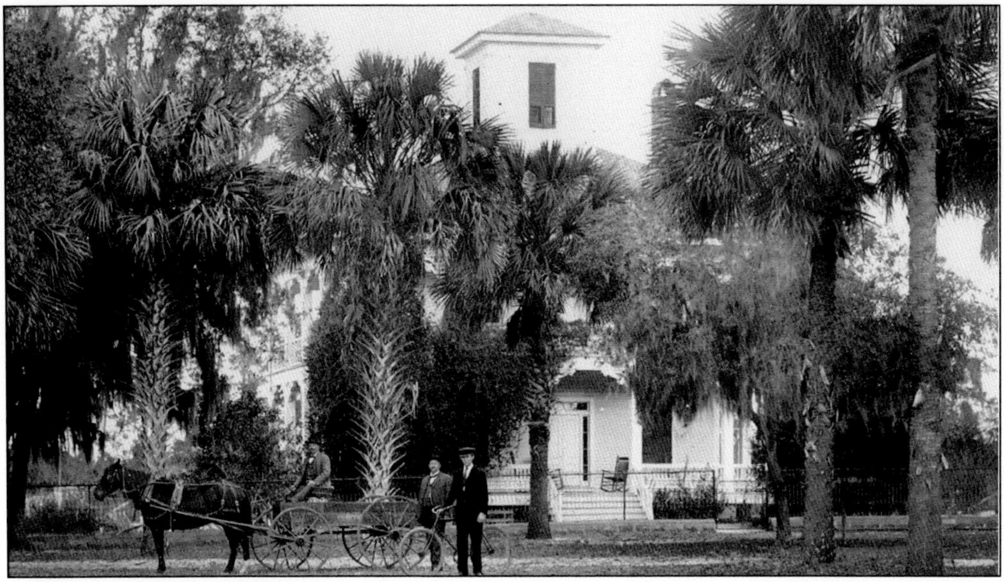

George C. Brantley settled in Mellonville sometime around 1868 and became a partner in a general store with M.J. Doyle. He married Ella A. Speer, the daughter of Dr. Algernon S. Speer, a Mellonville pioneer who had come to the area in the 1840s. Brantley built a two-story home east of Mellonville Avenue on the shore of Lake Monroe. John E. Pace, born in Georgia in 1854, came to Mellonville around 1878, the year Brantley died. In 1893 he married Brantley's widow, Ella, and acquired Brantley's home. His estate with its citrus groves and celery fields became known as Pace Park and later Pace's Acres. He became a partner in Doyle's store and by 1910 was one of the most successful businessmen in Sanford. Pace is credited as one of the first celery growers to employ the tile system of irrigation. He died in 1923.

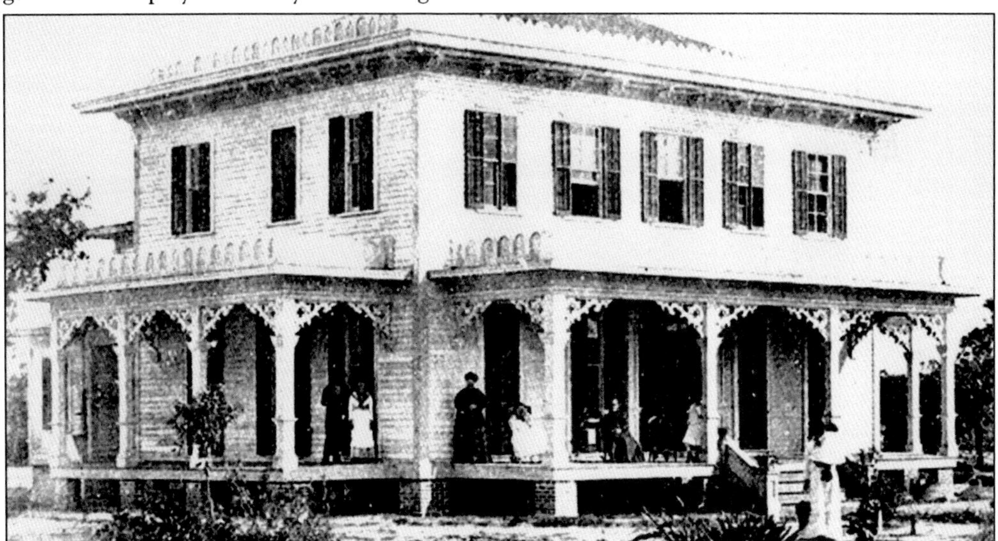

Michael J. Doyle immigrated to America from Ireland and came to Volusia County. During the Civil War, he enlisted in the Seventh Florida Infantry and was elected a first lieutenant. In 1866, he married Mary C. Speer, the sister of Ella Speer, and went into business with his brother-in-law George C. Brantley. He died in 1888. His two-story home on Orange Avenue in Mellonville vanished long ago. (Florida State Archives.)

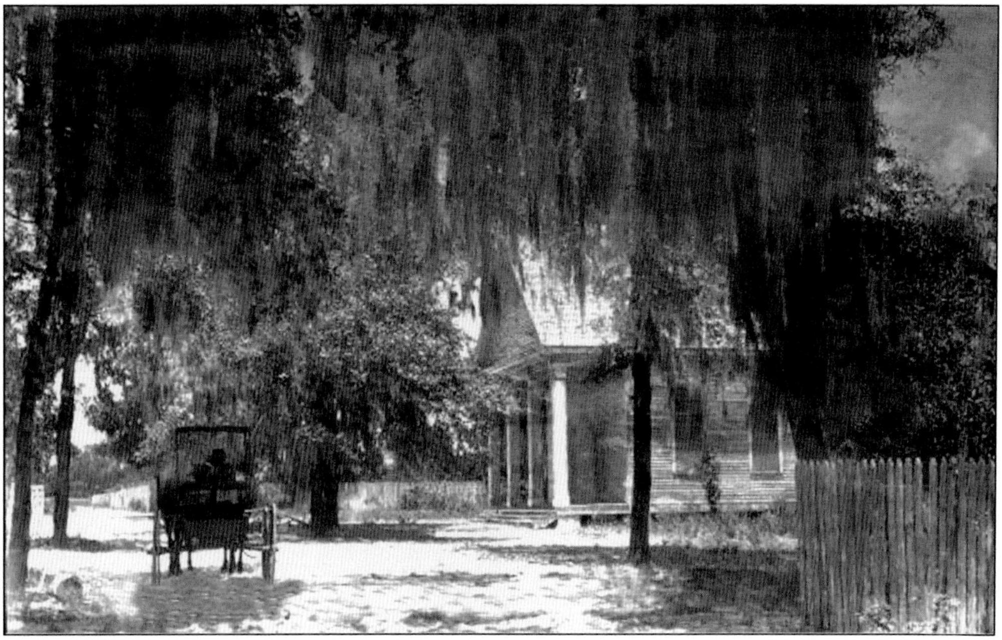

Ernest Chapel, the earliest Methodist church in the Sanford area, was known for its classical architecture with columns and a belfry. In 1874 the Mellonville Circuit was created and Rev. Robert Barnett arrived to minister to the 15 Methodists in the area. He stayed with the Wylly family at their fine home in Fort Reid. In 1875, Augustus J. Vaughn, a settler who had been a soldier at Fort Mellon, donated land for the construction of the chapel. (Florida State Archives.)

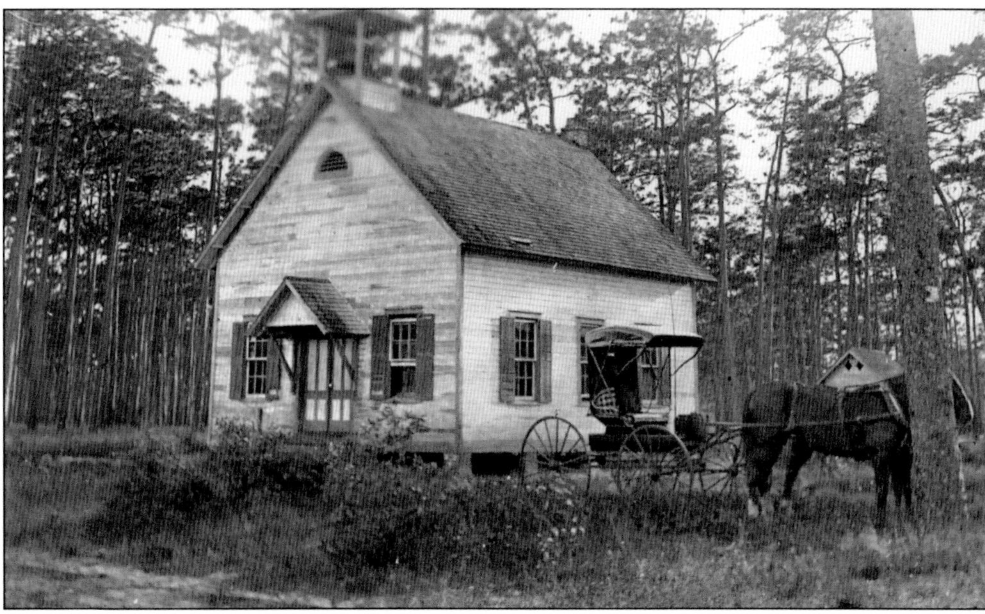

Silver Lake Presbyterian Church was established in 1878 in Fort Reid with William Telford as its first moderator. The community of Fort Reid grew up around an army post to the south of Fort Mellon. The neighborhood was cut in half in the 1940s with the construction of the Sanford Naval Air Station. Some of the oldest homes were lost at that time.

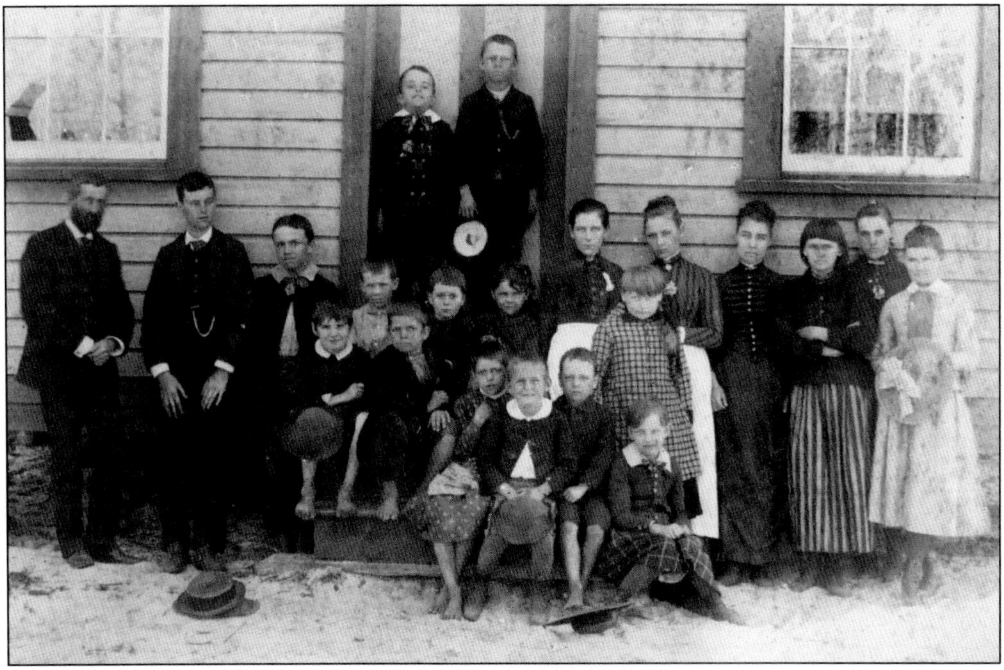

William Bingham Lynch and the pupils of the Fort Reid School are shown here *c.* 1886. The school at Fort Reid was the first in the area. Professor Lynch moved to Sanford in 1882. He became Principal of Schools and reorganized the Orange County school system.

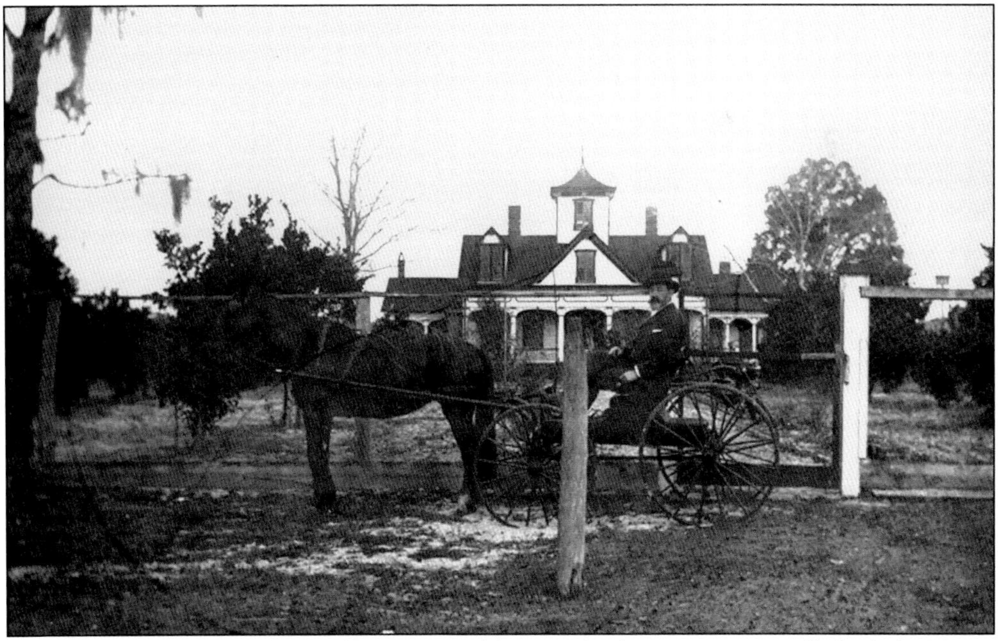

George W. Wylly sits in front of his Fort Reid home. The home was originally built for Hiram Potter, who was the official United States census taker. Today the house site is part of the Orlando-Sanford International Airport.

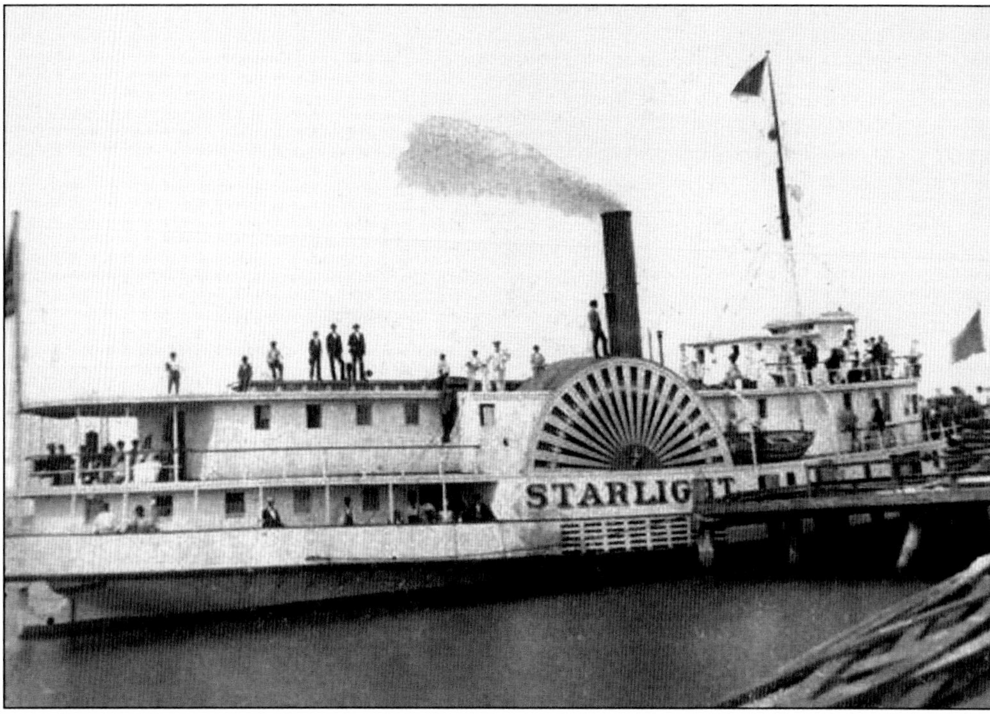

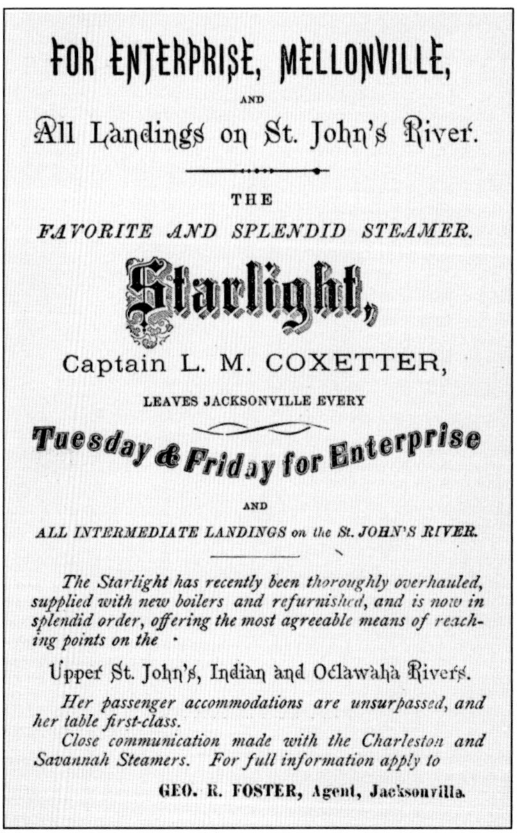

In 1847, the first commercial riverboats began making the run to and from Jacksonville. These were small, independently owned steamers that carried both passengers and freight. Algernon Speer of Mellonville owned three of these vessels, the *Hancock*, the *Sarah Spaulding*, and the *Tom Thumb.* A decade before the Civil War, Jacob Brock of Enterprise began his St. Johns River Line and put the first large boats into service. Following the war, a new era of steamboats brought settlers and tourists to Mellonville and Enterprise. One of the premiere steamers of this period was the 131-foot-long *Starlight*, a 261 gross-ton side-wheeler. Built in Portland, Maine in 1866, she could plow the St. Johns at 12 miles per hour. The *Starlight*'s end came on May 11, 1878 when she burned at the Sanford docks.

This advertisement for the *Starlight* was published in *Guide to Florida* by Rambler, 1873.

Two

The Gate City of South Florida

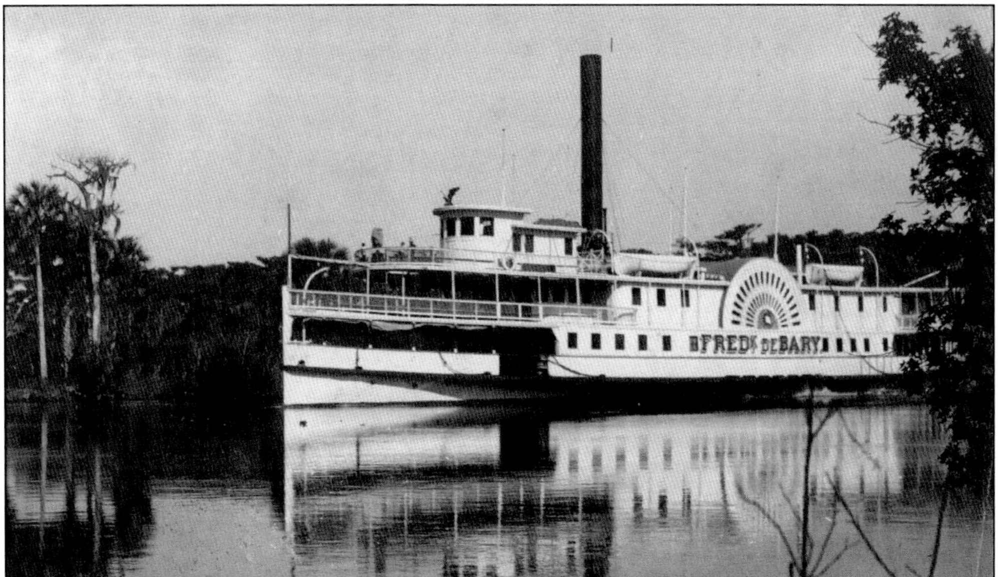

The St. Johns River, which flows north to Jacksonville, was advertised in the 1800s as "the Nile of America." Tourists and settlers were attracted by the exotic landscape, the healthy climate, and the abundant game and fish.

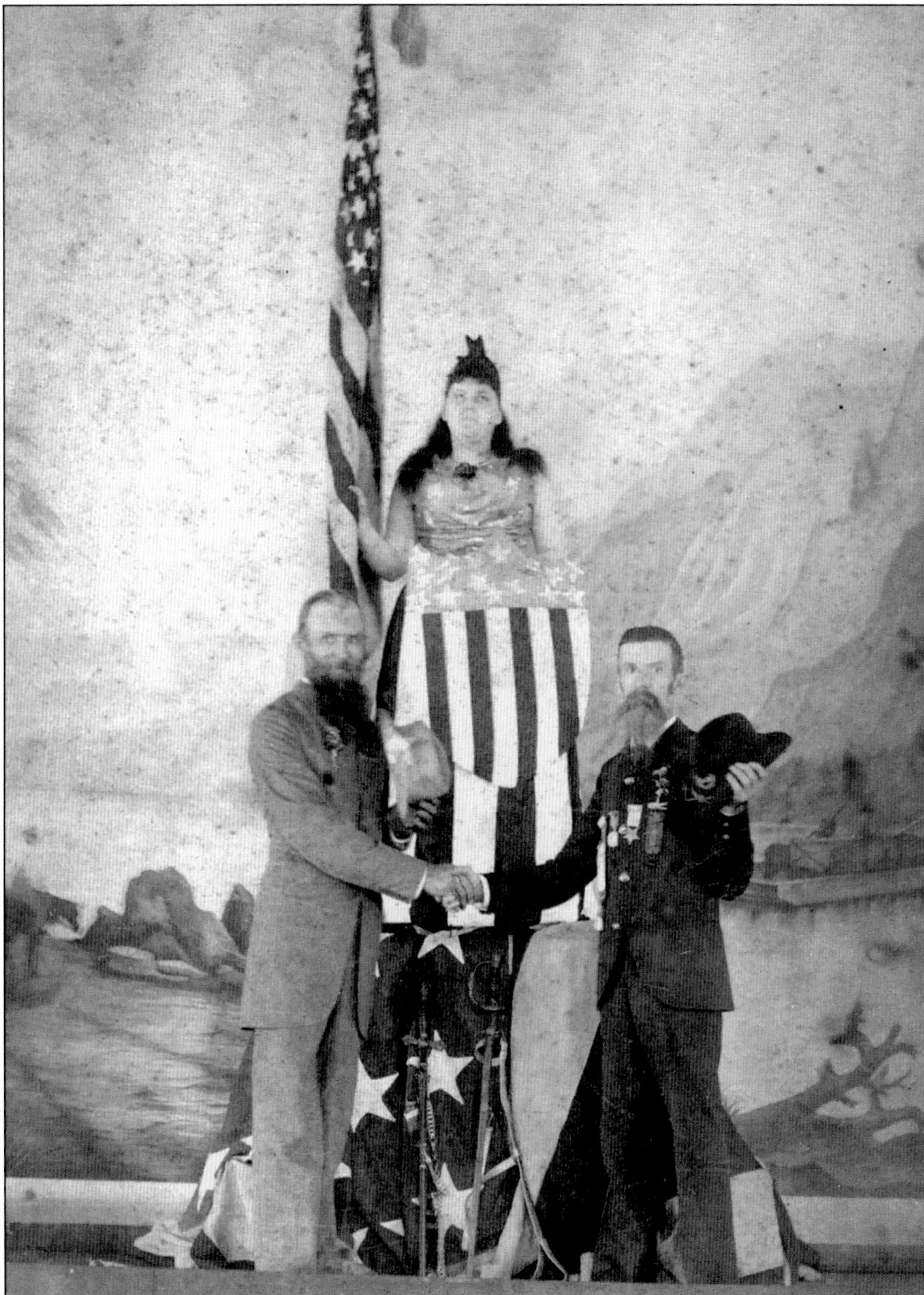

After the end of the Civil War, homesteaders, tourists, and land speculators from the North and South came to Central Florida. Men who were once enemies formed business partnerships on Florida's wild frontier. This relationship was celebrated in this tableau with Confederate veteran O.S. Tarver and Union veteran D.L. Way. This was probably part of a pageant in the 1890s marking an anniversary of the war's end.

Henry S. Sanford's first investment in Florida was a grove in St. Augustine that he purchased in 1867. In 1870, he and his wife Gertrude journeyed to Florida on a pleasure trip which was to include searching for investment opportunities. They traveled up river to Mellonville. General Sanford immediately recognized the strategic value of Lake Monroe and envisioned a "Gate City of South Florida," which would open up the state's interior to immigration and development. Mrs. Sanford was never as enchanted with the possibilities of Florida. A Philadelphia born socialite, her life was the social whirl of Brussels. She did, however, take on the founding of Holy Cross Episcopal Church as a personal project.

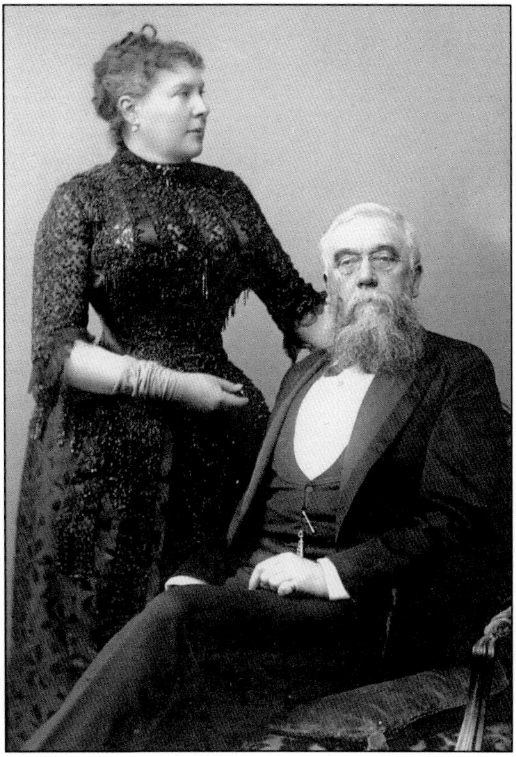

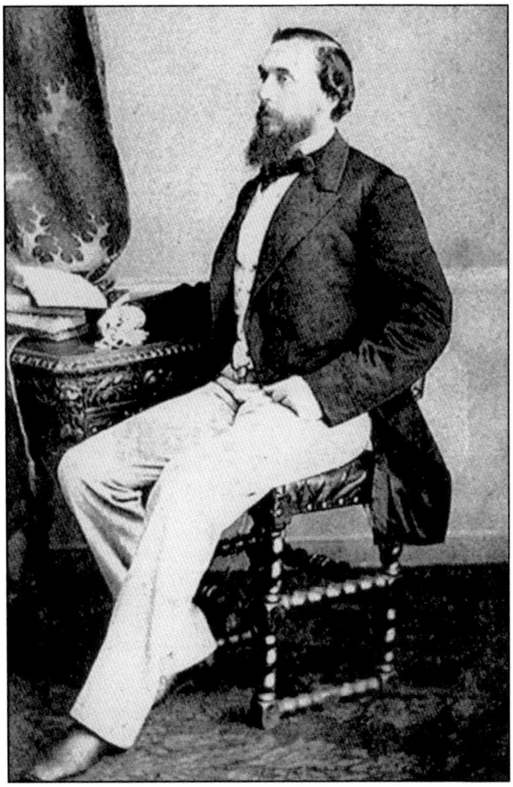

Henry S. Sanford was born in 1823 and spent his childhood years in Derby, Connecticut where his father amassed a fortune manufacturing carpet tacks. Upon his father's death in 1841, he took his inheritance and embarked on a career in the diplomatic service. During the Lincoln administration he received an appointment to Brussels, Belgium. From that post he supervised a surveillance network undermining Confederate activity in Europe. He married Gertrude Dupuy in 1864 and they had eight children. During the war he was given the honorary title of general. In the 1880s he became enmeshed in the creation of the Belgian Congo and it is for this that he is best known in history.

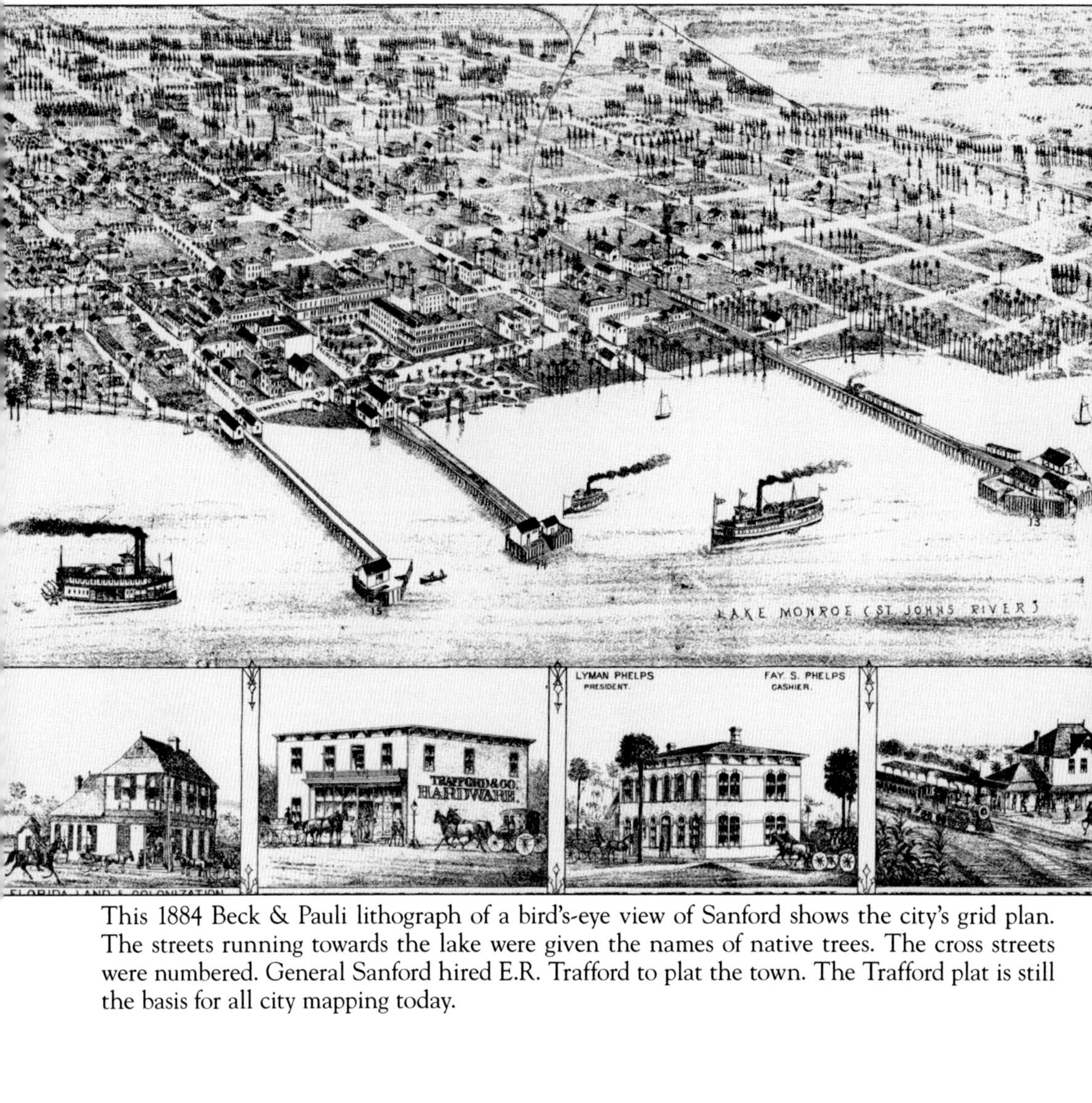

This 1884 Beck & Pauli lithograph of a bird's-eye view of Sanford shows the city's grid plan. The streets running towards the lake were given the names of native trees. The cross streets were numbered. General Sanford hired E.R. Trafford to plat the town. The Trafford plat is still the basis for all city mapping today.

Holy Cross Episcopal Church was built through the efforts of Gertrude Dupuy Sanford. The Sanfords' daughter, Ethel, was married in this church in 1892. The first church was destroyed by a hurricane in 1880, the second, pictured here, burned in 1923. The present church was built in 1924.

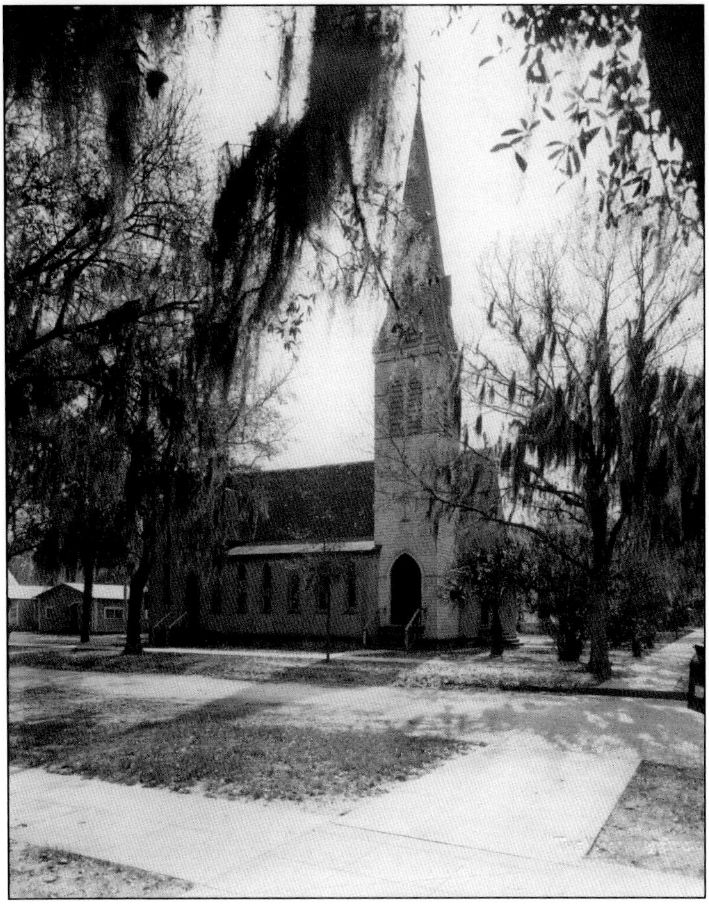

As part of his city planning, Henry Sanford set aside land for churches, parks, and schools. Five of the original parks remain today. One of these, now known as Centennial Park, included a bandstand where concerts were given by the city band.

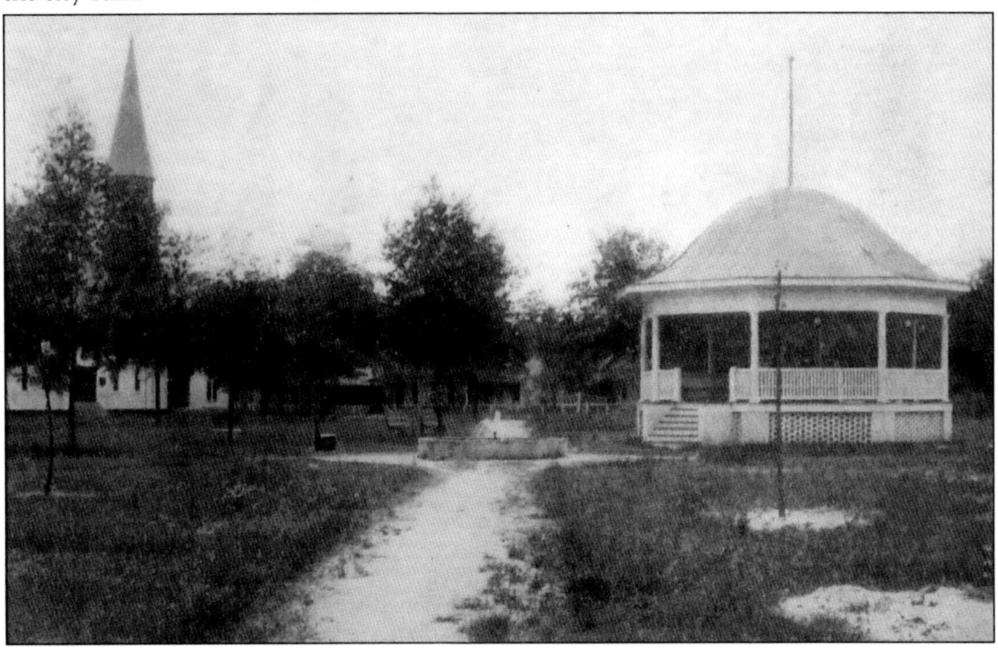

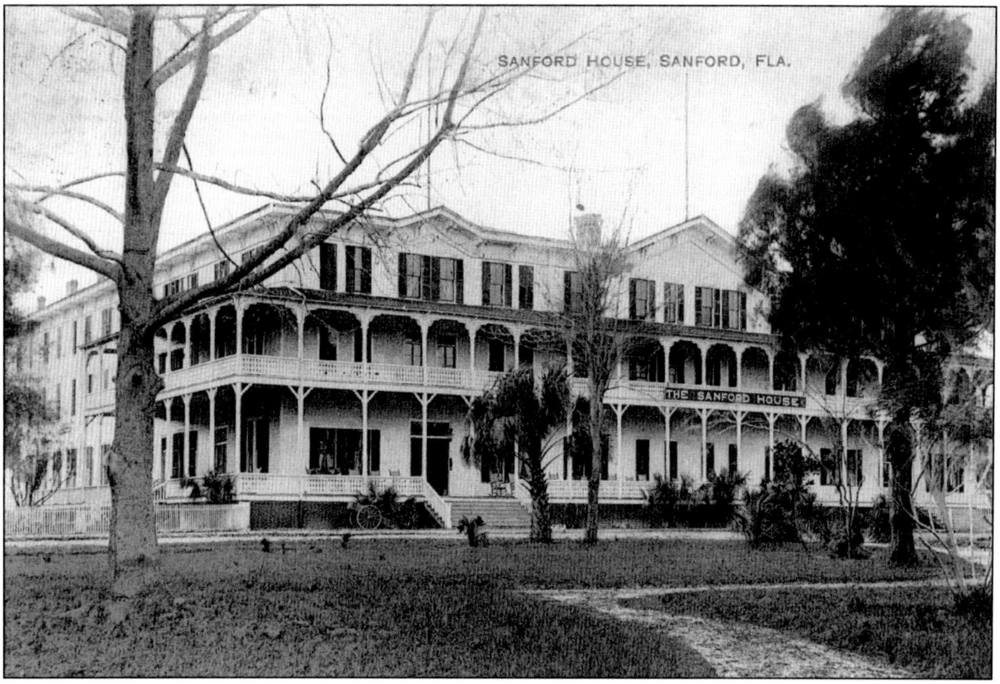

The Sanford House Hotel was built in 1875 by Henry Sanford to attract tourists to the city. The hotel, which could accommodate 150 guests, faced the waterfront on Commercial Street.

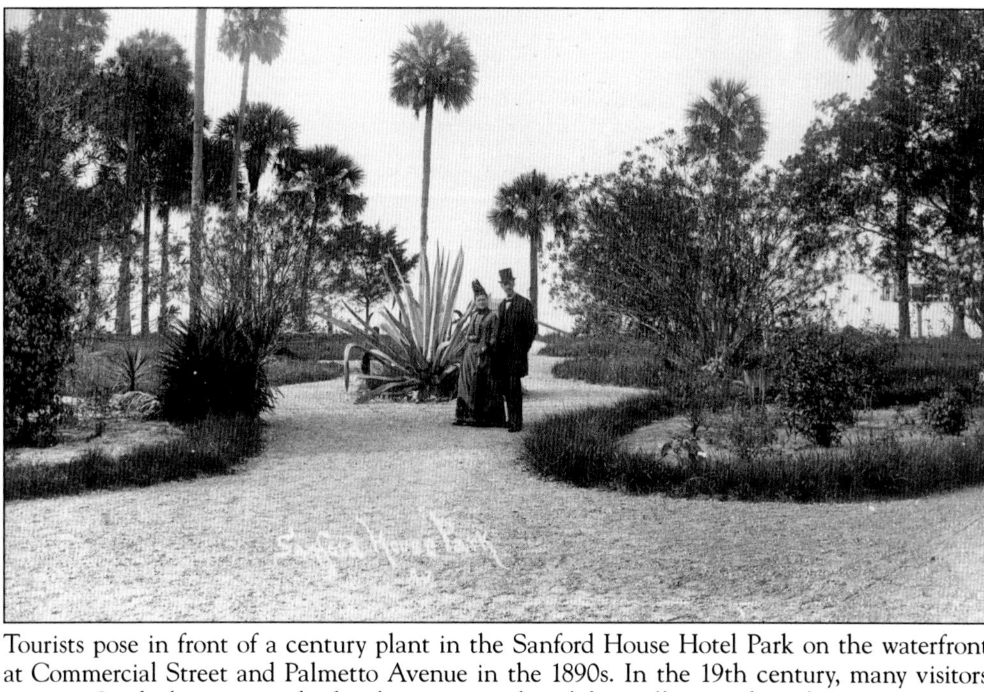

Tourists pose in front of a century plant in the Sanford House Hotel Park on the waterfront at Commercial Street and Palmetto Avenue in the 1890s. In the 19th century, many visitors came to Sanford to escape the harsh winters and coal fire pollution of northern cities. Some with a variety of ailments came seeking the reputed curative power of Sanford's sulfur springs and pine-scented air.

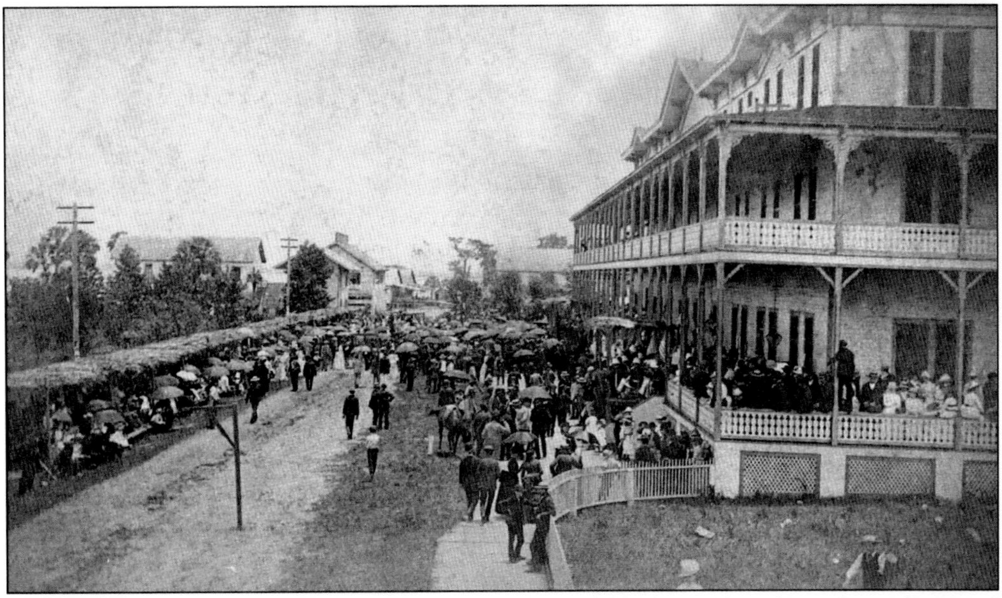

The Sanford House Hotel was once the center of city celebrations. This photo shows the crowd at a Fourth of July celebration on Commercial Street in 1887. The crowd here is probably waiting for the riding tournament to begin.

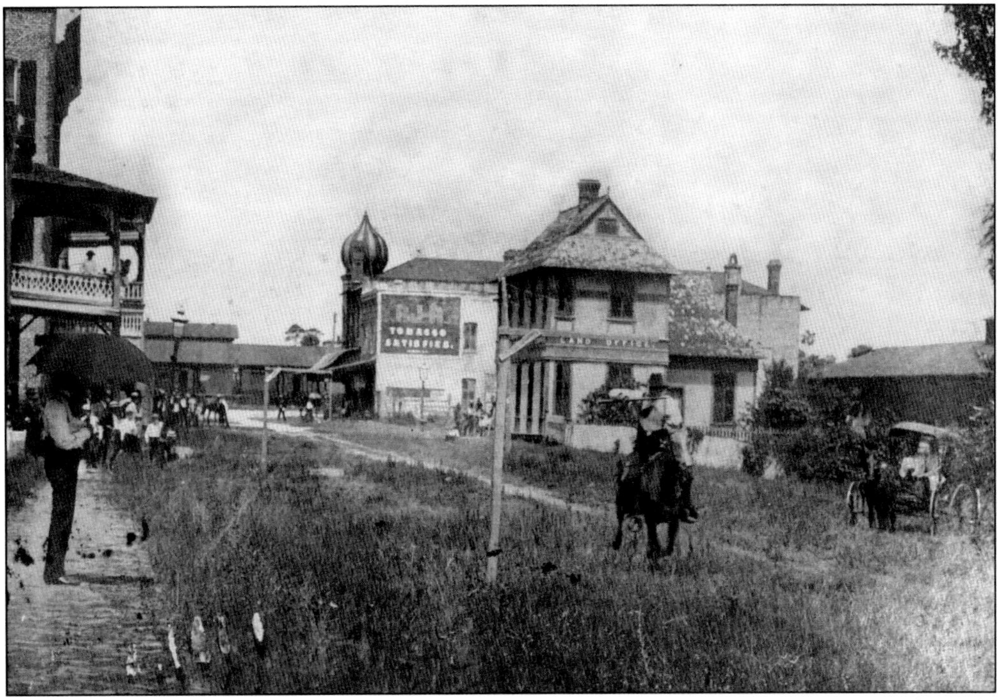

For many years, a substantial cattle industry thrived in the country around Sanford with cattle grazing on the prairies along the St. Johns River. Local ranches, like those of the Camerons and the Becks, employed cowboys locally called cowmen. The cowmen often showed off their skills during special events in Sanford. Here a cowman in full gallop spears a ring.

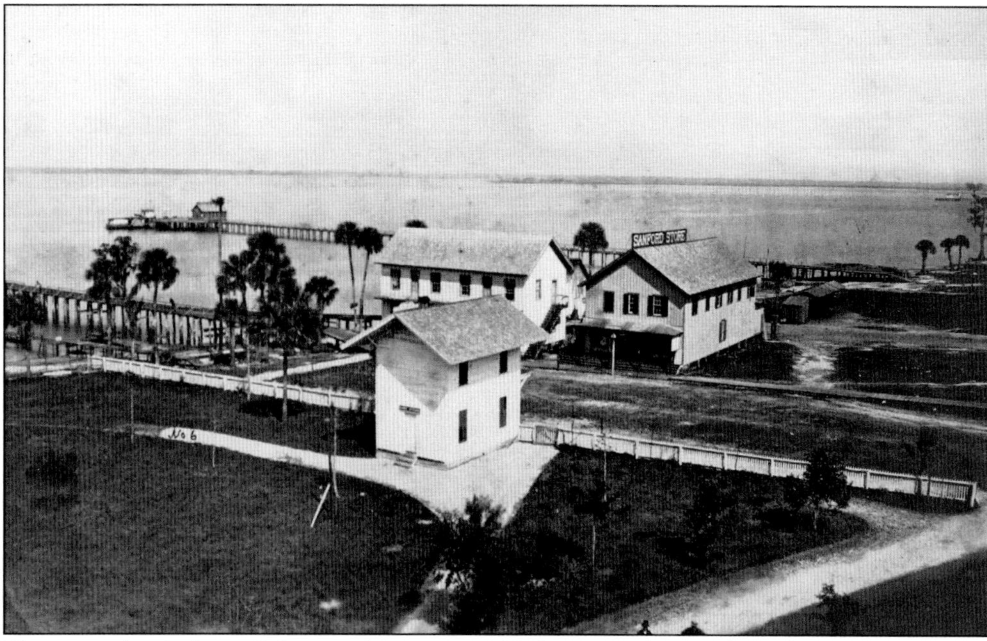

These are the docks at Palmetto Avenue in 1882. In 1882, the riverboat docks at the base of Palmetto Avenue included the city's telegraph office and Henry Sanford's company store.

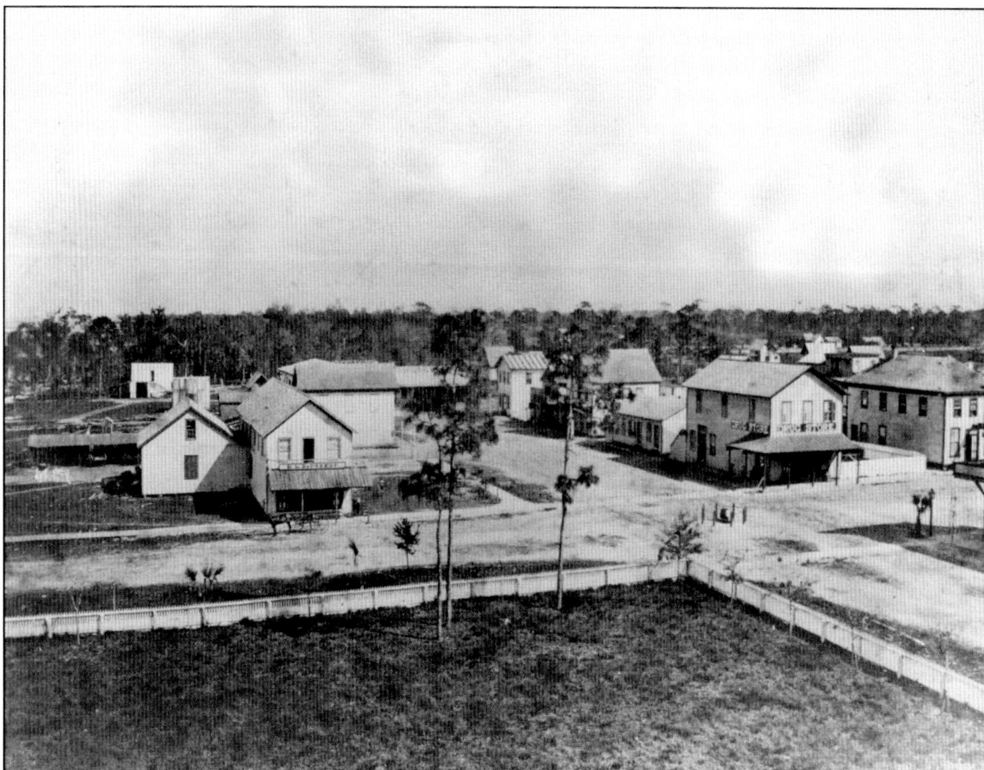

This is Palmetto Avenue at First Street looking east in 1882. First Street ended at Sanford Avenue at this time. A fountain sits in the intersection for watering horses.

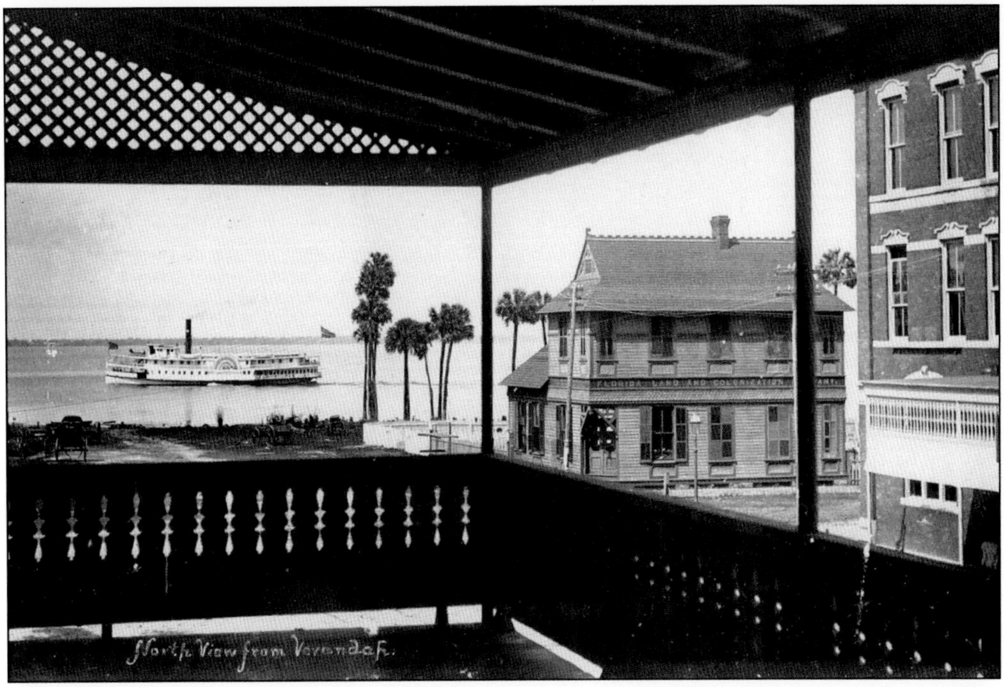

Henry Sanford organized the Florida Land and Colonization Company in London in 1880. The company's land office stood on the northeast corner of Commercial Street and North Park Avenue. This photo was taken from photographer J.C. Ensminger's balcony.

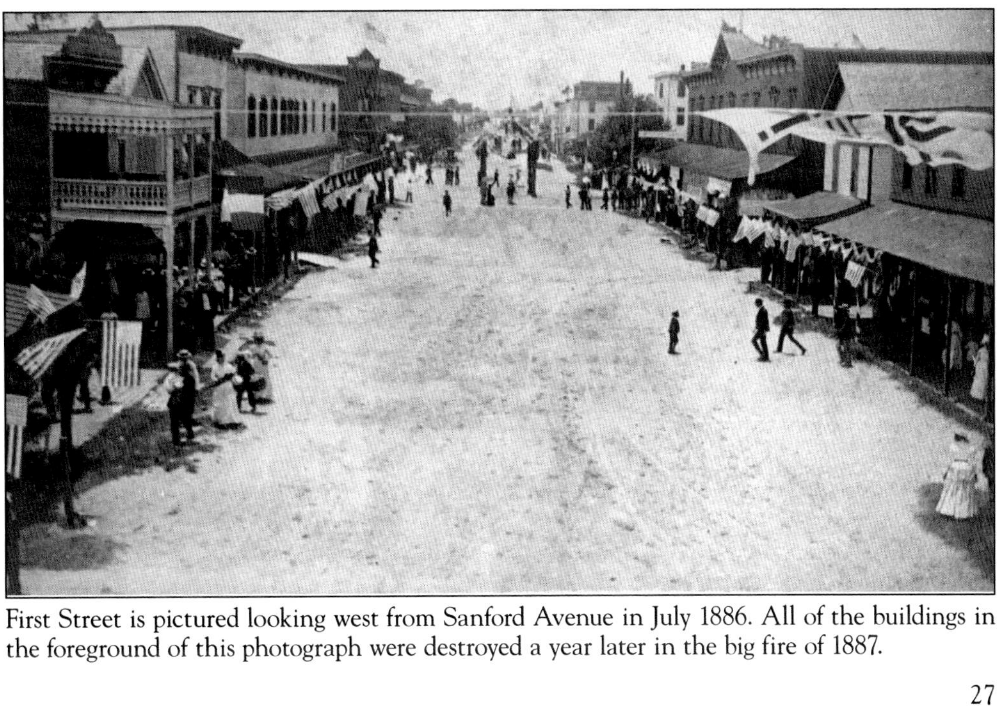

First Street is pictured looking west from Sanford Avenue in July 1886. All of the buildings in the foreground of this photograph were destroyed a year later in the big fire of 1887.

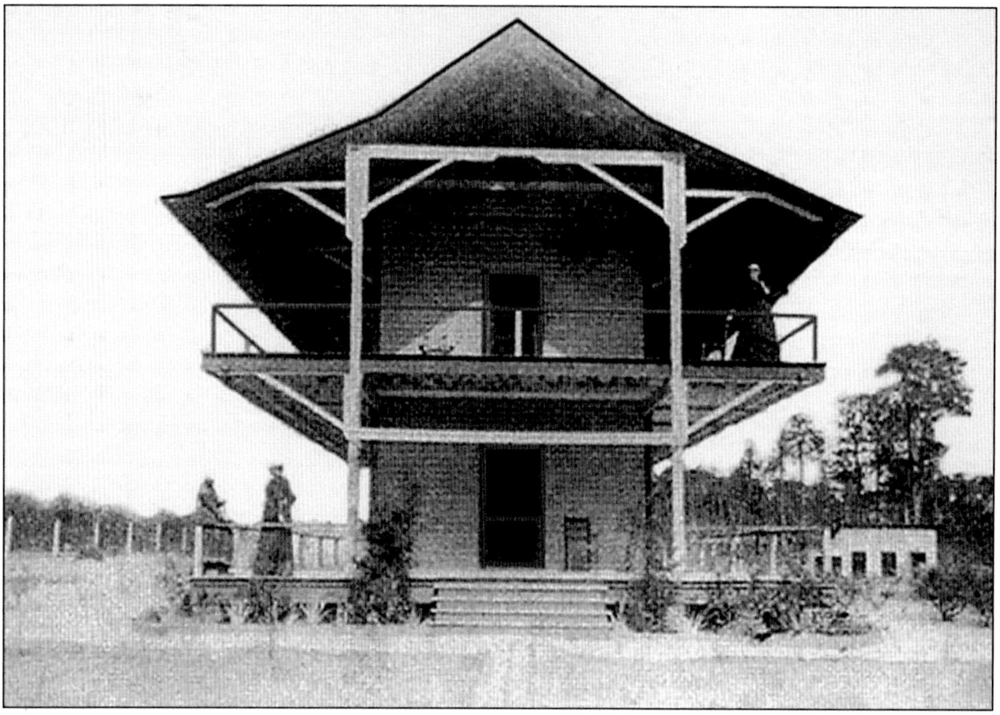

Shown here is "the Lodge" at Henry Sanford's grove, Belair. This home was built in 1889 for Henry S. Sanford Jr., who lived in Sanford for two years working as his father's agent. When General and Mrs. Sanford visited town they stayed at the Sanford House Hotel or with their friend Charles Amory, who had an estate near the grove.

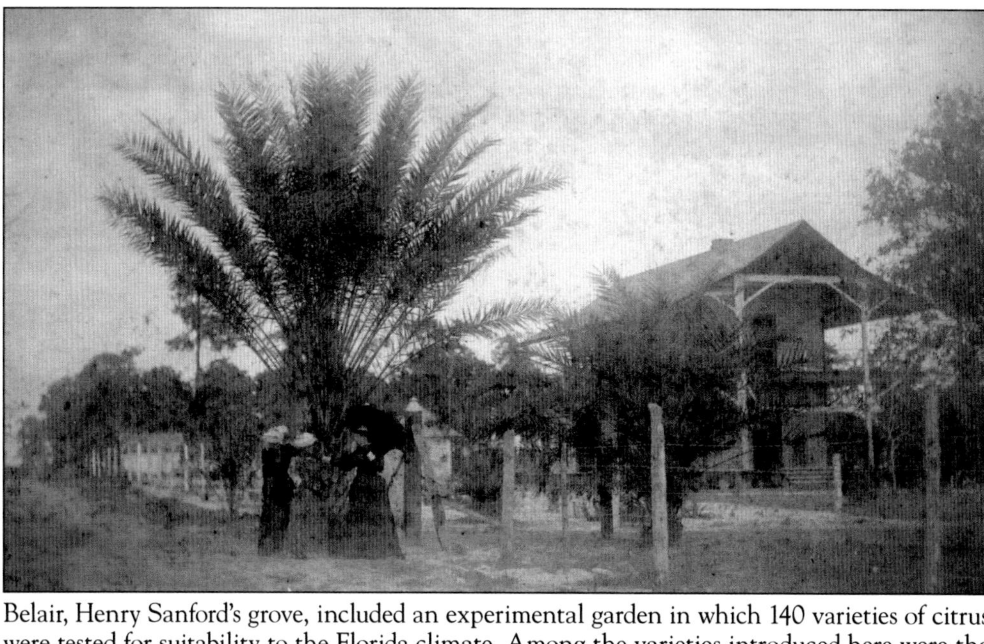

Belair, Henry Sanford's grove, included an experimental garden in which 140 varieties of citrus were tested for suitability to the Florida climate. Among the varieties introduced here were the Jaffa and Valencia oranges.

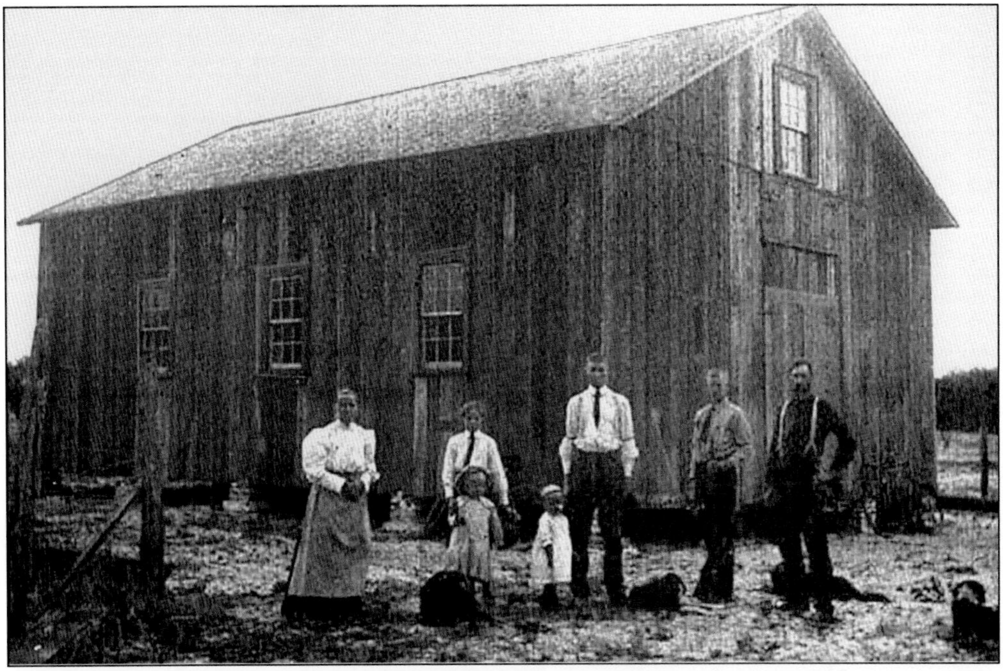

In 1871, Henry Sanford began importing laborers from Sweden under the Contract Labor Law to work at his Belair Grove and Experimental Gardens. In 1878, these immigrants established the New Upsala Colony, Florida's earliest and largest Swedish settlement. The Scandinavian Hall, pictured above, served this community as a public meeting house and social center.

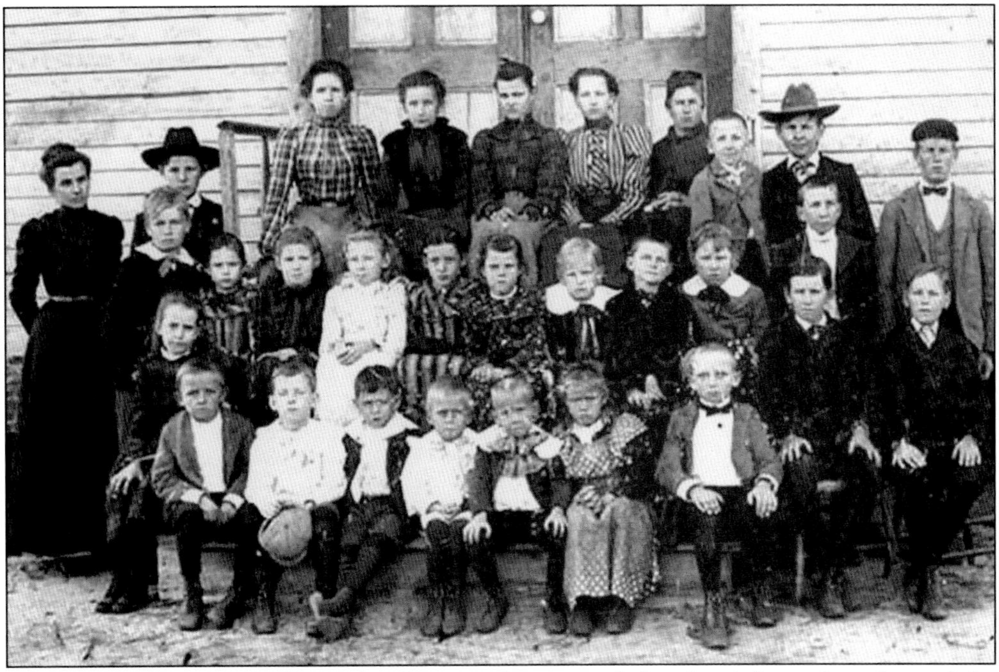

Teacher Josephine Jacobs (later Mrs. Stenstrom) poses with her Swedish pupils in front of the New Upsala School. Many of the children in this 1878 photograph represent the first American generation of the New Upsala colony. (Courtesy of Bettye Smith.)

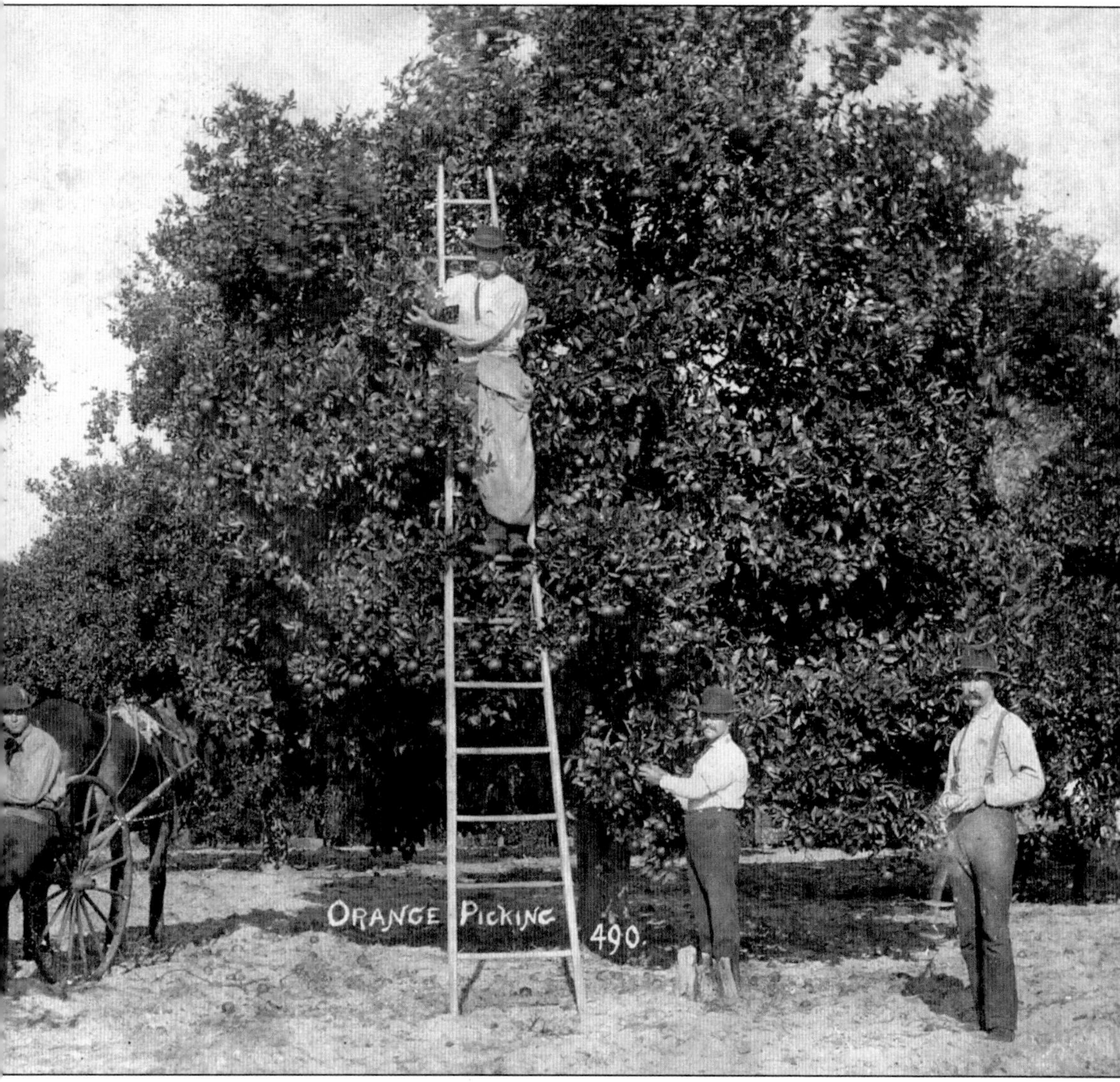

Picking oranges from the top of a swaying ladder supported only by branches was no easy task in 1890. Similar ladders are still used today. From the earliest days the Sanford area was famous for its groves. The Speer Grove outside Mellonville was mentioned in early guidebooks. With improvements brought by Henry Sanford, citrus became the basis of the city's economy until the Great Freeze of 1894 and 1895.

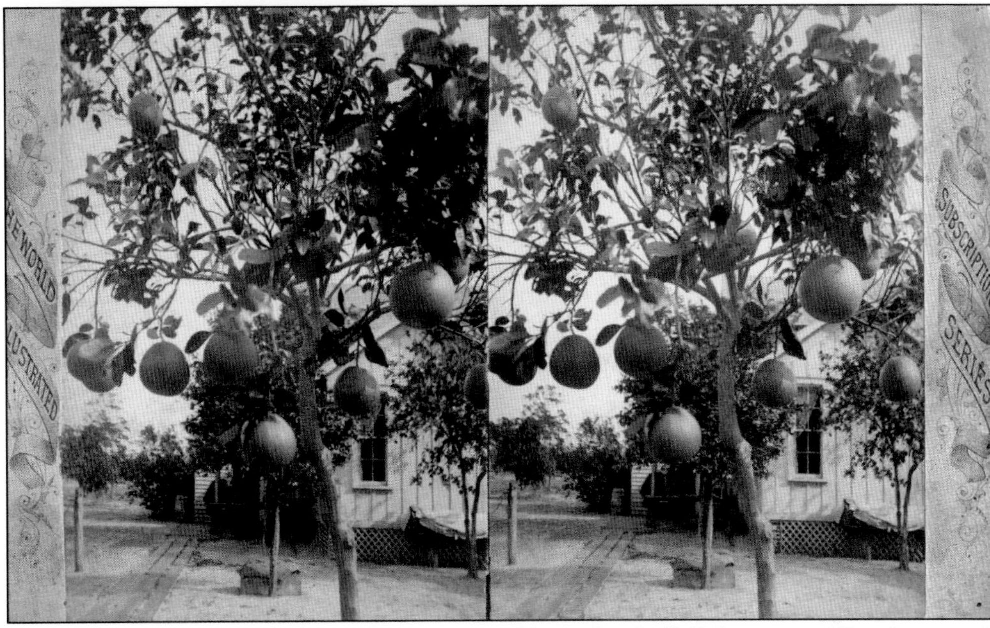

This is a stereoscope card of grapefruit grown at Henry Sanford's Belair grove. The photograph on this card would appear to be three dimensional when viewed through a stereoscope.

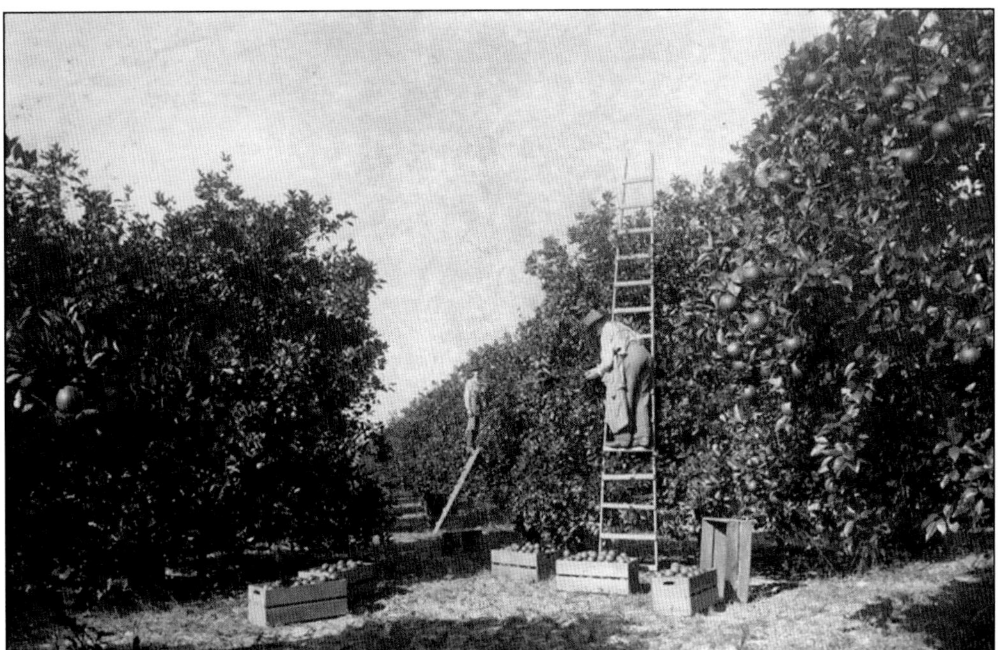

These workers are harvesting oranges in 1890. Bags were slung over the workers shoulder for holding the oranges while on the ladder. A later improved bag had a bottom that opened so the fruit could be dropped into field crates.

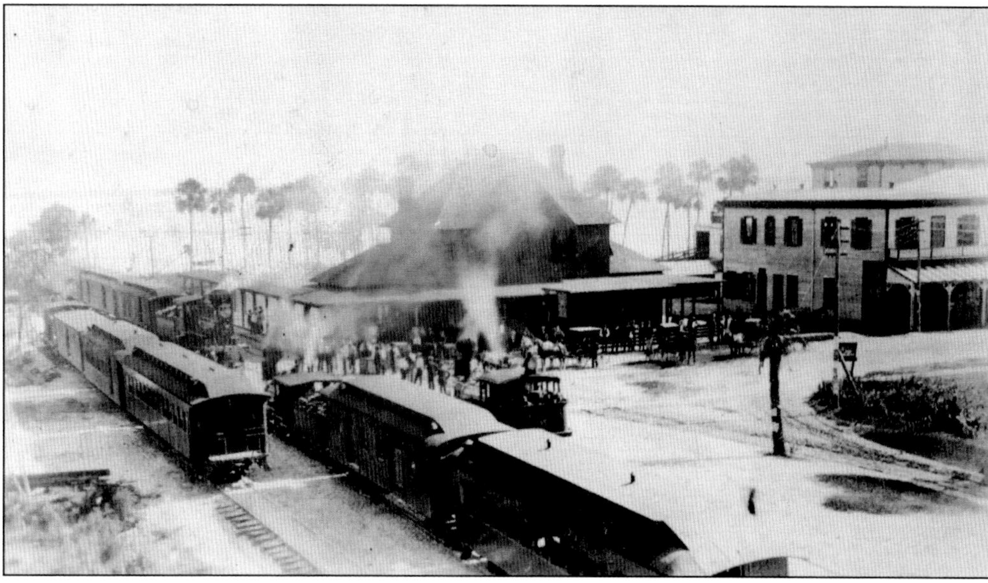

On January 10, 1880, former President Ulysses S. Grant participated in the groundbreaking ceremony for the South Florida Railroad. Beginning with only 10 miles of track between Sanford and Longwood, this was Central Florida's first operating railroad. Within six months the line was running to Orlando. In 1883, Henry B. Plant bought three-fifth's ownership in the South Florida Railroad, making it part of his Plant System and the Plant Investment Company.

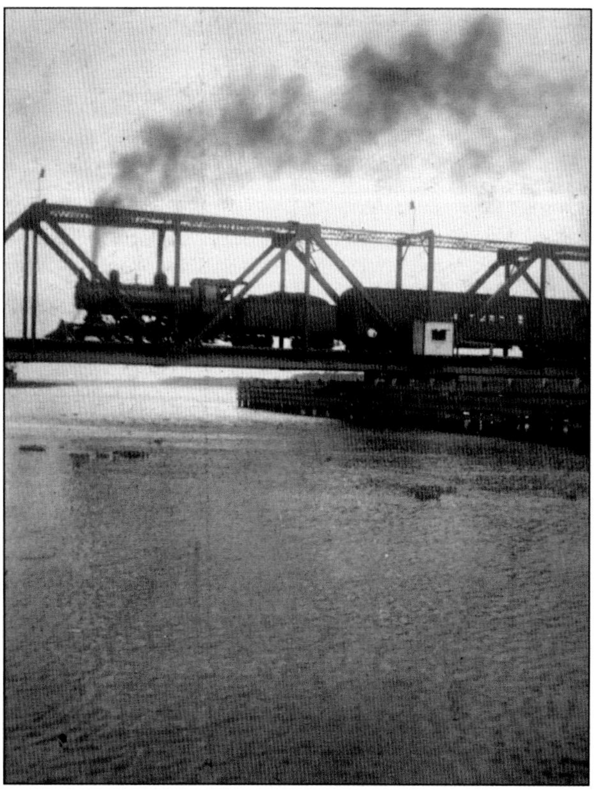

In 1886 the Jacksonville, Tampa and Key West Railroad (JT&KW) built the Thrasher Ferry railroad bridge across the St. Johns River. The bridge tied together a continuous rail route across the state from Jacksonville to Tampa. While this railroad bridge made it possible to go from Jacksonville to Tampa in a single day, it also began the decline of Sanford's era of steamboat passenger travel. (Courtesy of Library of Congress.)

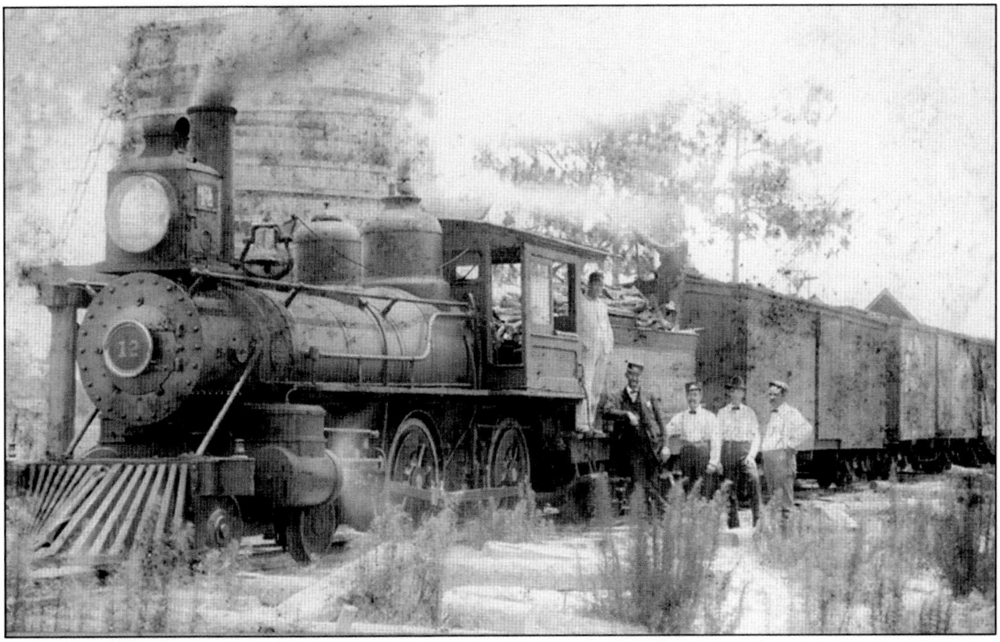

John Anderson was a conductor for the Orange Belt Railroad. Built in 1887 by Russian immigrant Peter Demens, the Orange Belt had its own depot in Sanford. It was one of many railroad companies to service Sanford. In 1893, it was reorganized as the Sanford and St. Petersburg Railroad. This was the nation's longest narrow-gauge line and the last one to operate in Florida. It ceased operations in 1896 after being bought out by the Henry B. Plant System.

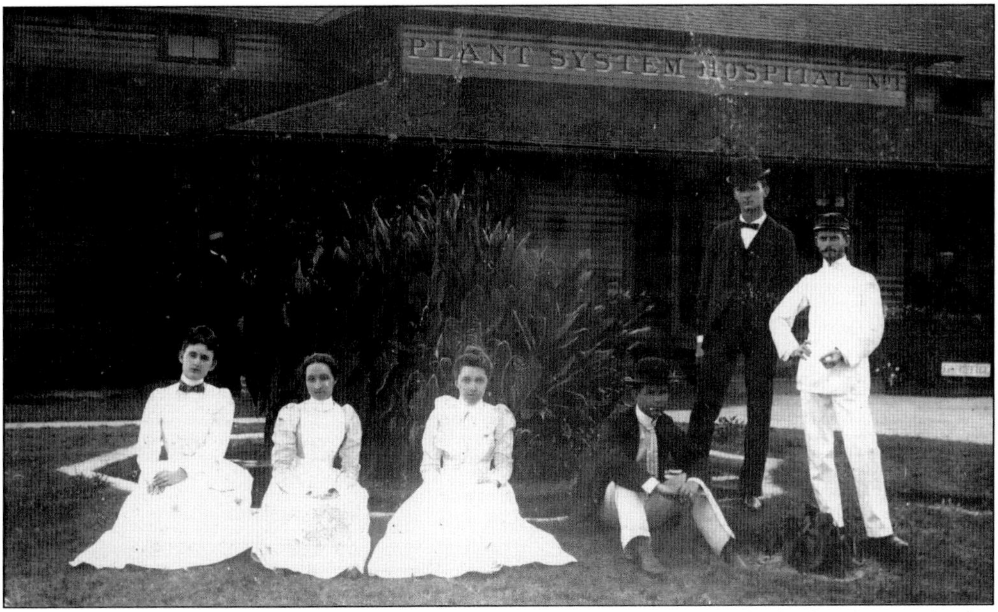

Plant System Hospital #1, seen here in an 1892 photograph, was Sanford's first hospital. The hospital was later moved to Waycross, Georgia.

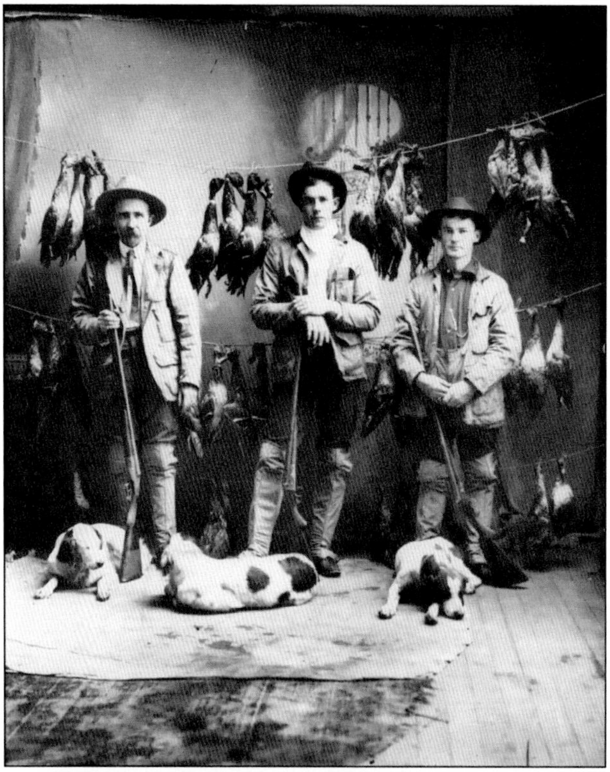

Hunting was a popular pastime for early tourists in Sanford. Native birds were prized as trophies and for the feathers which were used to decorate ladies hats. Henry Sanford, who had enjoyed shooting birds and alligators on his first visit, expressed concern in the late 1880s that the wild birds might disappear altogether.

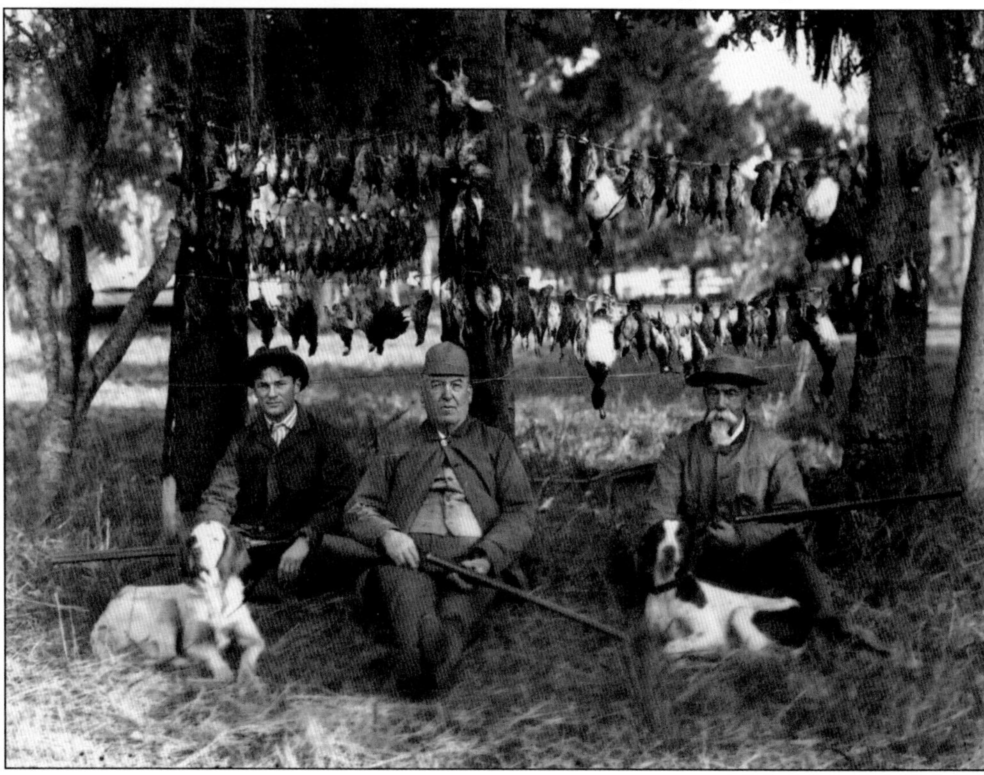

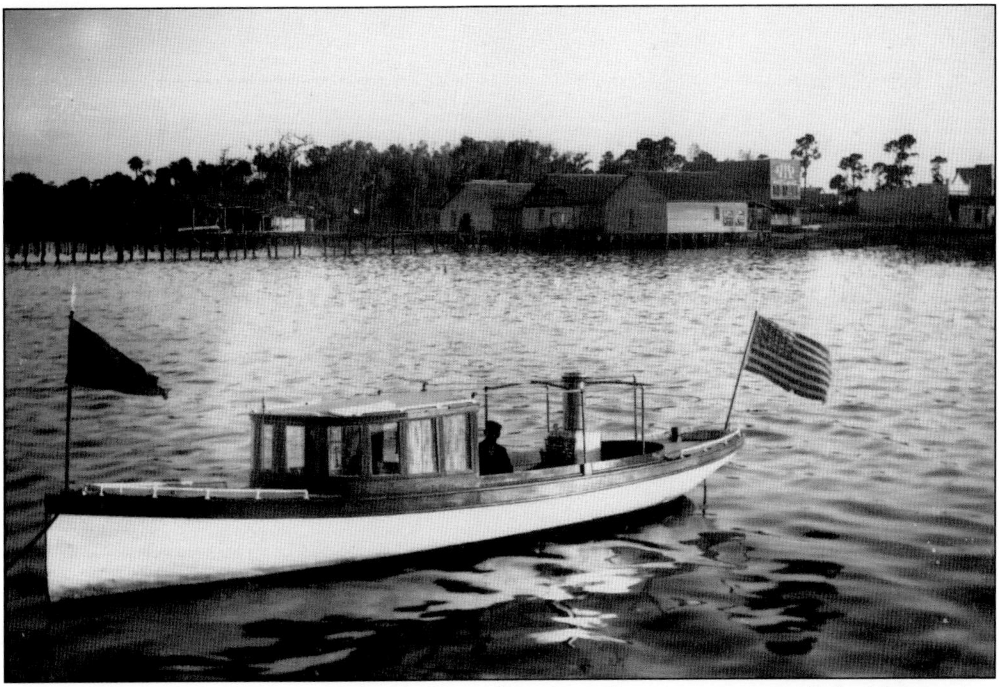

Steam launches like this one run by Mr. Paganhart ferried passengers across Lake Monroe.

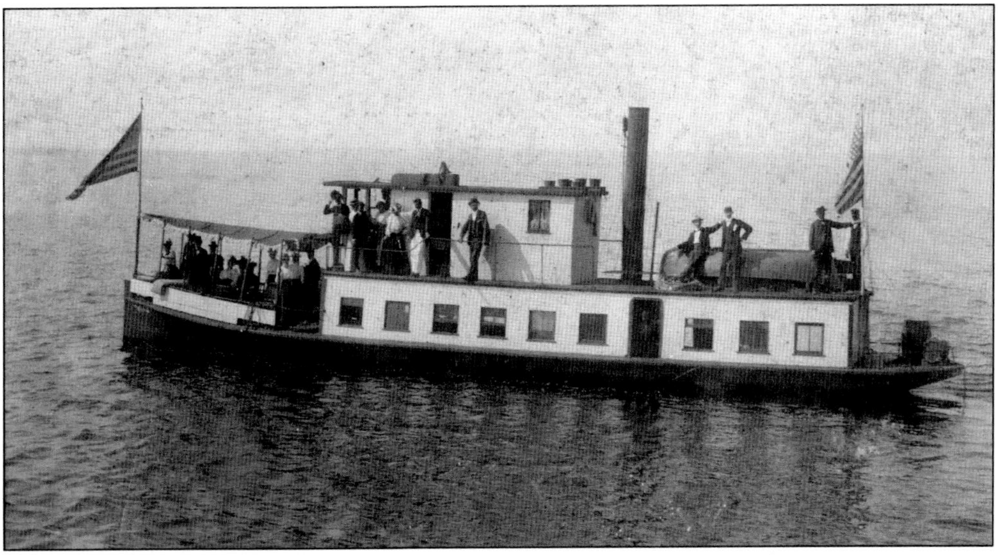

The steamboats plying the St. Johns River came in all sizes. Here the riverboat *Enterprise* is seen on Lake Monroe on March 22, 1899.

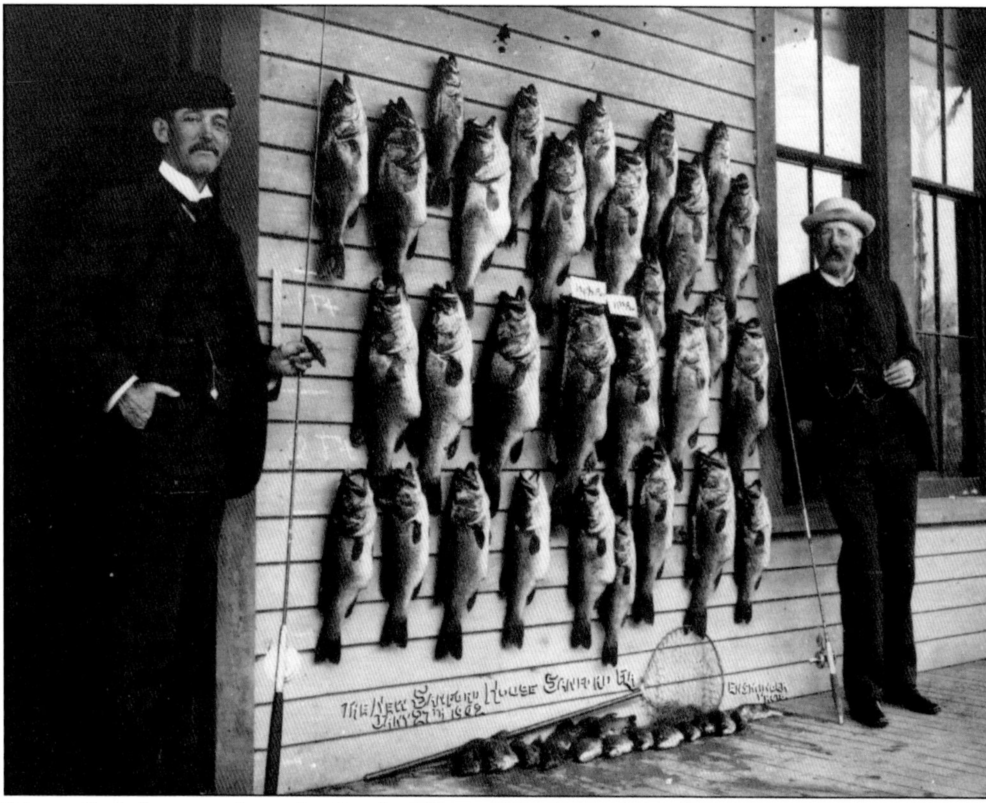

The wall of the veranda at the Sanford House Hotel must have been constantly covered with scales from the prize catches of visiting fishermen.

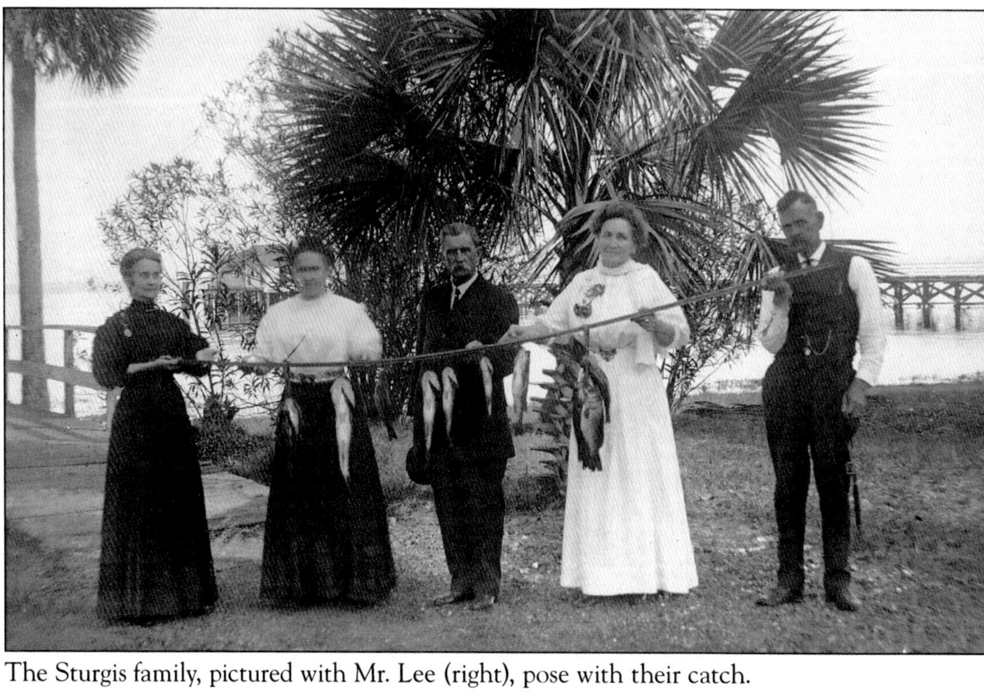

The Sturgis family, pictured with Mr. Lee (right), pose with their catch.

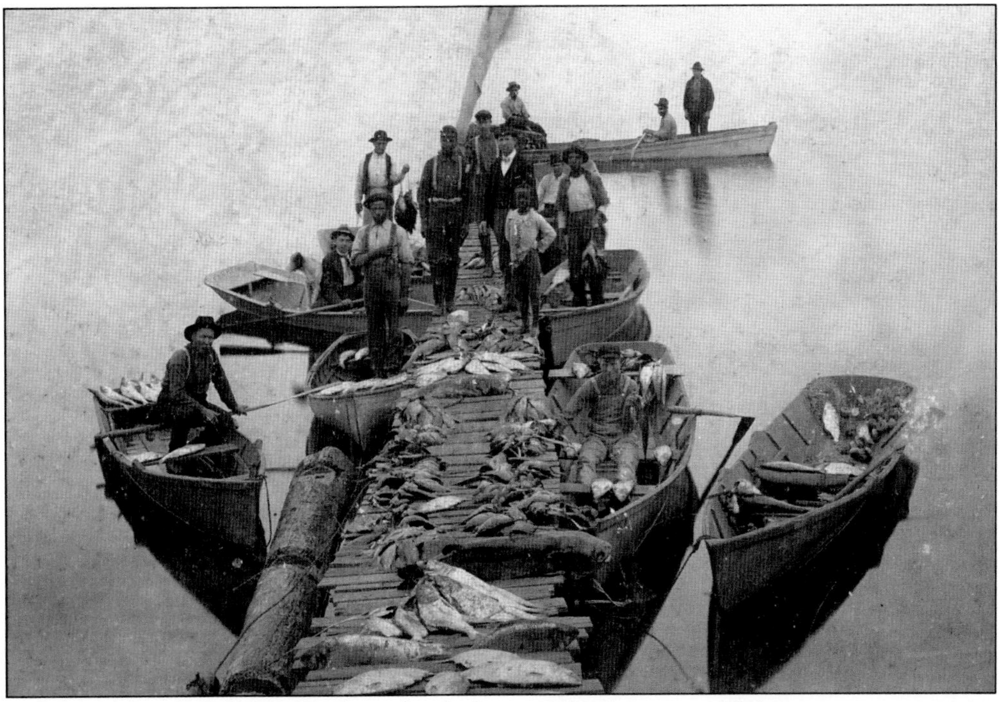

Shad fishermen bring their catch to the docks in 1890. Commercial fishing was an important part of Sanford's early business economy. Fish houses sat along the banks of Lake Monroe. The fish were packed in barrels for shipment north on riverboats.

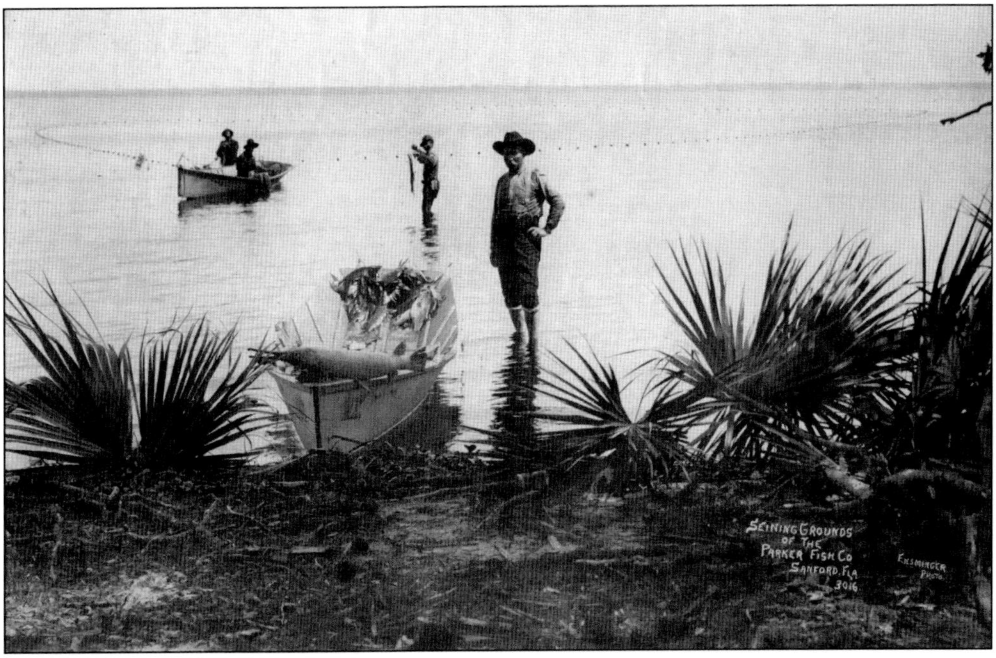

This Ensminger photo from the 1890s shows commercial fishermen using sein nets in Lake Monroe.

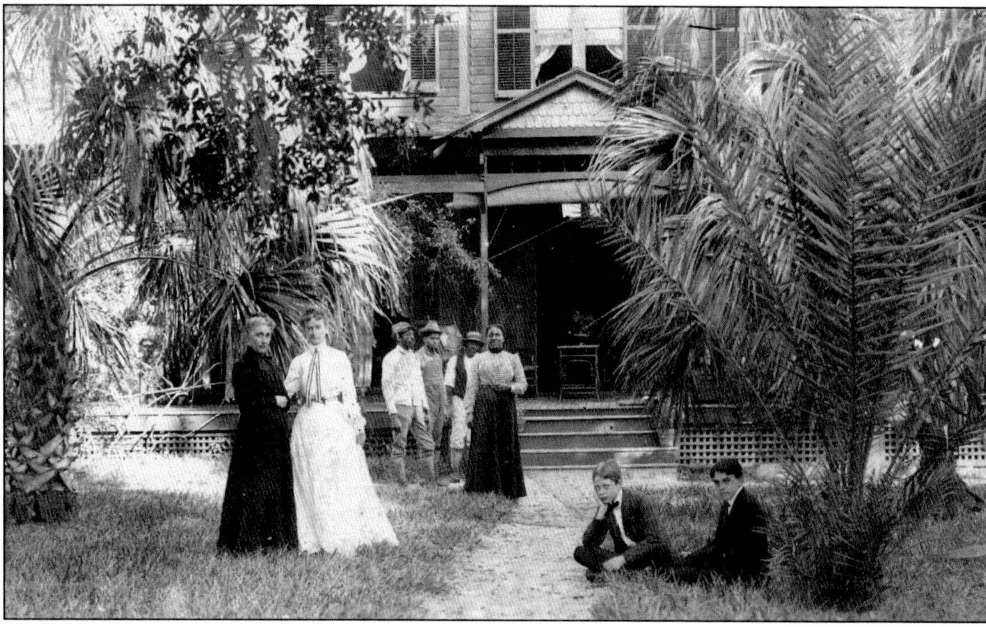

The Henry L. DeForest home, known as "The Palms" and located on Aldean Drive, was built by a cousin of Henry S. Sanford. Henry DeForest was born a few doors down from the childhood home of Henry Sanford in Derby, Connecticut. He came to Florida in 1870 seeking a healthy climate. For many years he acted as an agent for Sanford. By the 1880s, he was a prominent businessman and grove owner. He built several commercial buildings in the downtown.

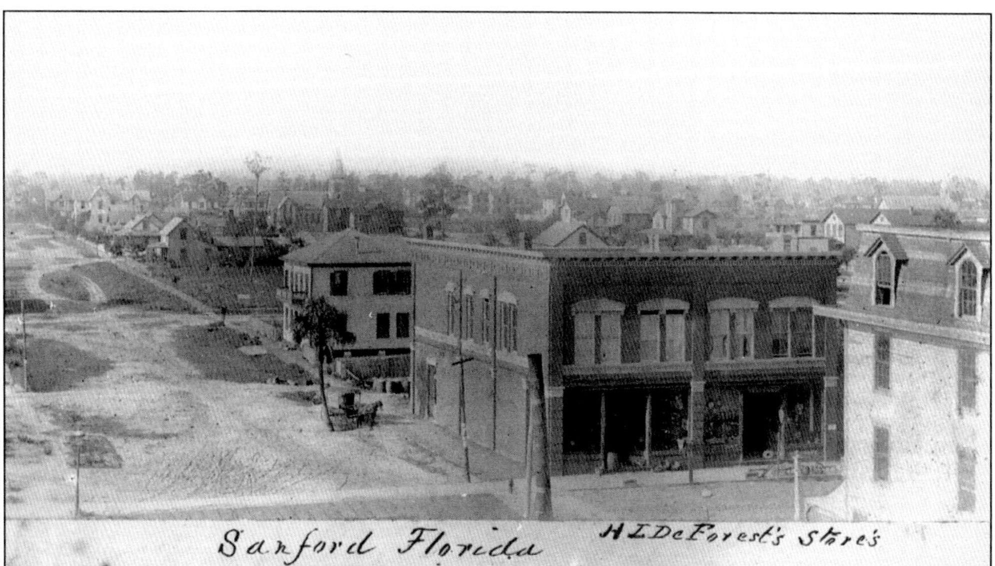

The DeForest Block, the second oldest brick building in downtown Sanford, was built in 1887 by Henry DeForest as a general store. The big fire of September 1887 stopped at this building. The building is best remembered for its 61 years as Touchton's Drugstore.

W.J. Hill was among Sanford's most colorful characters. Born in London in 1842, he immigrated to New York in the summer of 1873. Seeking warmer climes, he moved south and ended up in Sanford. He made his first "home" in two wooden barrels on the shores of Lake Monroe. He later took up residence in a discarded piano crate. In 1877, as the "voting inspector," Hill played a part in the incorporation of Sanford as a city. At the time there were only eight eligible voters living in town. To insure enough votes favoring incorporation, Hill extended the voting district to include the Swedes of the New Upsala colony. In 1880, former President Grant came to town for the groundbreaking ceremony of the South Florida Railroad. W.J. Hill followed the former president around and picked up his discarded cigar stubs, which he later sold as souvenirs for 25¢ a piece. Hill was a true entrepreneur who went on to own several orange groves and businesses. He is best remembered for Hill's Hardware and Lumber Company.

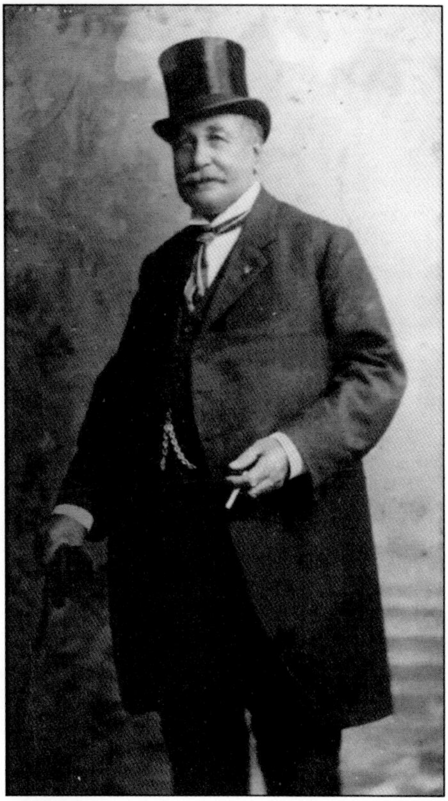

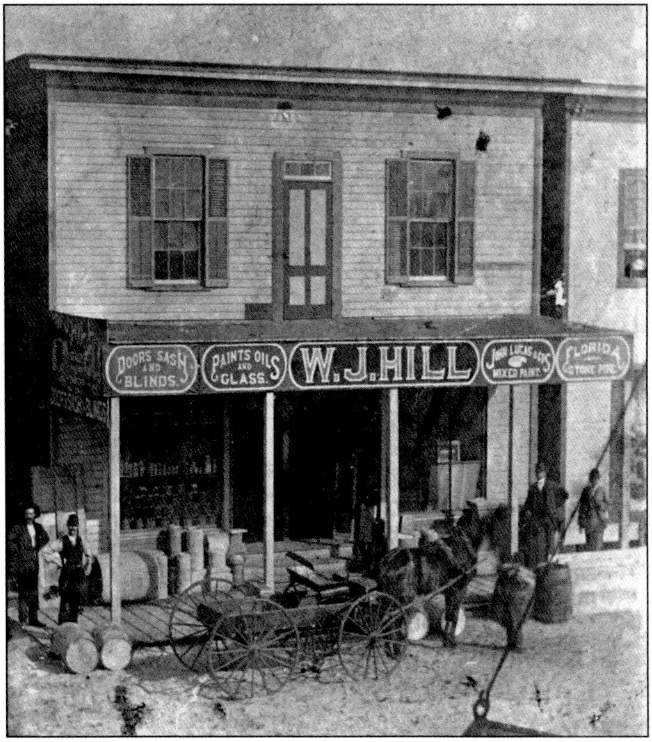

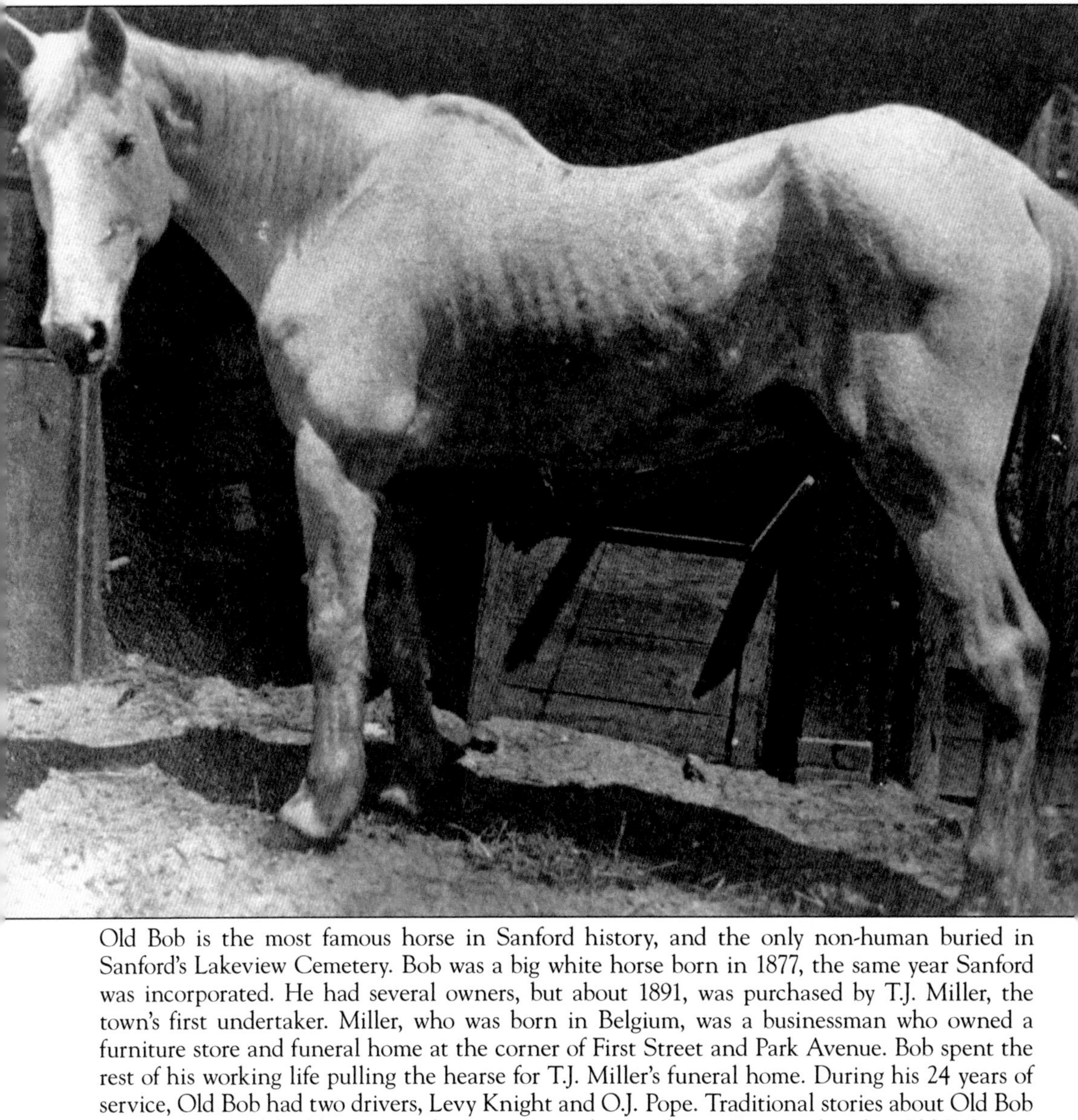

Old Bob is the most famous horse in Sanford history, and the only non-human buried in Sanford's Lakeview Cemetery. Bob was a big white horse born in 1877, the same year Sanford was incorporated. He had several owners, but about 1891, was purchased by T.J. Miller, the town's first undertaker. Miller, who was born in Belgium, was a businessman who owned a furniture store and funeral home at the corner of First Street and Park Avenue. Bob spent the rest of his working life pulling the hearse for T.J. Miller's funeral home. During his 24 years of service, Old Bob had two drivers, Levy Knight and O.J. Pope. Traditional stories about Old Bob say that he could find his way to the cemetery without a driver. For two decades, Old Bob gave many Sanford citizens their "last ride." In 1913, the same year that Sanford became the county seat for the new county of Seminole, Old Bob was retired to pasture. In 1914 at age 37, Old Bob died and was buried with his former "passengers" in Lakeview Cemetery.

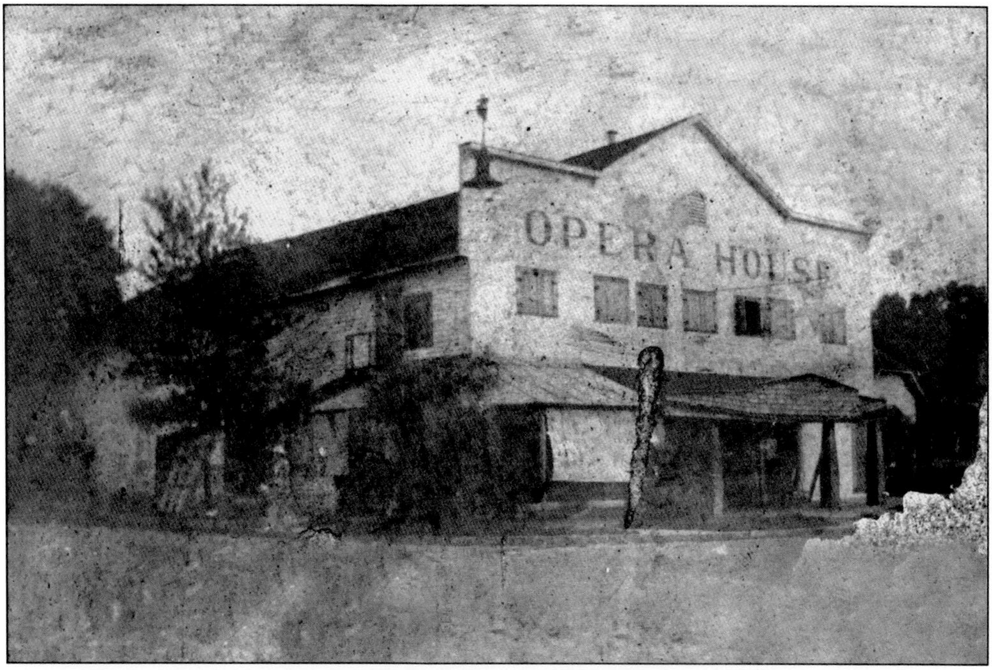

The Opera House stood on the southeast corner of Magnolia Avenue and Second Street. It was replaced by the Milane Theatre in the 1920s.

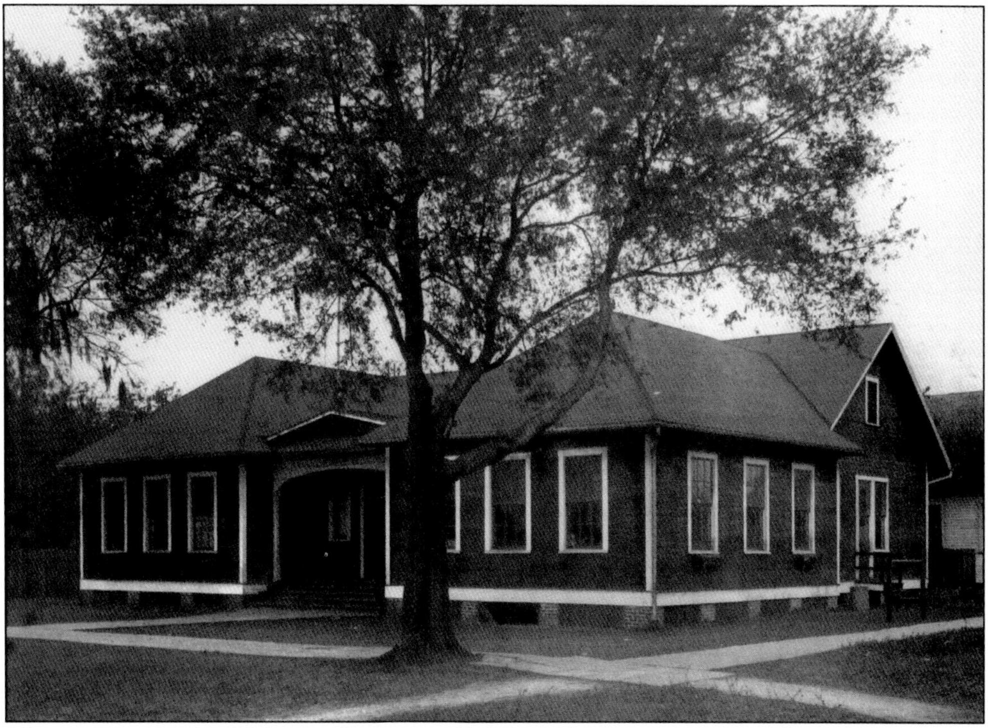
The Little Red School House, also once called Eastside Primary, is the oldest school building still standing in Sanford. The school was built in 1883 on the corner of Sixth Street and Palmetto Avenue.

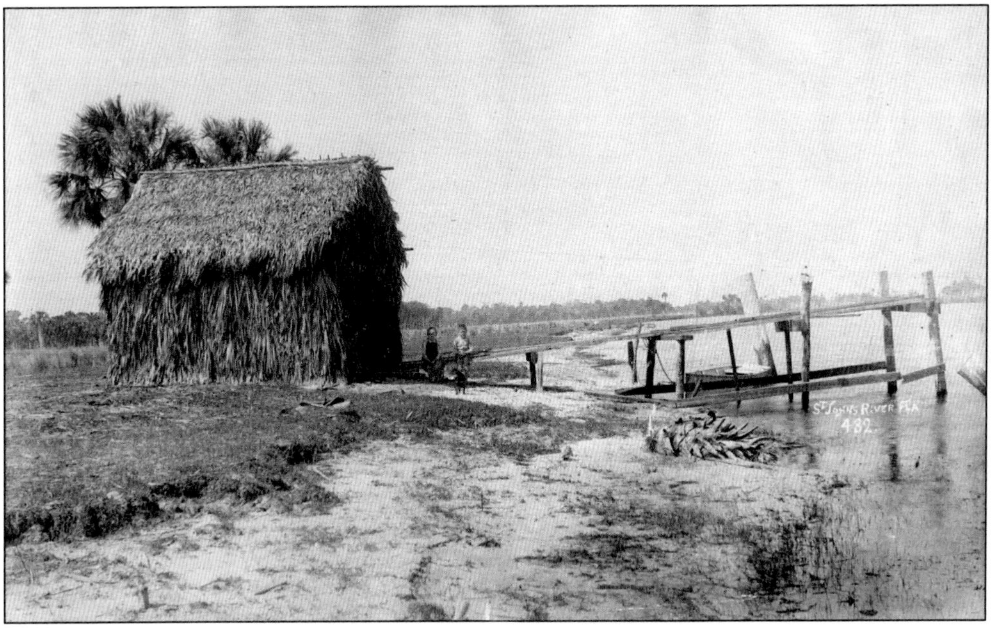

For many early pioneers arriving in the area, the common dwelling was a shack made of palmetto fronds woven together over a wooden frame

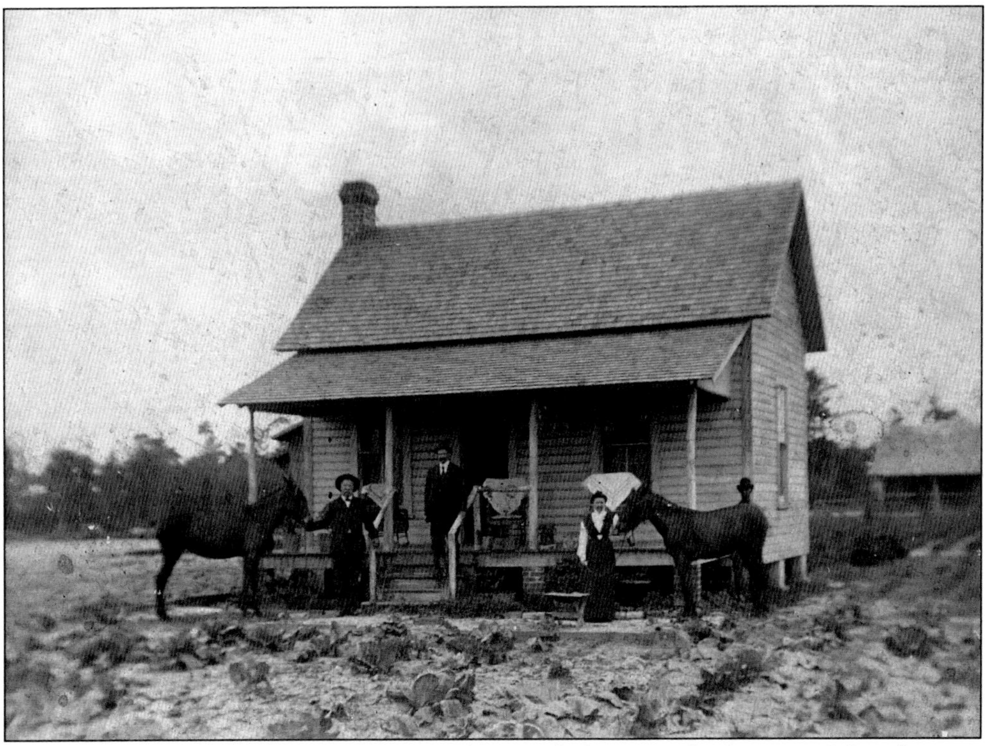
William J. McBride and his wife Mary were early east side farmers with a home on Celery Avenue.

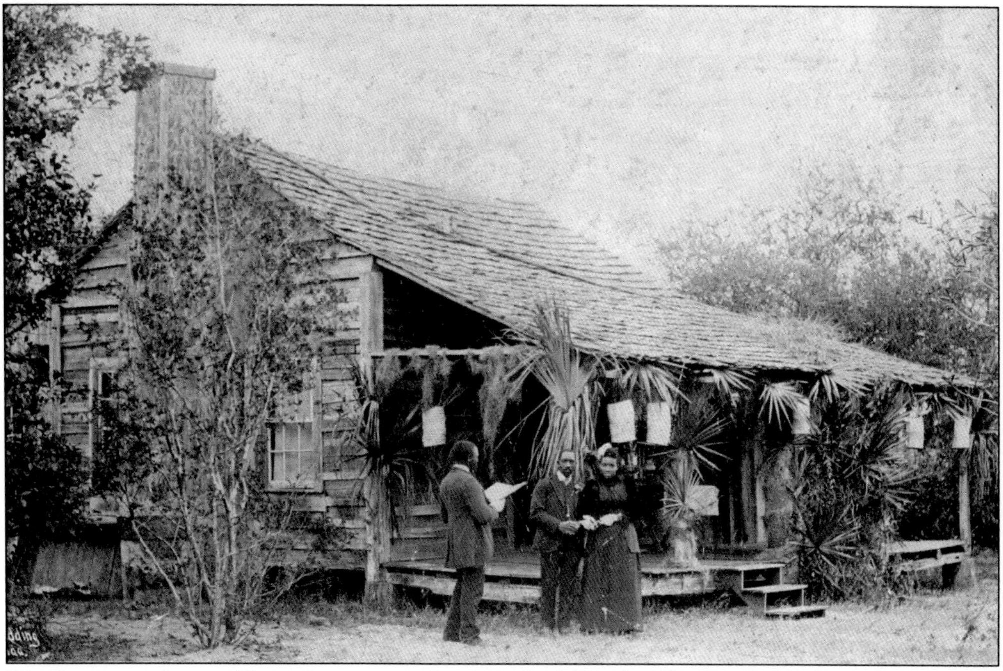

The house in this wedding photo is a style typical of Florida. The porch has been decorated in Florida style with palm fronds and Spanish moss.

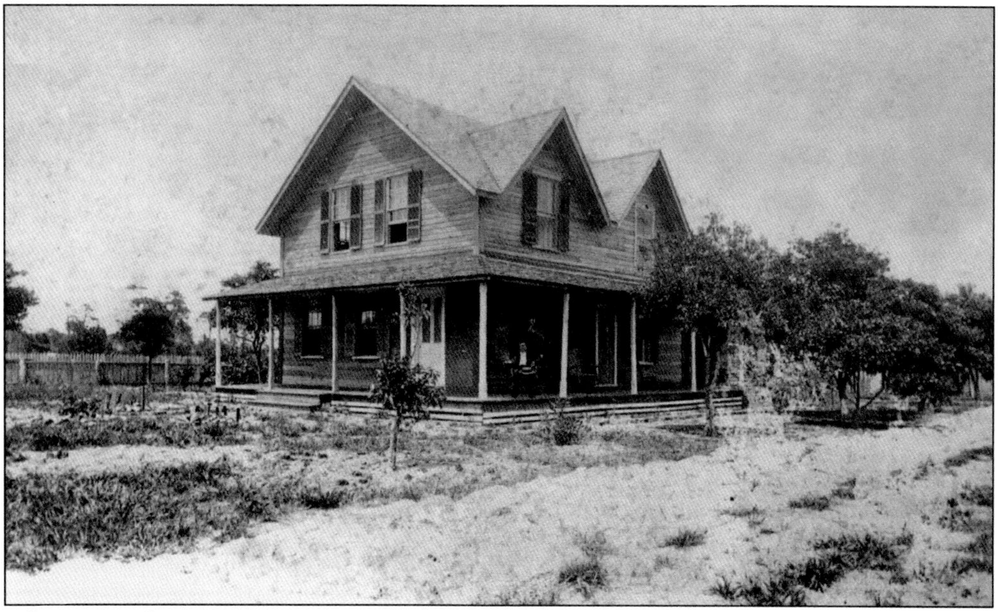

Albert H. and Mattie Crippen's home was in the Silver Lake settlement. Mr. Crippen owned a piano store near the depot.

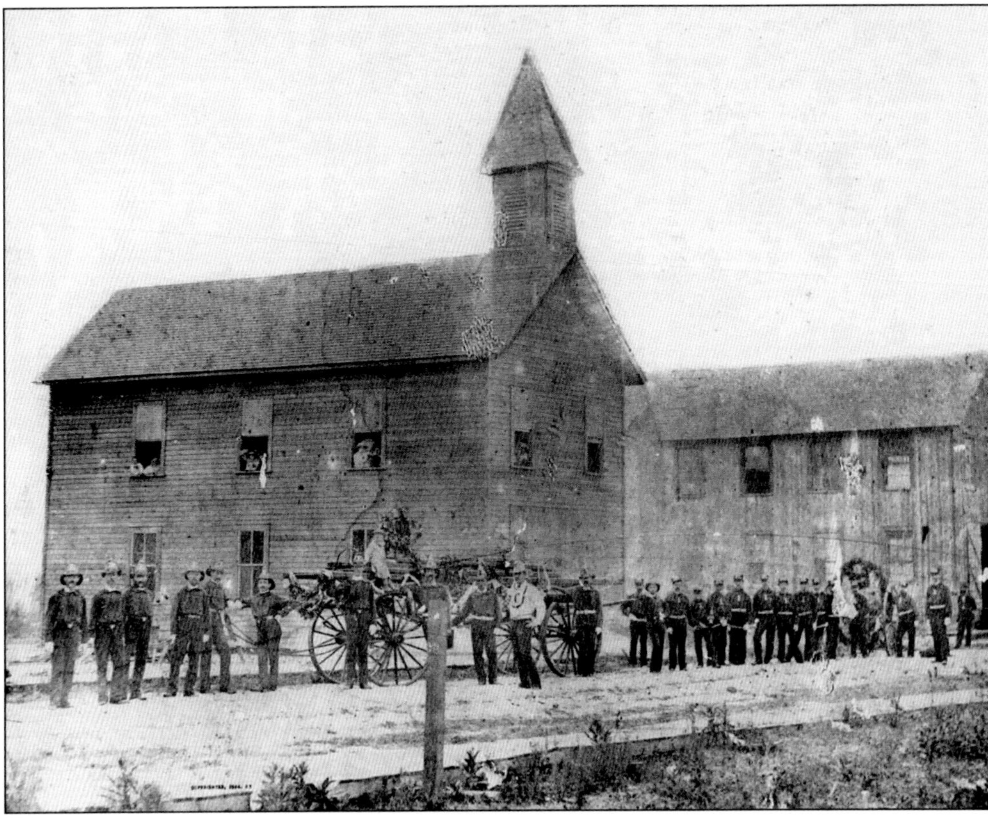

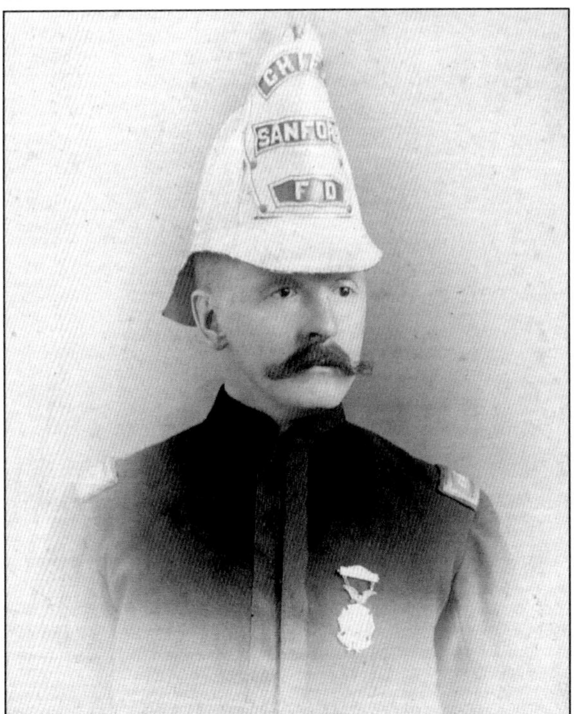

The Sanford Fire Department was established in 1873. Hook and Ladder Company #1 and Hose Company #1 were formed by the city council in 1883. The department had 35 firemen at that time. A fire station on Sanford Avenue was dedicated with a parade on January 1, 1884. The first firefighter to fall in the line of duty was Harry Ashton, who died in 1888 in a fire at the Deforest Block.

Harry Papworth came to Sanford from England. He was one of the city's first fire chiefs.

Two Sanford firemen and the department mascot posed for photographer J.C. Ensminger in 1890. The fire department dogs ran along side fire trucks to protect the horses.

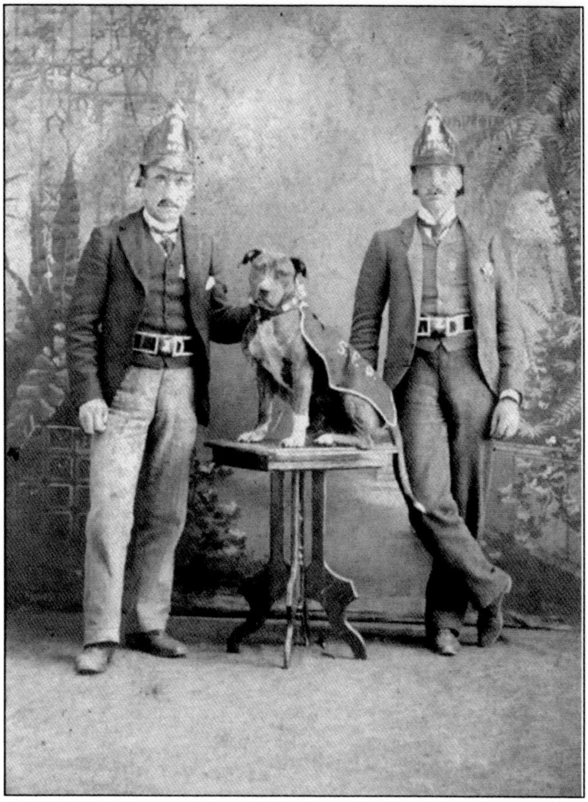

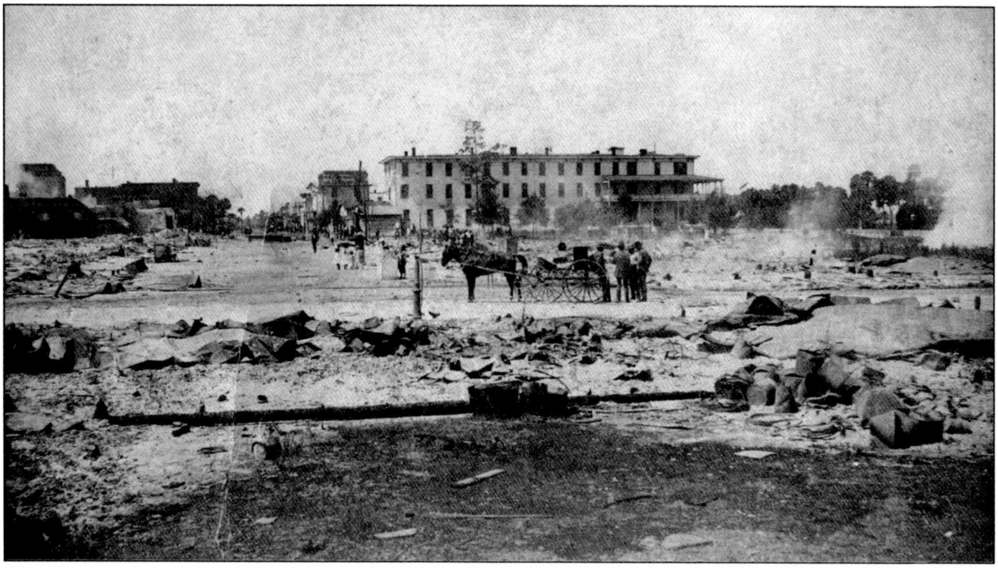

This is a view of First Street looking west after the big fire of 1887. Four blocks of Sanford's commercial district were destroyed before the fire could be contained. The fire began in Altree's Bakery on First Street in the early morning hours of September 27. The Sanford House Hotel, in the center of the photo, was saved by placing wet blankets on the roof.

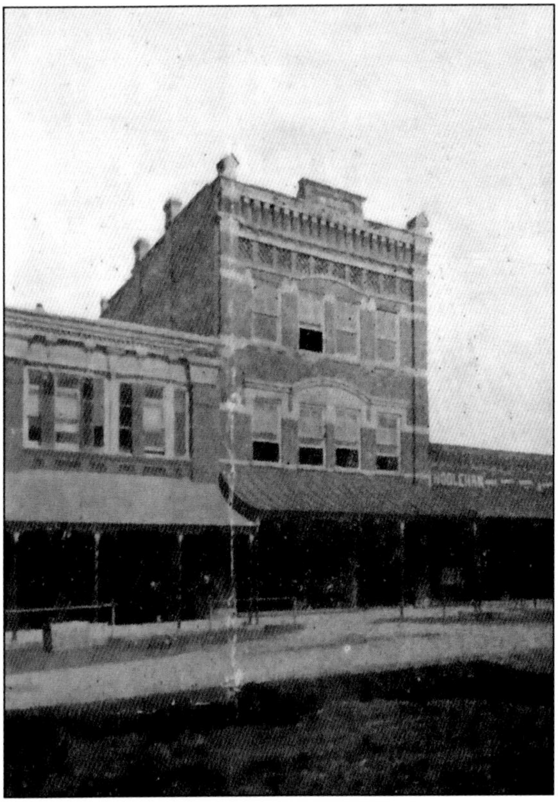

M.K. Hester and Mr. Samuel W. Shepard had this building constructed after the September 1887 fire that swept through downtown Sanford. The top floor was condemned and removed in 1928. The block served as a fire station from 1890 to 1974 and also housed the city hall, police station, and jail at one time. The building was renovated for use as a private residence in the 1990s.

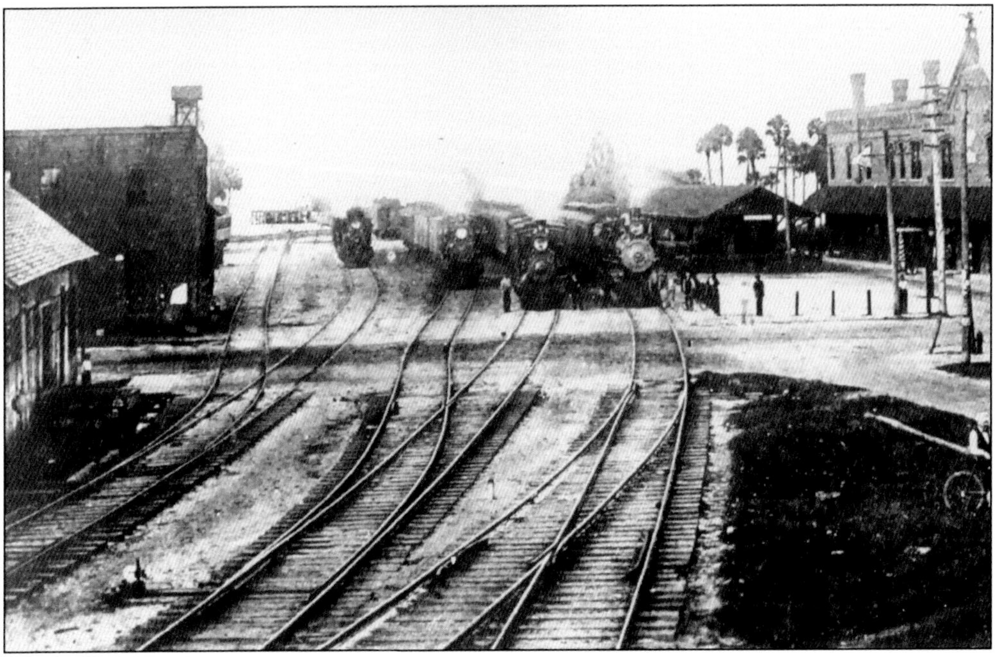

This is Railroad Way (North Oak Avenue) looking north at West First Street, c. 1912. The distant buildings are the South Florida Railroad Depot and Plant Investment Company (PICO) offices and shops built in 1887. The Hill Hardware building appears in the right foreground.

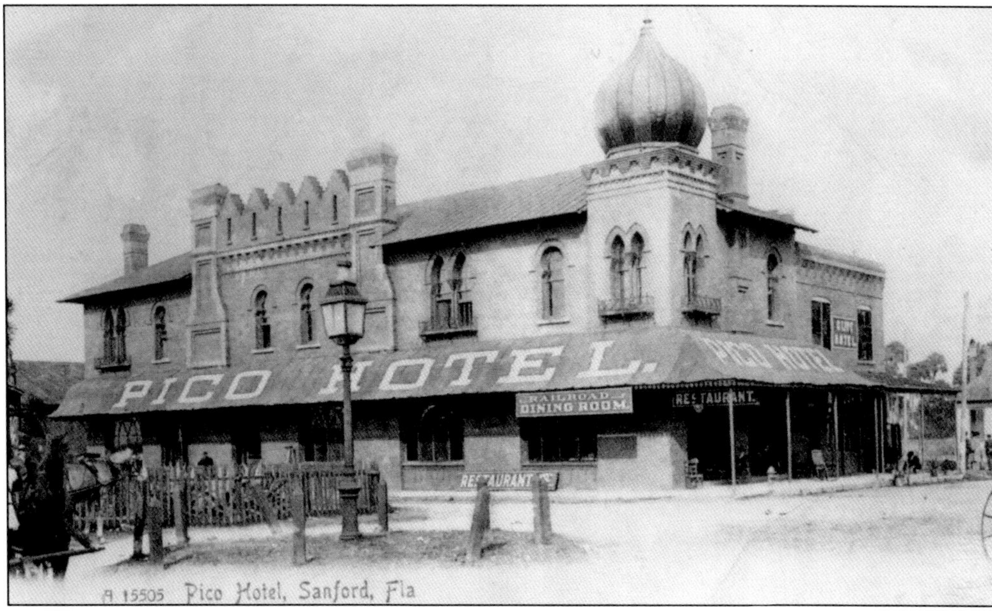

In 1887, the Plant Investment Company (PICO) built a hotel, a railroad depot, and an office building on what is now North Oak Avenue but was then known as Railroad Way. The fancy brick hotel with Turkish design served the railroad and steamboat passengers. The restaurant was run for many years by the Takach family. By 1900, the Plant System controlled all railroads entering Sanford.

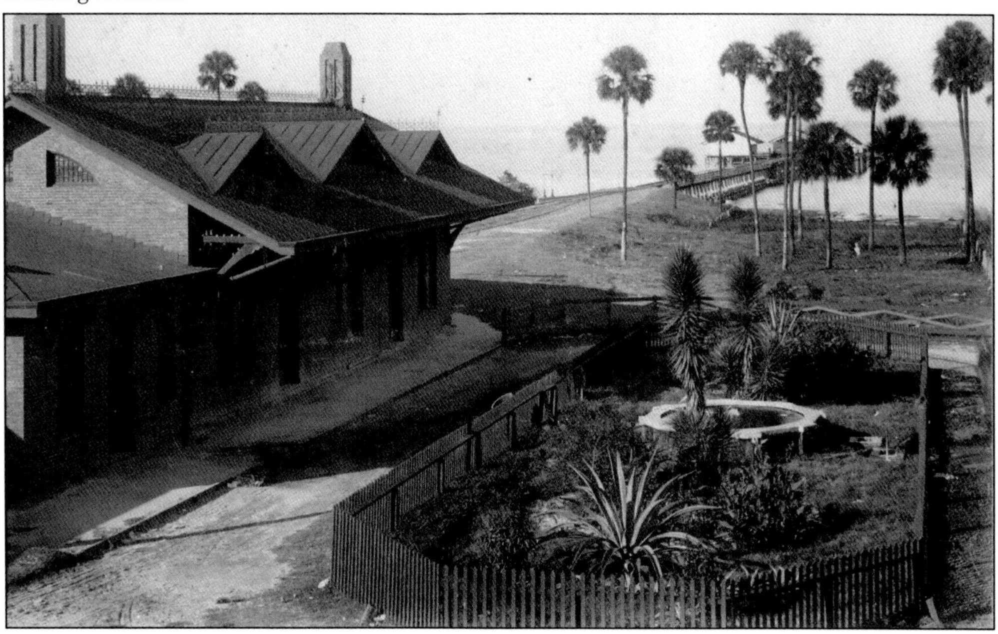

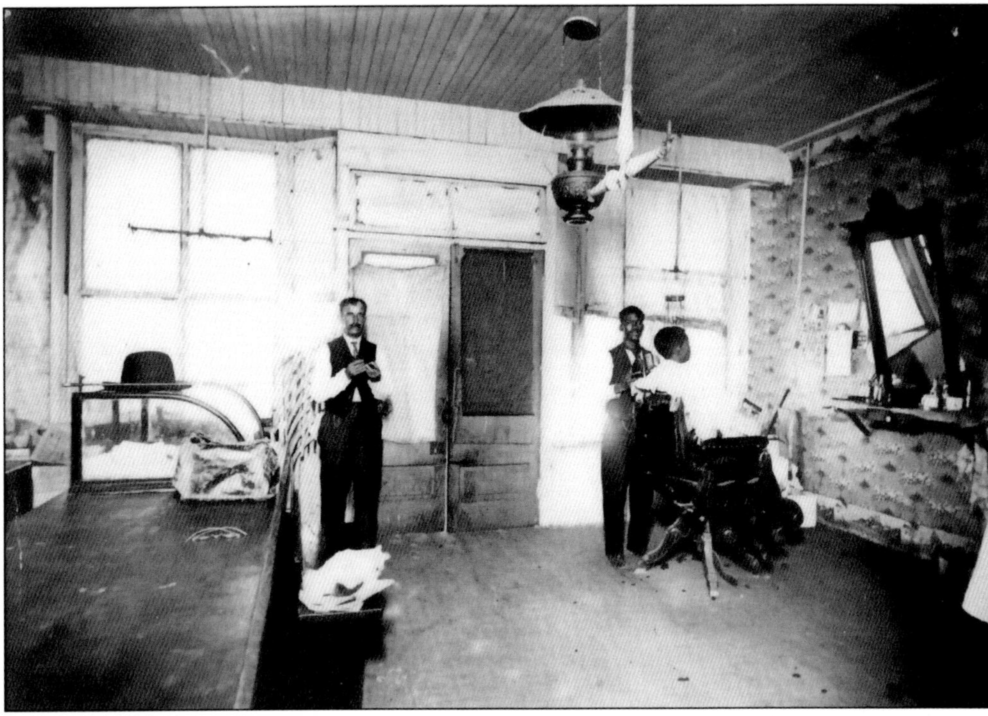

Frank Eaverly was an African-American barber with a shop located at 110 Sanford Avenue at Commercial. His shop also repaired watches.

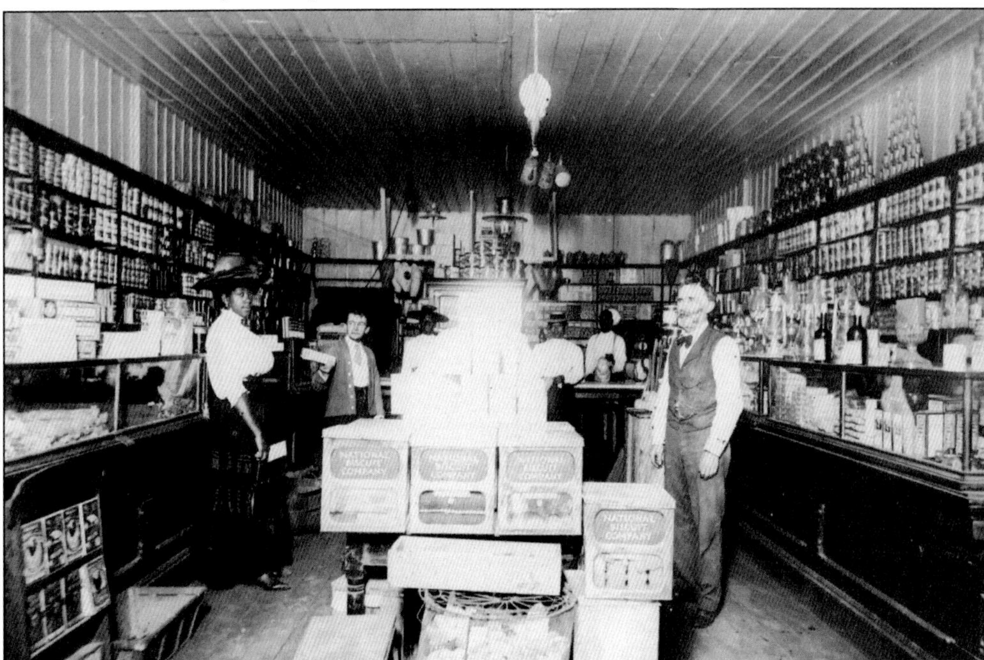

Sanford Avenue was a major commercial and residential street for the black community for much of Sanford's history. J.B. Williams's store, shown here in 1914, was located at the corner of Third Street and Sanford Avenue.

Rev. John Hurston was pastor of Zion Hope Baptist Church in Georgetown in 1910. His daughter, Zora Neale Hurston, spent part of her youth in Sanford and returned to the city in the 1930s. She wrote her first published novel, *Jonah's Gourd Vine*, while living in Georgetown.

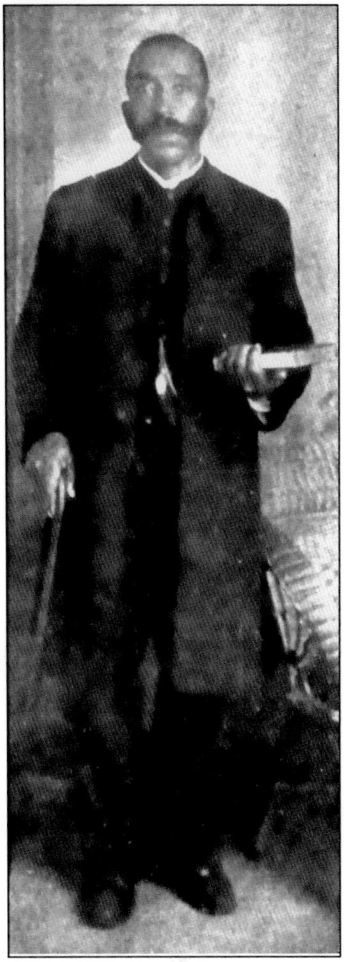

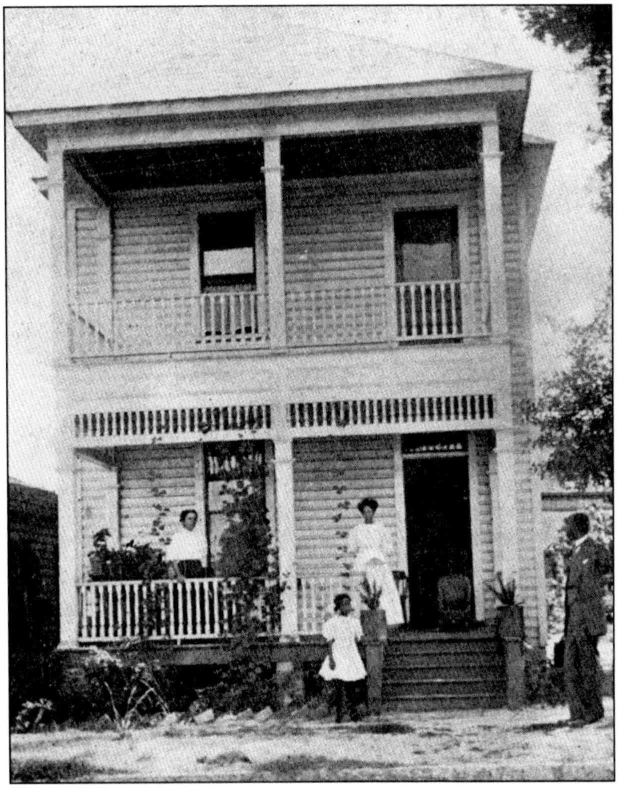

Henry Sanford created the African-American neighborhood of Georgetown to foster the growth of a black middle class in Sanford during the era of Reconstruction. The "Harris Nest," the home of Frank and Montez Harris on Second Street and Cypress Avenue, was enlarged over the years as the couple prospered.

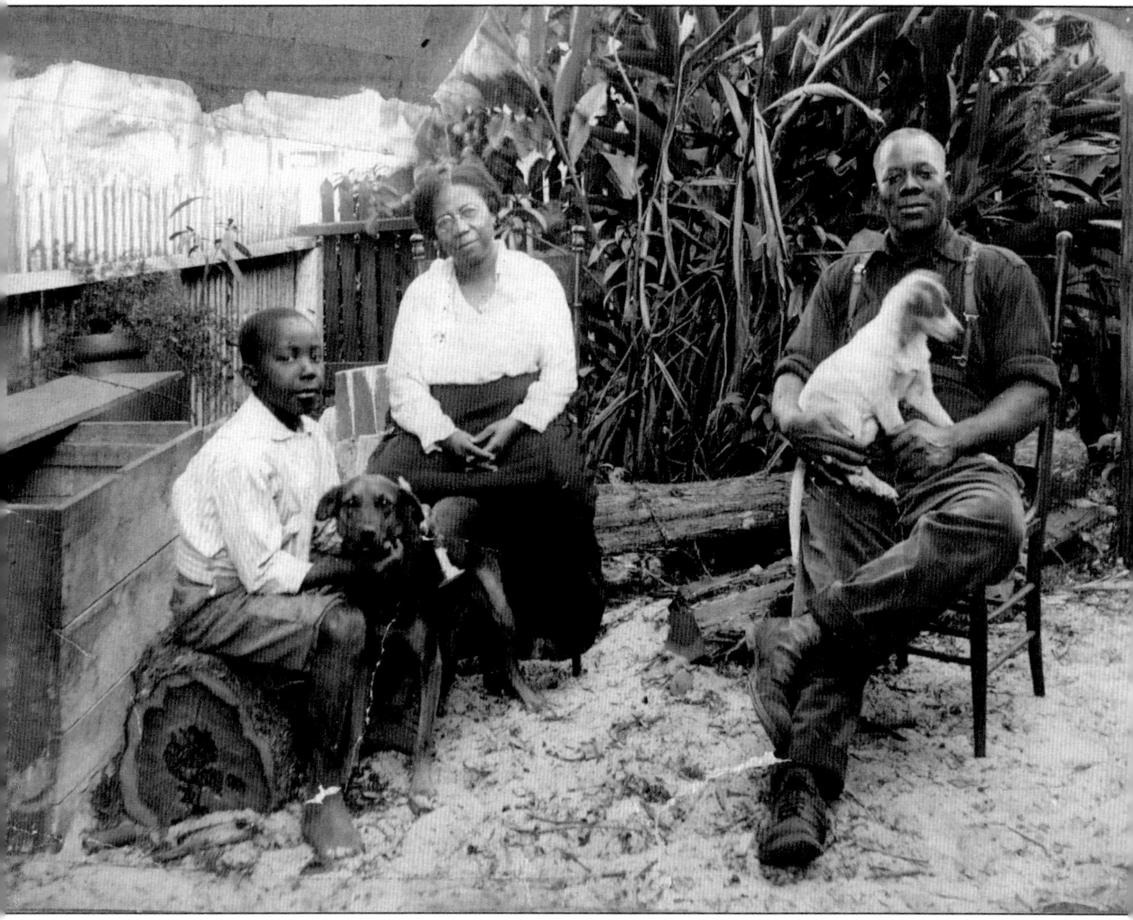

William B. Boykin was the postmaster of the African-American town of Goldsboro, incorporated in 1891. This photograph of Boykin, his wife Rosa, and his son Raleigh was taken in the back yard of their home on Thirteenth Street. Goldsboro was annexed by the city of Sanford in 1911.

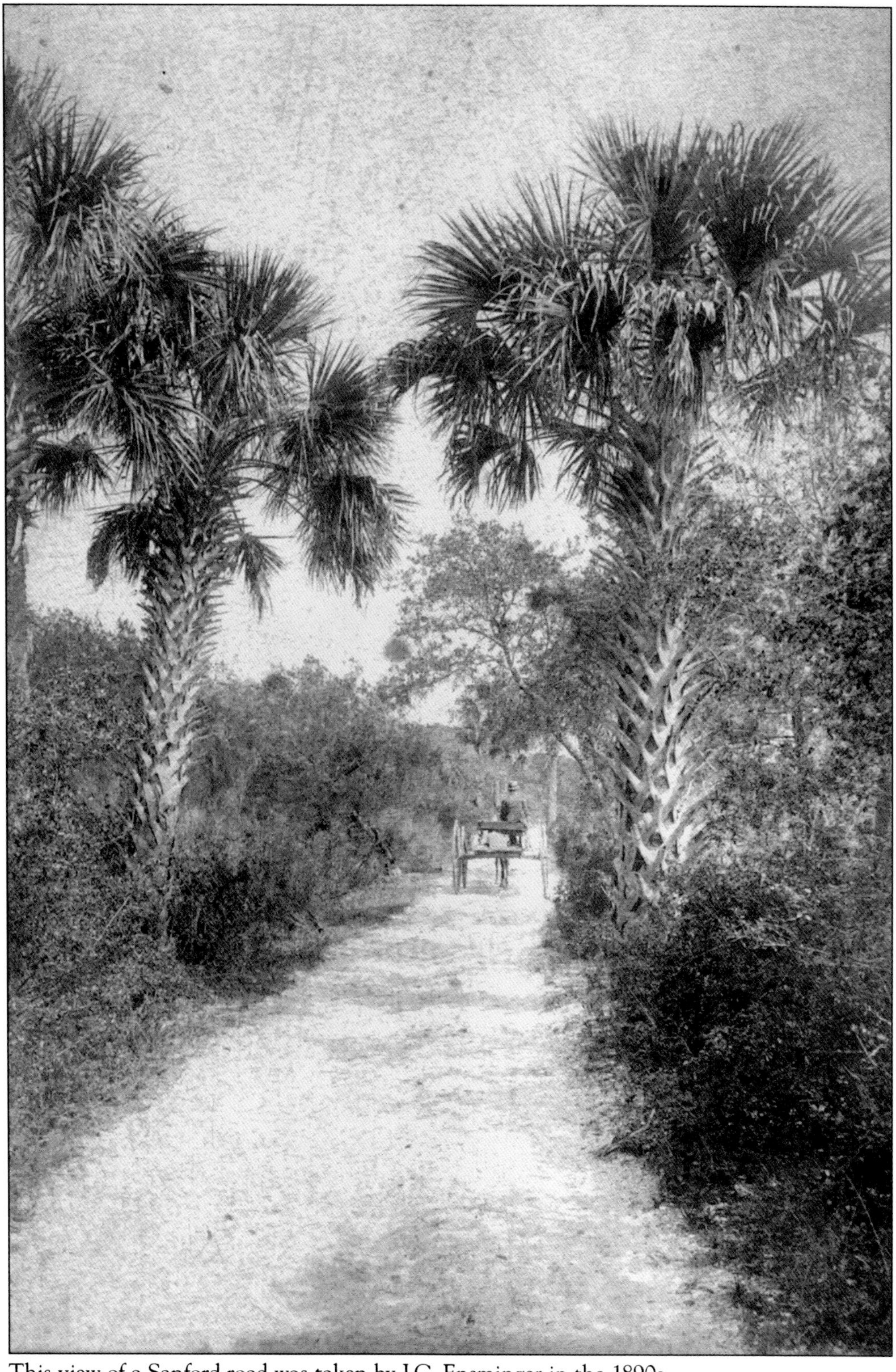

This view of a Sanford road was taken by J.C. Ensminger in the 1890s.

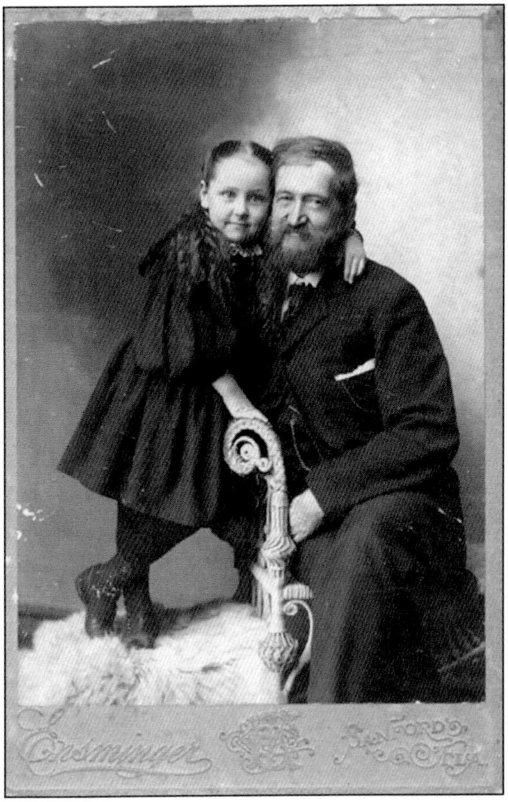

Photographer Jefferson Clay Ensminger was born in Ohio and came to Sanford in 1885. He was well known for his landscape and flower photography. Henry Plant, who owned buildings near the Ensminger studio, was so impressed with his work that he made him the official photographer of the Plant Railway System.

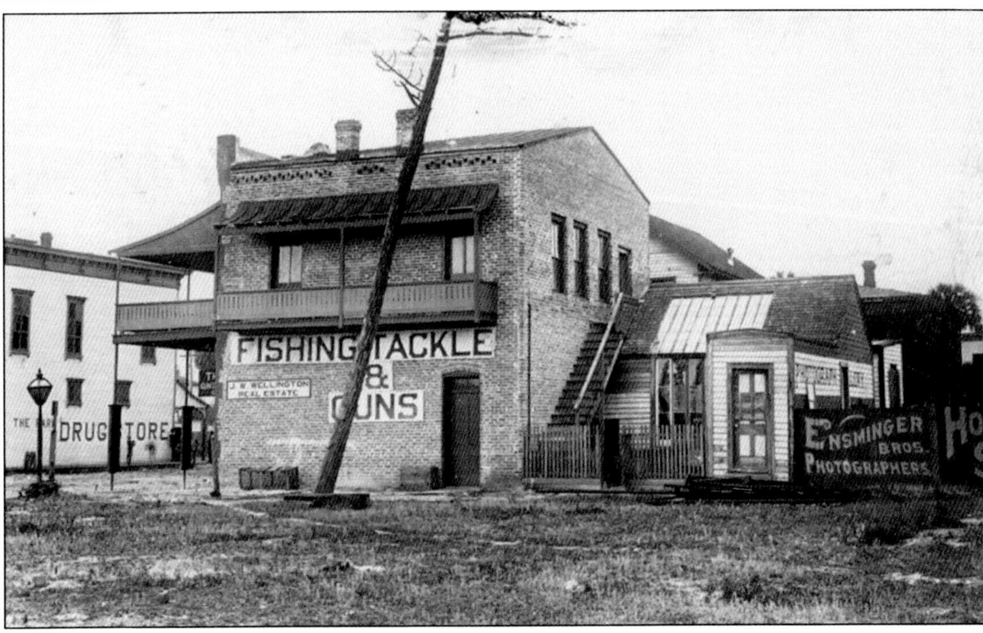

Pictured here is Ensminger Brothers photography studio, c. 1890, located on the west side of North Park Avenue. The Ensminger Block was built about 1888 by J.C. Ensminger. The business was known as Ensminger Bros., although his brother, J.M. Ensminger, had his studio in Independence, Iowa.

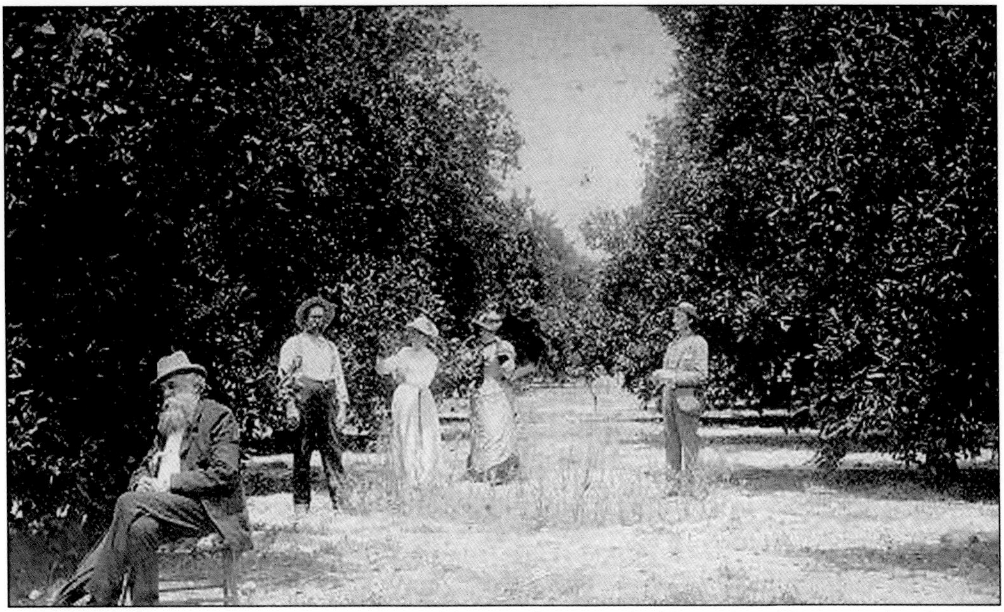

Henry Sanford spent his last months of life at Belair. He died May 21, 1891 immediately after arriving in Healing Springs, Virginia to undergo treatment for kidney disease. His heir Harry, pictured on the right, died of a lung ailment in October of that same year.

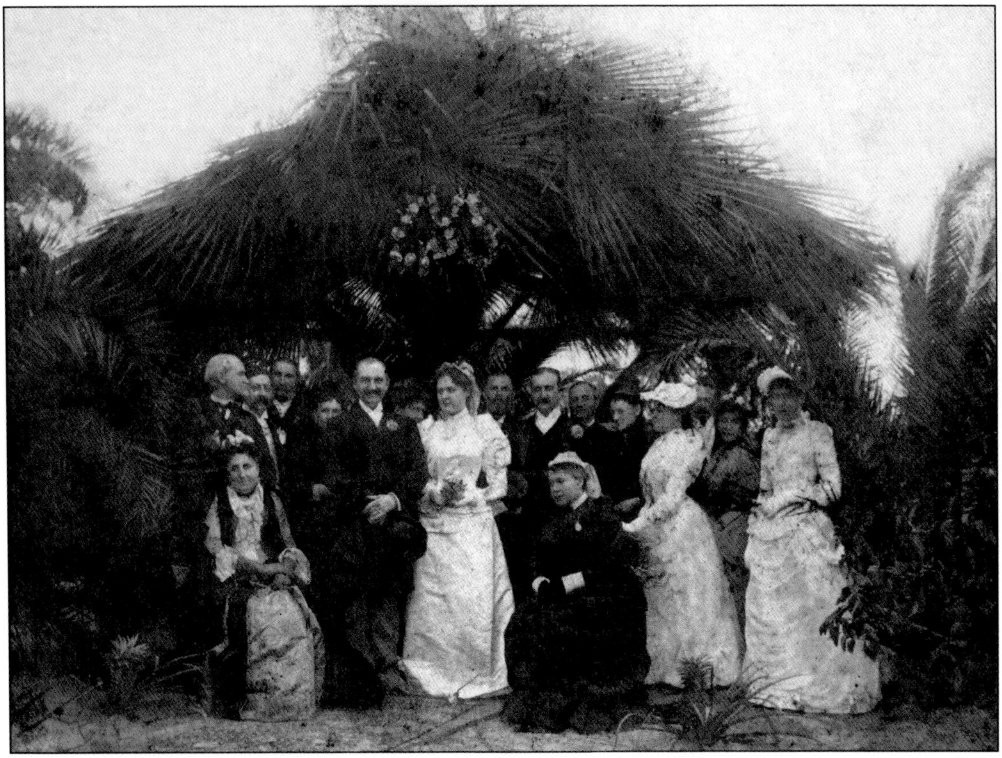

The wedding reception of Ethel and John Sanford was held at Belair after a ceremony at Holy Cross. John, a distant cousin of Henry Sanford, acquired Belair from his mother-in-law and sold it to the Chase brothers in 1902.

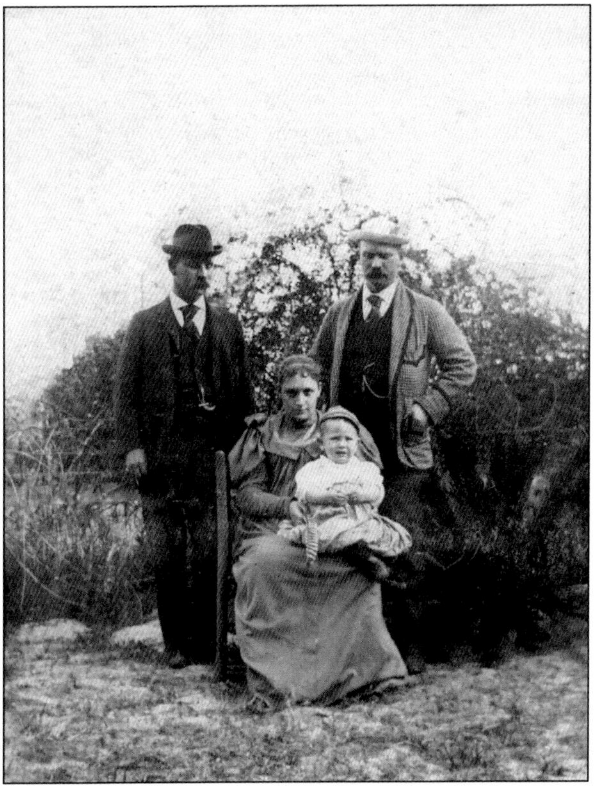

In 1878, Sydney O. Chase came to Florida from Philadelphia after reading about Sanford in *Scribner's Magazine*. Joshua C. Chase joined his brother in 1884 and they formed Chase and Co. This Ensminger photograph shows Sydney on the left and Joshua on the right with his wife, Jeanie Whitner Chase, and baby.

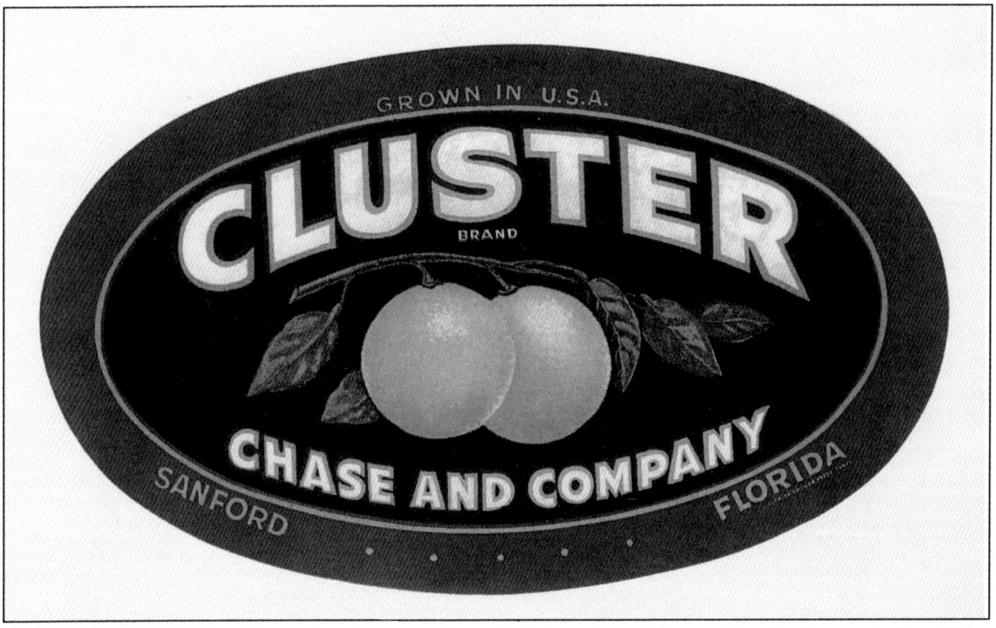

On April 1, 1902 the Chase brothers purchased Belair from Henry Sanford's son-in-law. The company became a leader and innovator in citrus and celery. The company still exists today as Sunniland Corporation which was named for Chase and Co.'s top brand of produce.

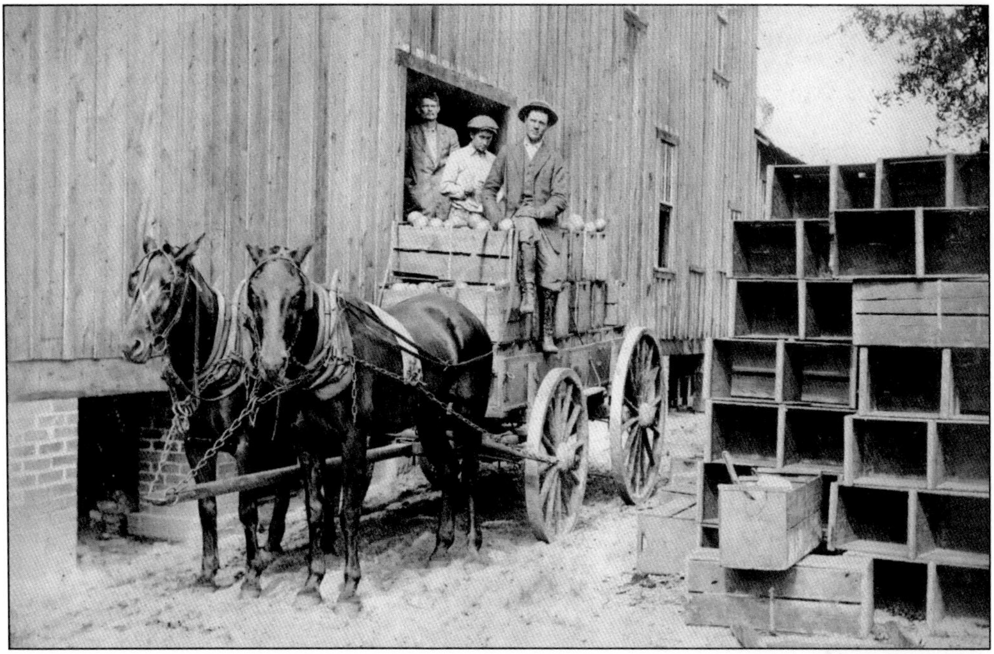

Citrus was brought to the Chase and Co. packinghouse in field crates. It was then sorted and packed for shipment. The fruit was packed under different labels according to its quality. Henry Sanford introduced the concept of shipping premium fruit as gifts. This fruit was individually wrapped in tissue before being boxed.

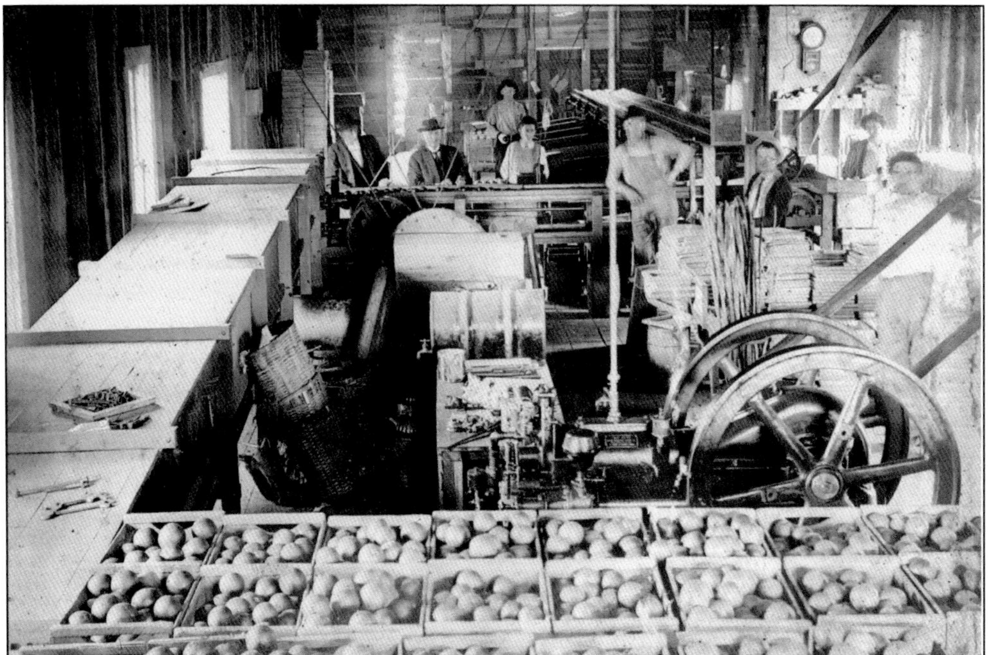

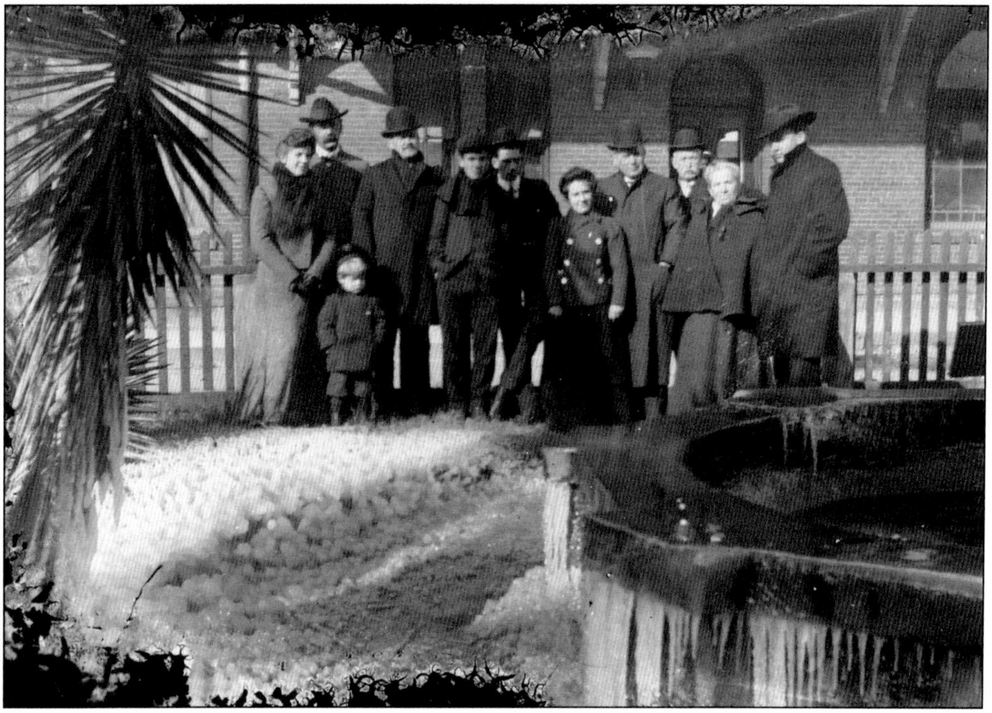

In the winter of 1894–1895, a series of freezes destroyed the citrus trees in Central Florida. Sanford growers began to search for a different crop and settled upon celery.

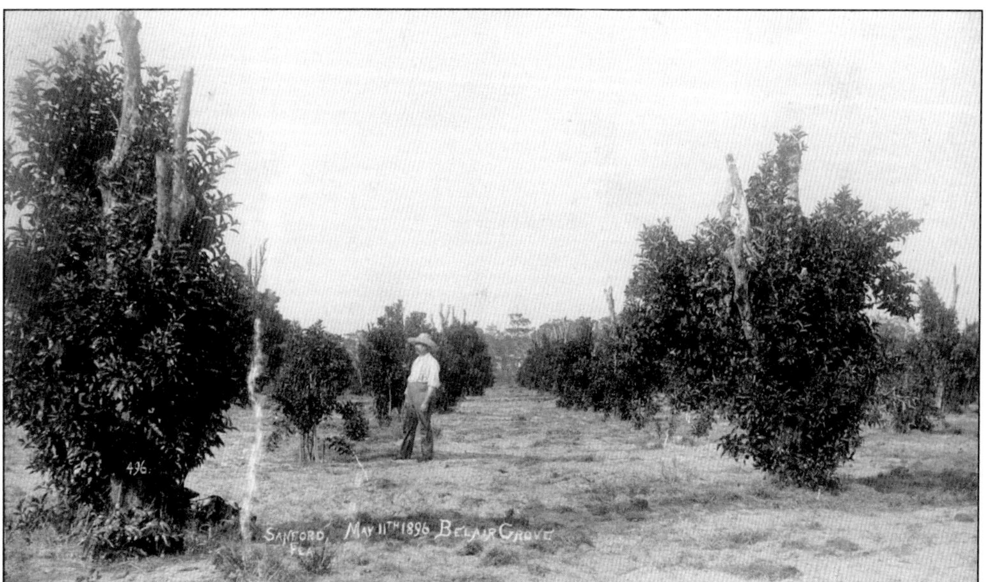

After the Great Freeze, it fell to Donald Houston, grove manager, to bring back the severely damaged trees at Belair.

Three

The Celery City

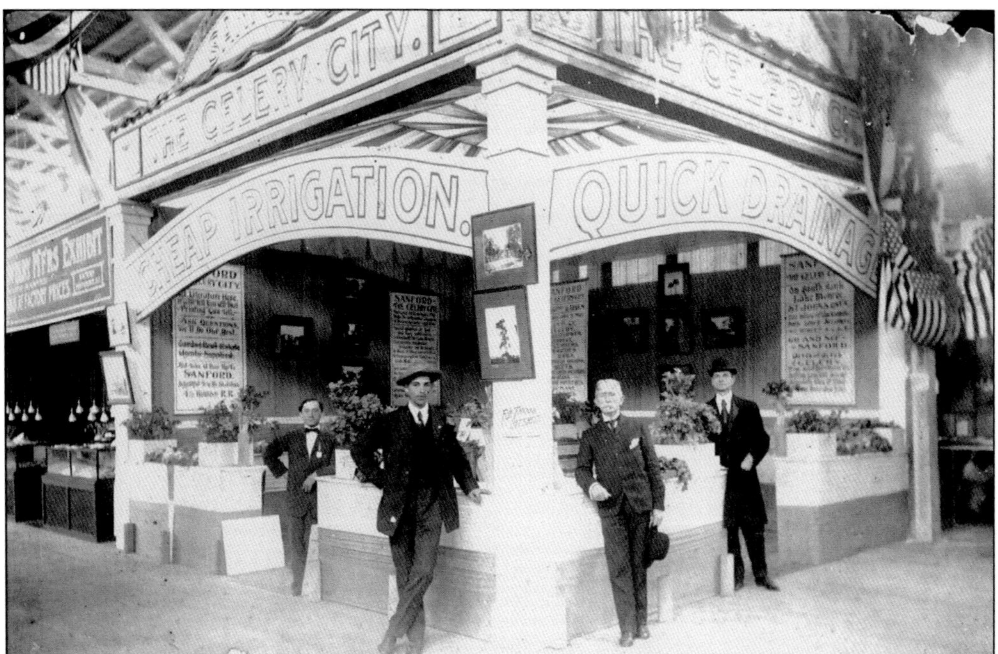

By 1908, Sanford was becoming famous for the success of its celery and was known as "The Celery City." Sanford farmers were great boosters of their town. Elaborate displays were created for fairs and agricultural exhibitions.

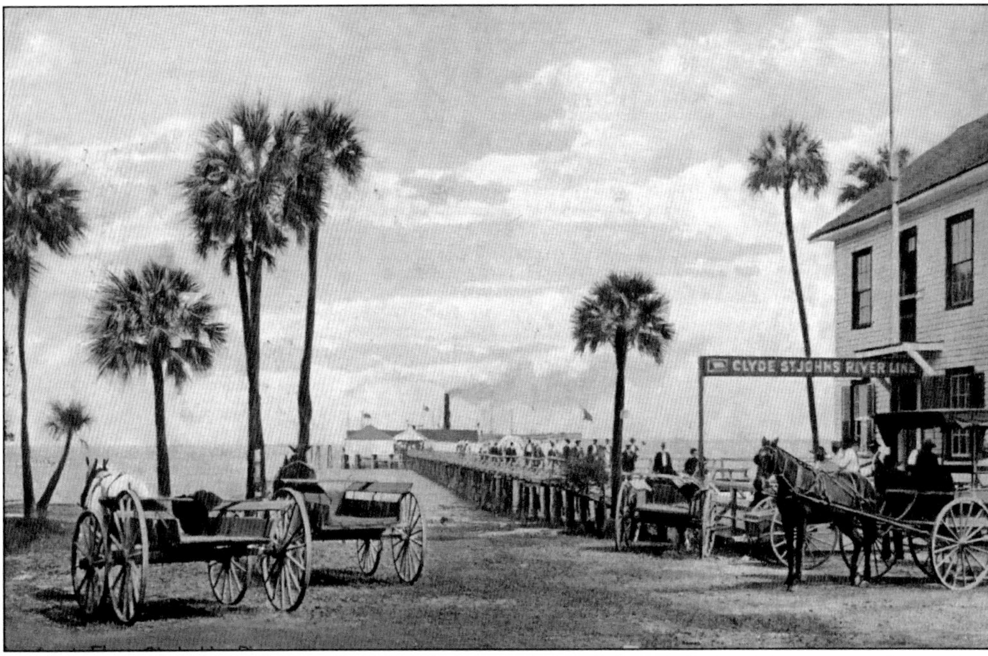

The Clyde Line steamboat company's dock went far out into Lake Monroe at the end of Palmetto Avenue. Water hyacinths would sometimes float in towards shore, clogging the area around the dock.

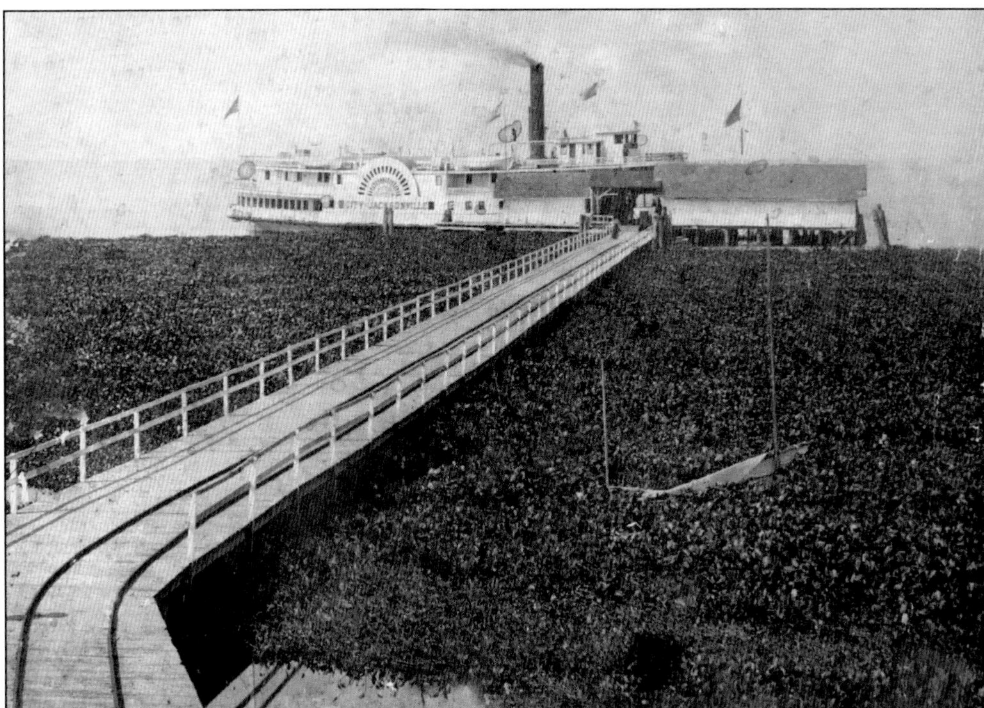

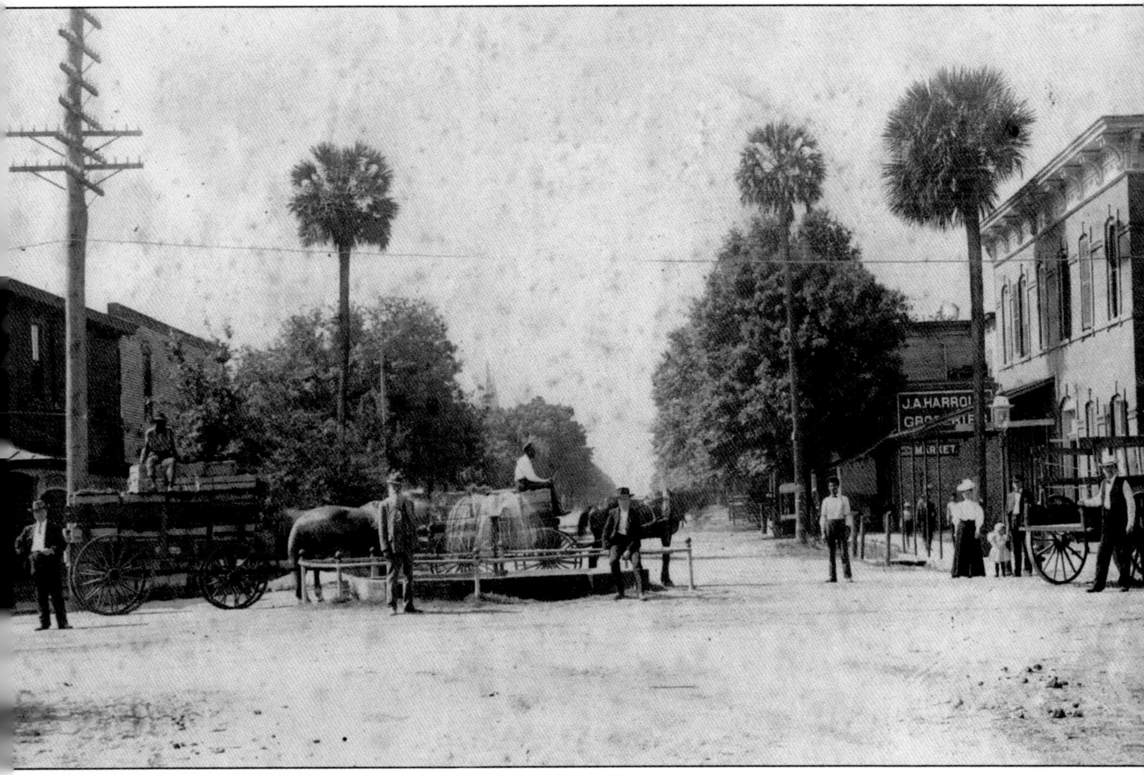

The fountain at Park Avenue and First Street in 1900 took advantage of the free flowing artesian wells under Sanford. The Lyman Bank, visible on the right, was the first brick building in Sanford and was constructed in 1884. Rollins College was chartered in an upstairs room.

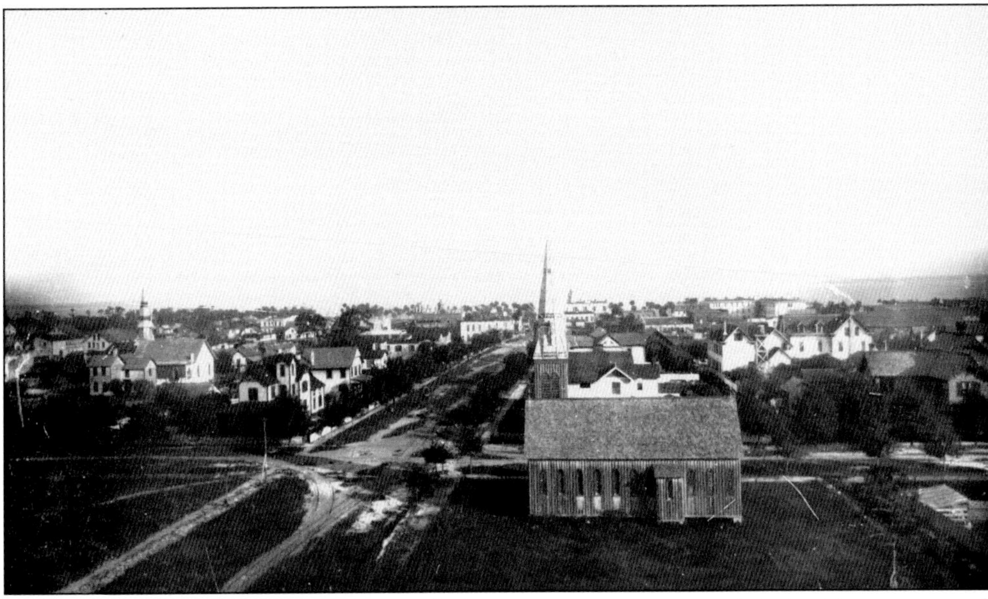

When Sanford's street plan was designed, the streets running towards Lake Monroe were all named avenues and were given the names of local trees with a few exceptions. Park Avenue, shown here, was planned as a major thoroughfare with many of the largest churches and homes. French Avenue was named for Dr. Seth French who is said to have cut the road through to the lake with his military sword.

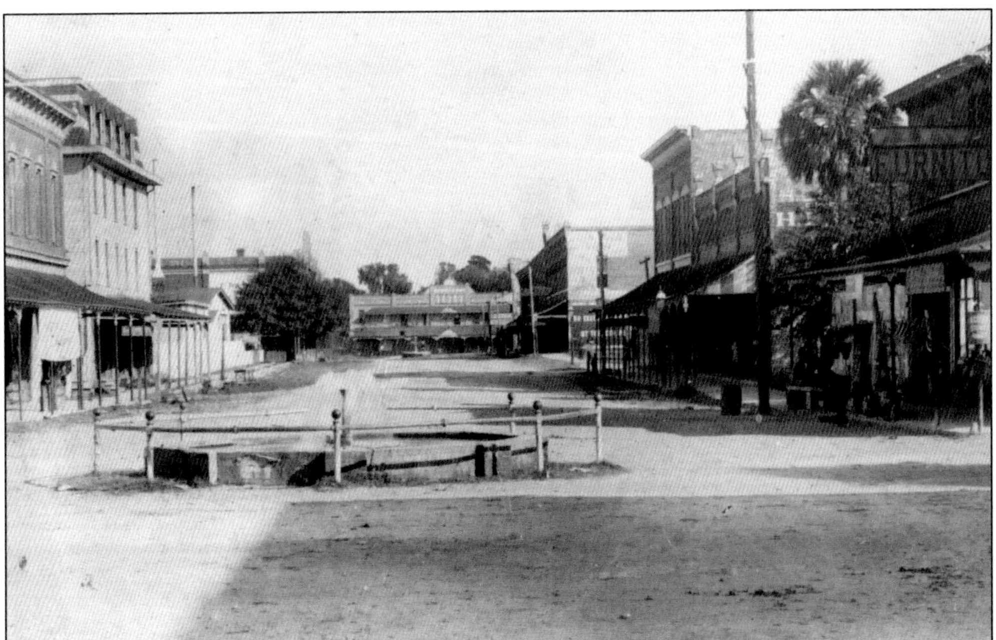

In 1900, First Street ended at Sanford Avenue. The street was not extended to the east until the completion of the bulkhead in the mid 1920s.

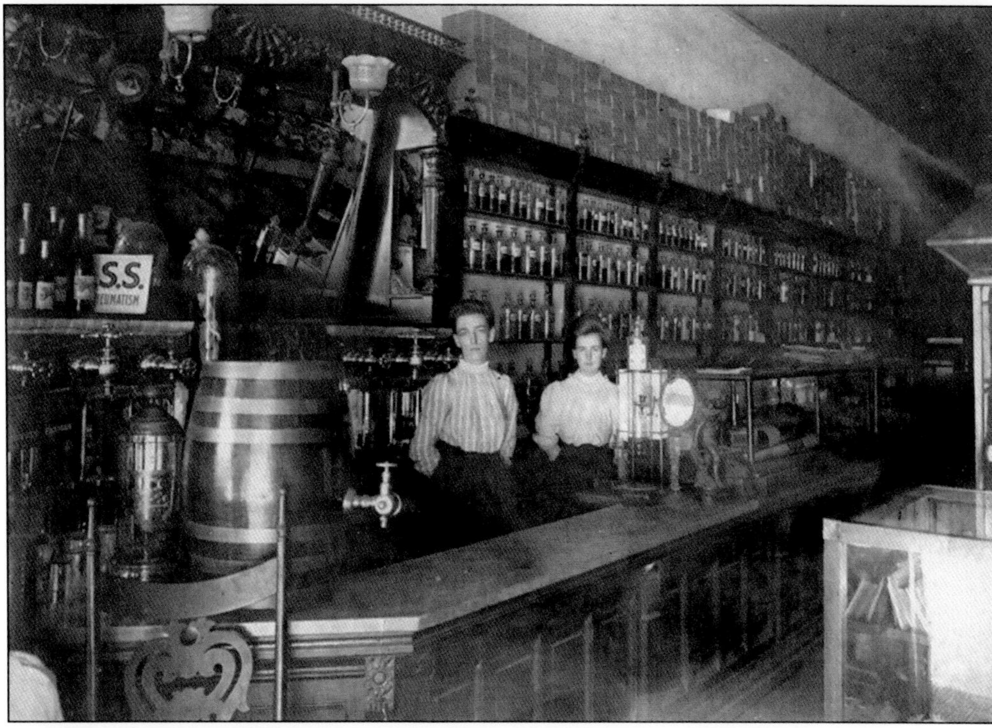

In 1900, Alma and Mabel Saint worked behind the counter in William "Doc" Aldridge's drugstore on West First Street. Aldridge came to Sanford in 1878 and was the pharmacist at Plant System Hospital #1.

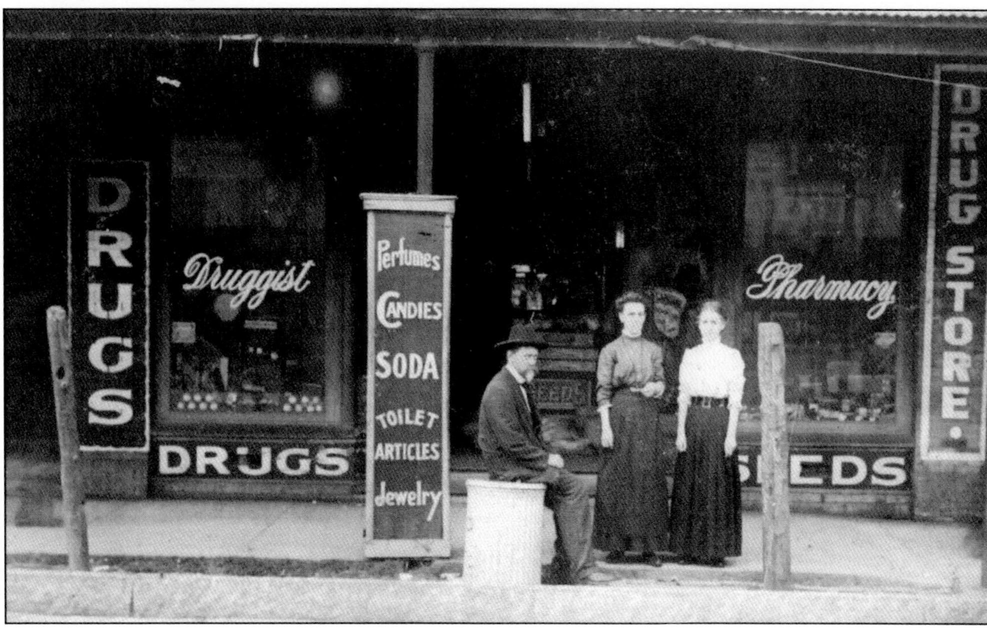

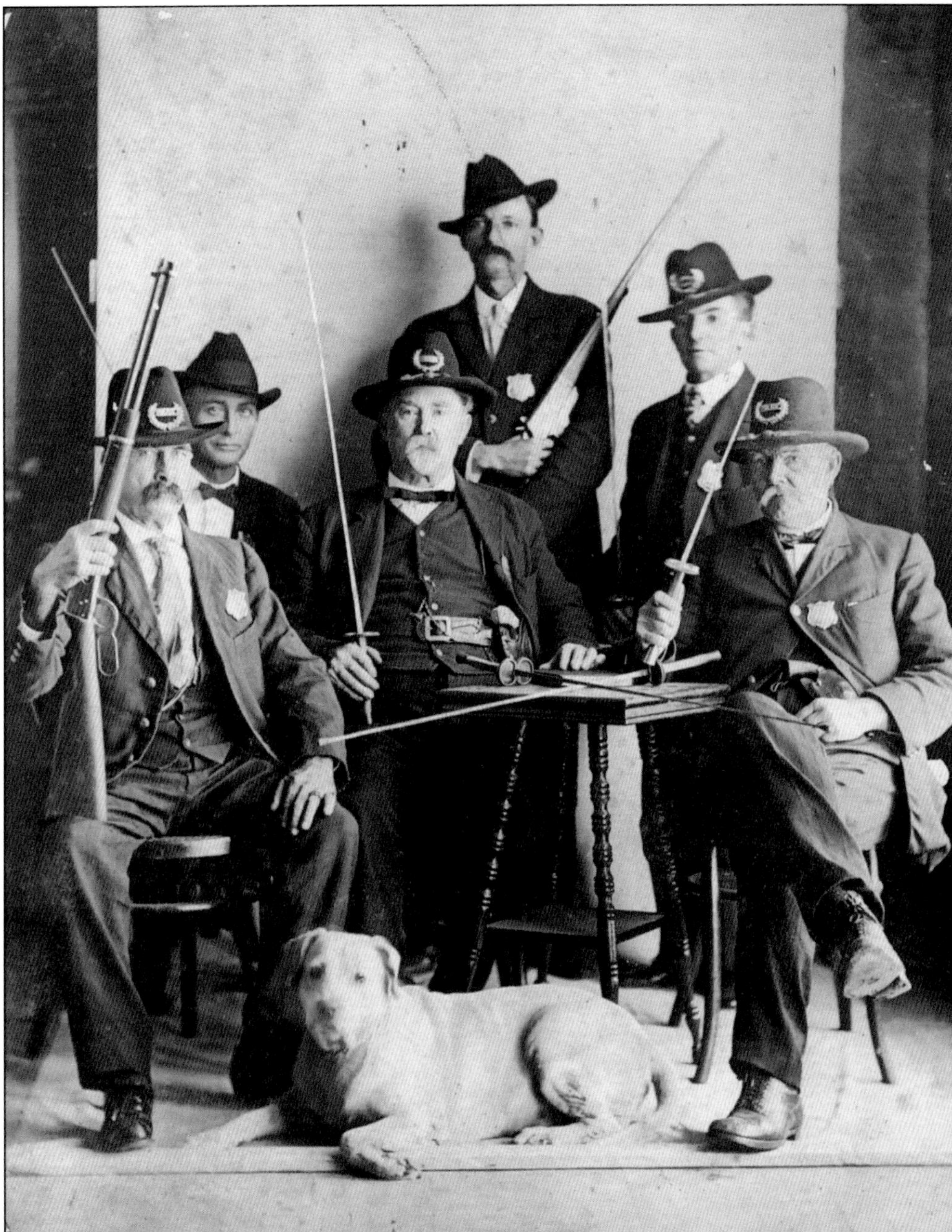

Marshal William Green Smith, seen here in the center, and the Sanford Police Department were well equipped to fight crime in 1900.

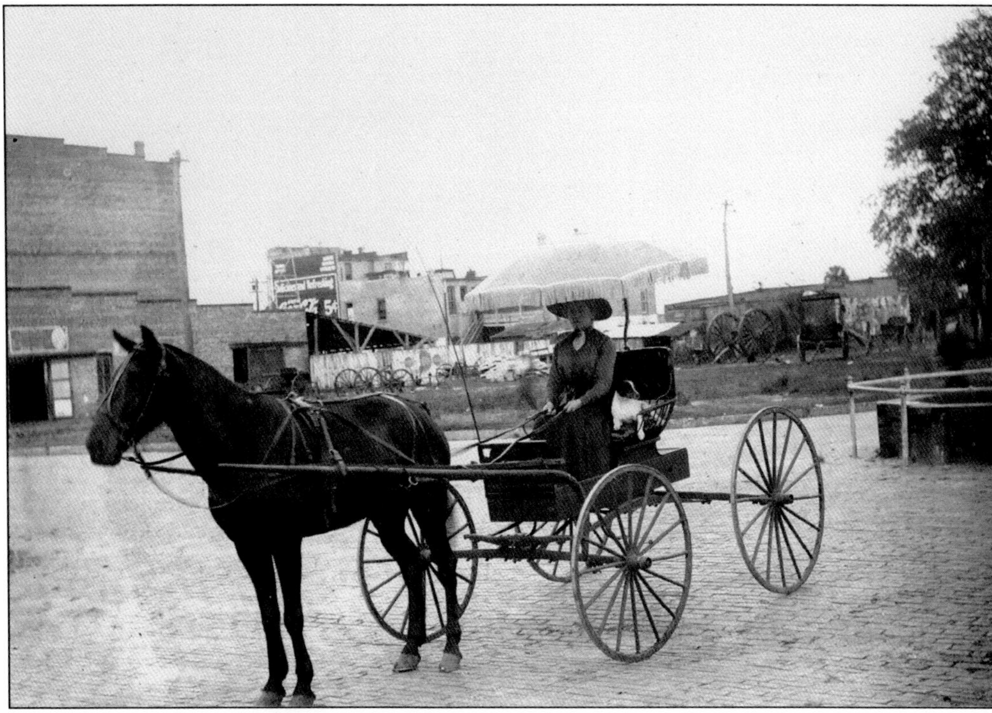

Livery stables were an important business downtown in 1900 when wagons and buggies were common. E.E. Brady had a livery stable with a large side yard on Palmetto Avenue near Second Street. A fountain fed by an artesian well stood in the center of this nearby intersection and was used to water the horses. (Courtesy of Sophie Shoemaker.)

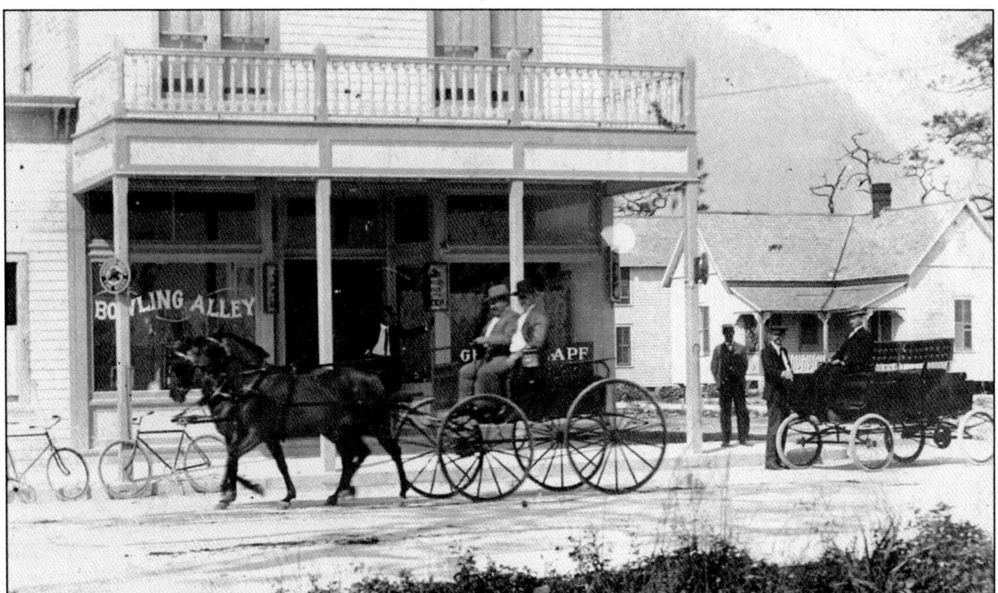

Early automobiles like this motor buggy began to appear in Sanford at the turn of the 20th century. George Zapf's store on Park Avenue promoted Anheuser-Busch beer, bottled locally by Joseph Zapf. (Courtesy of Sophie Shoemaker.)

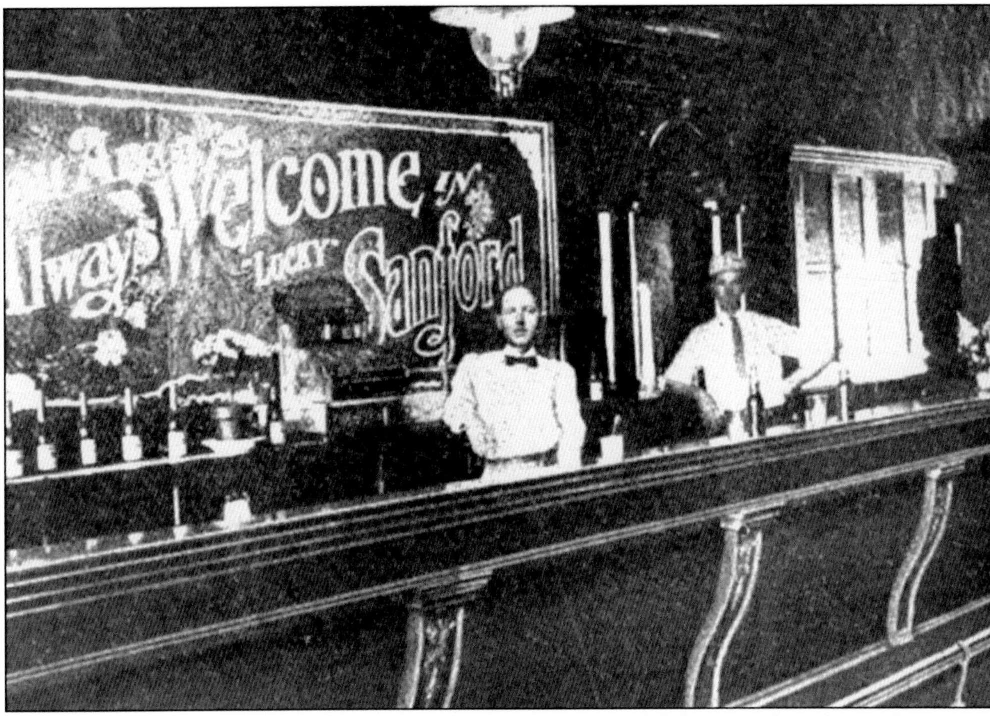

There was a time when a fine locally-made cigar could be purchased in downtown Sanford. Among the brands manufactured by J.J. Mauser in 1910 were "Lucky Sanford" and "Banker's Choice."

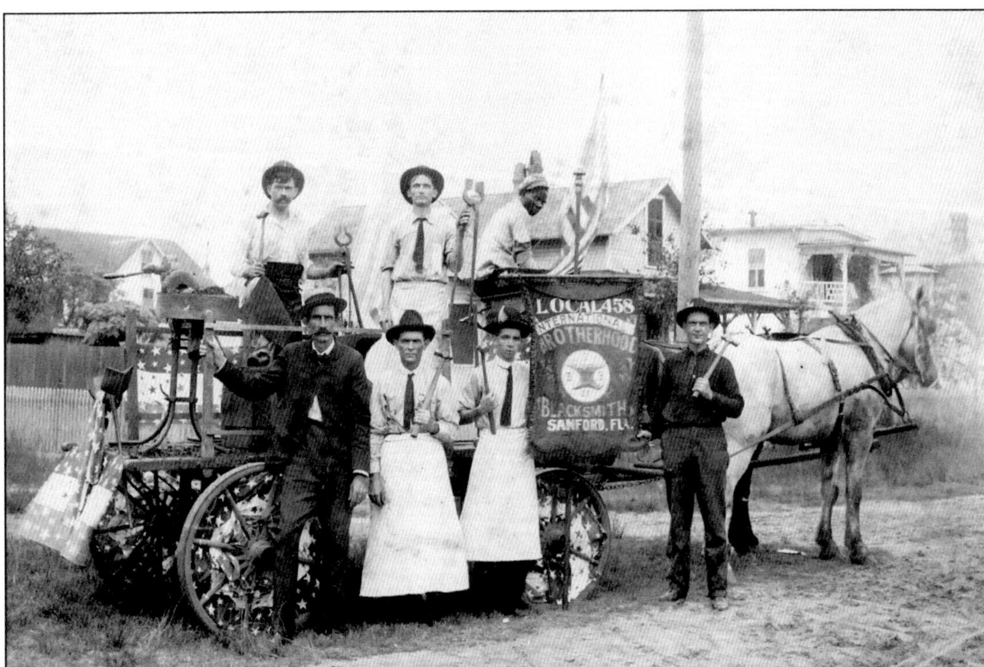

Parades were popular events in Sanford. Groups such as the local Brotherhood of Blacksmiths would elaborately decorate wagons and later automobiles. (Courtesy of Sophie Shoemaker.)

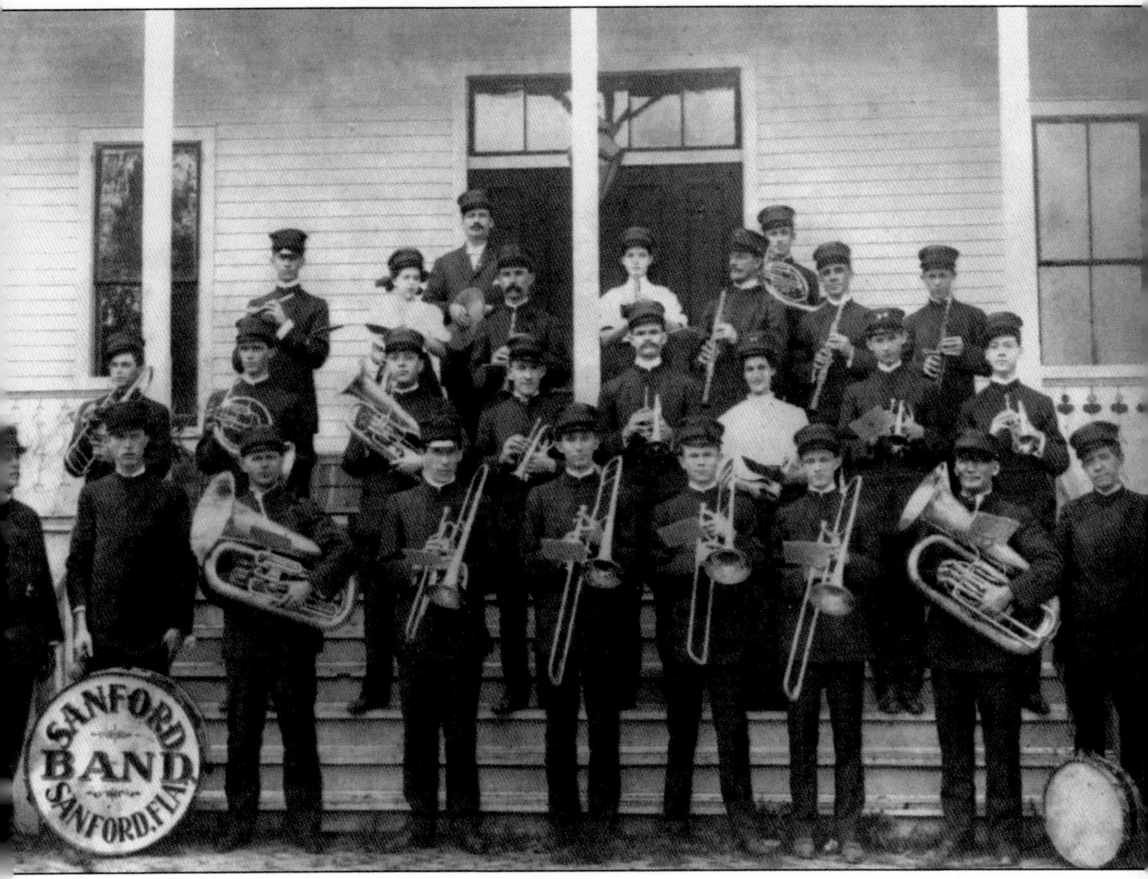

The Sanford City Band as seen in this 1907 photograph was a Stumon family business. Bandmaster James Monroe Stumon is on the far left and his daughters Jessie, Junnie, and Jossie are in the second and third rows.

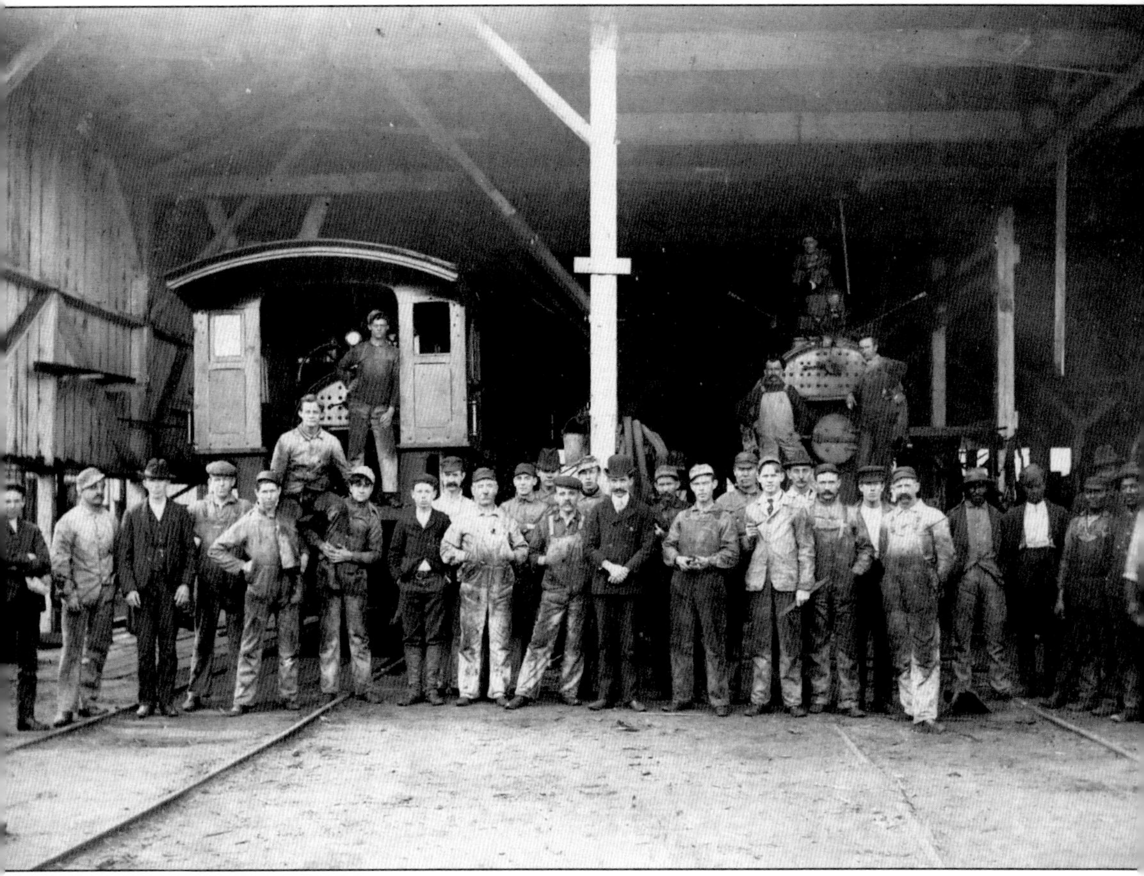

The Atlantic Coast Line railroad shops were located on West Seventh Street in 1910, when this photograph was taken.

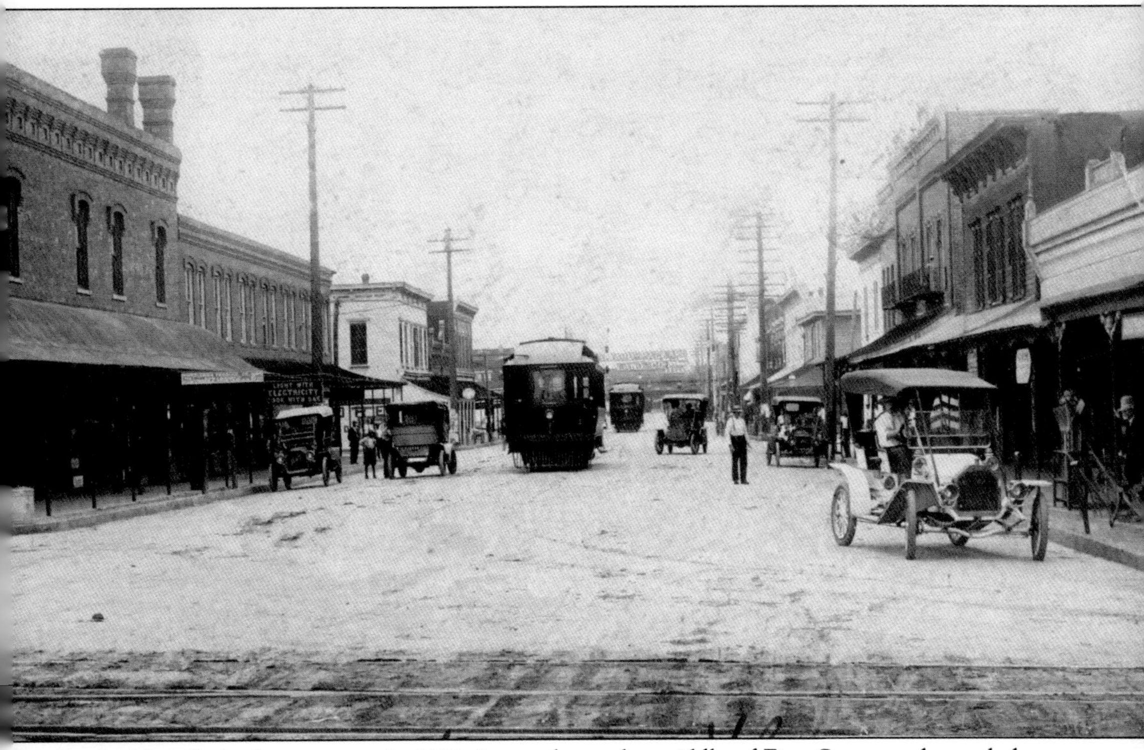

Sanford briefly had a streetcar in 1910. It ran down the middle of First Street and traveled to the outlying farm communities.

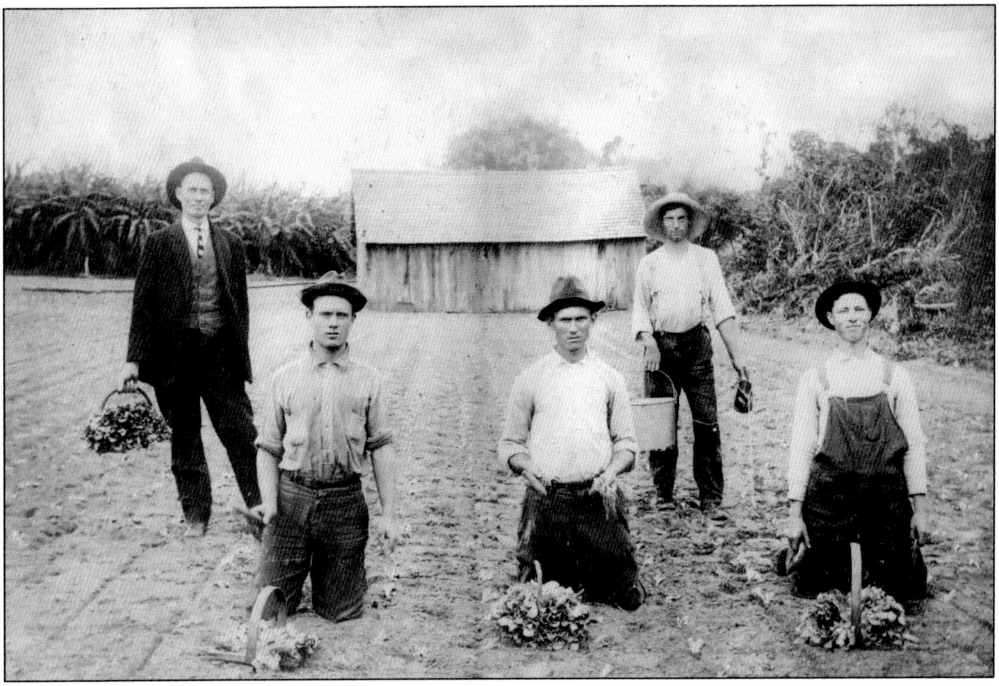

Celery was planted by crews of laborers crawling on their hands and knees to set each plant individually. A mechanical setter was developed in the 1930s but it still required the human touch.

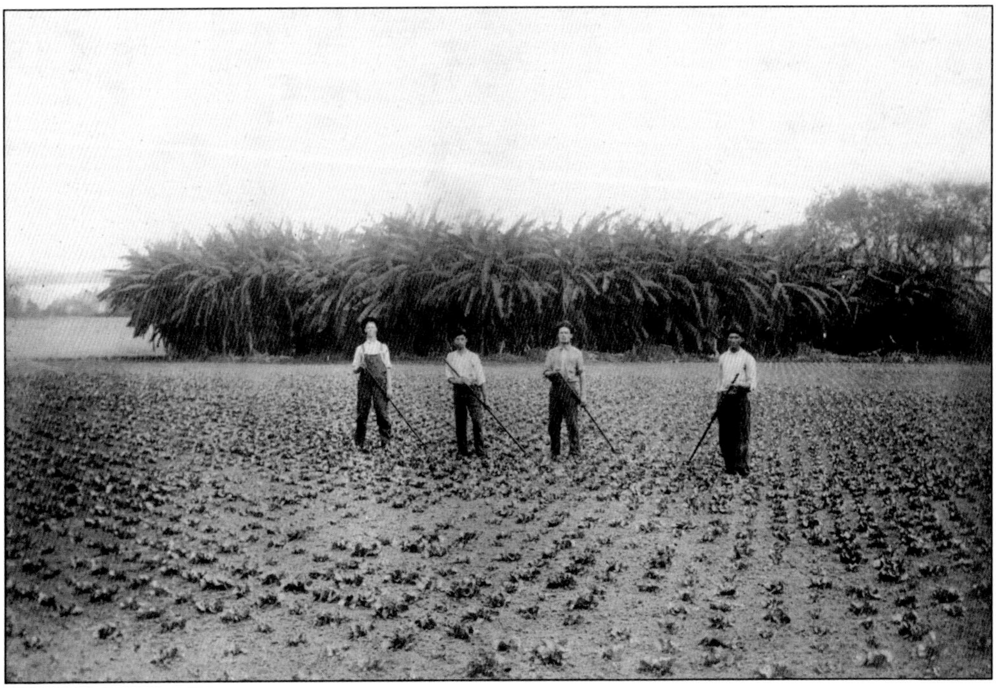

Some Sanford farmers used banana plants as wind breaks as shown in this photograph of a lettuce field.

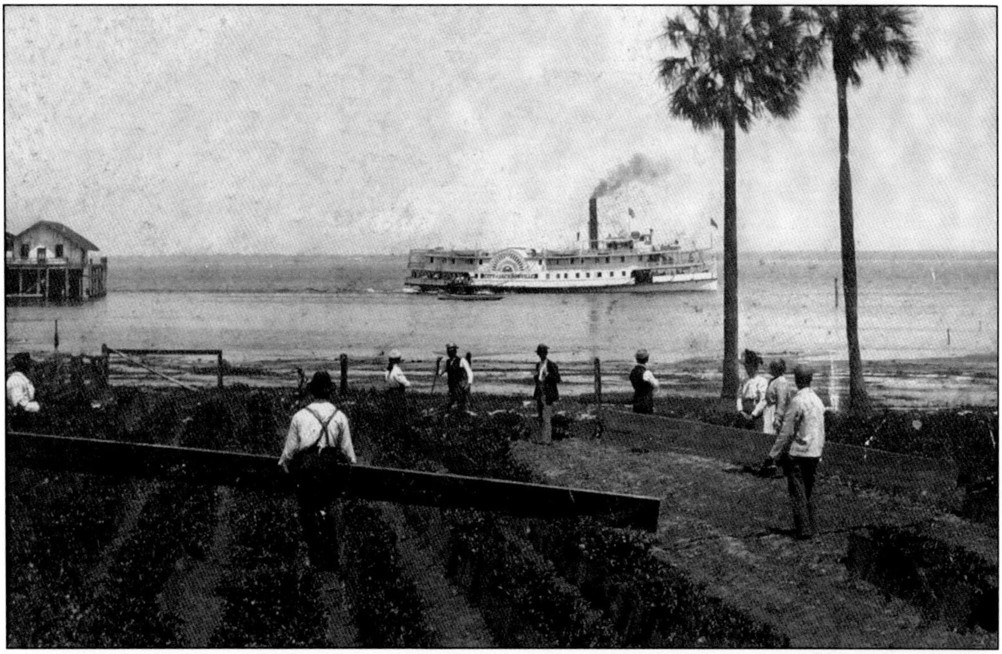

"Boarding up" celery involved securing long cypress planks along the rows of plants. With sunlight blocked out, this bleaching produced a tender celery.

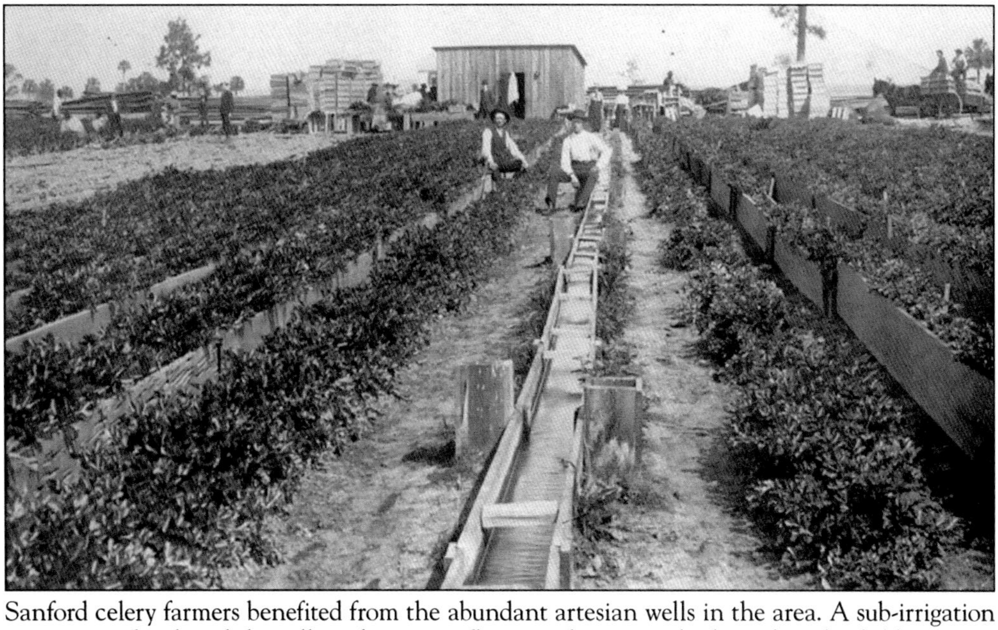

Sanford celery farmers benefited from the abundant artesian wells in the area. A sub-irrigation system was developed that allowed water to flow evenly across tiles buried in the fields.

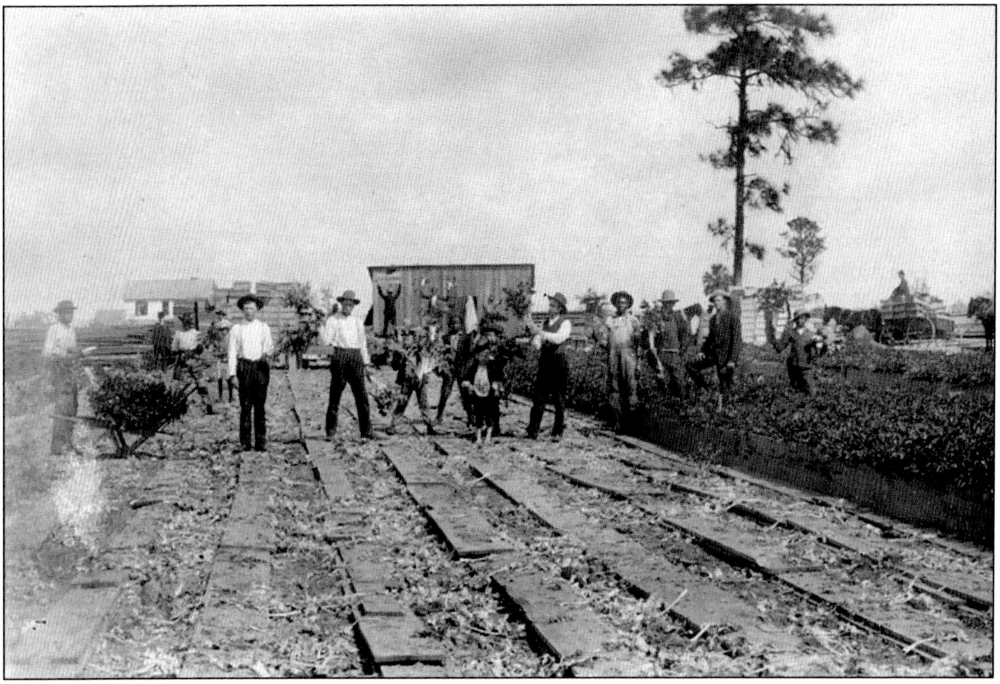

This celery field has been harvested. The boards will be stacked and stored for the next crop.

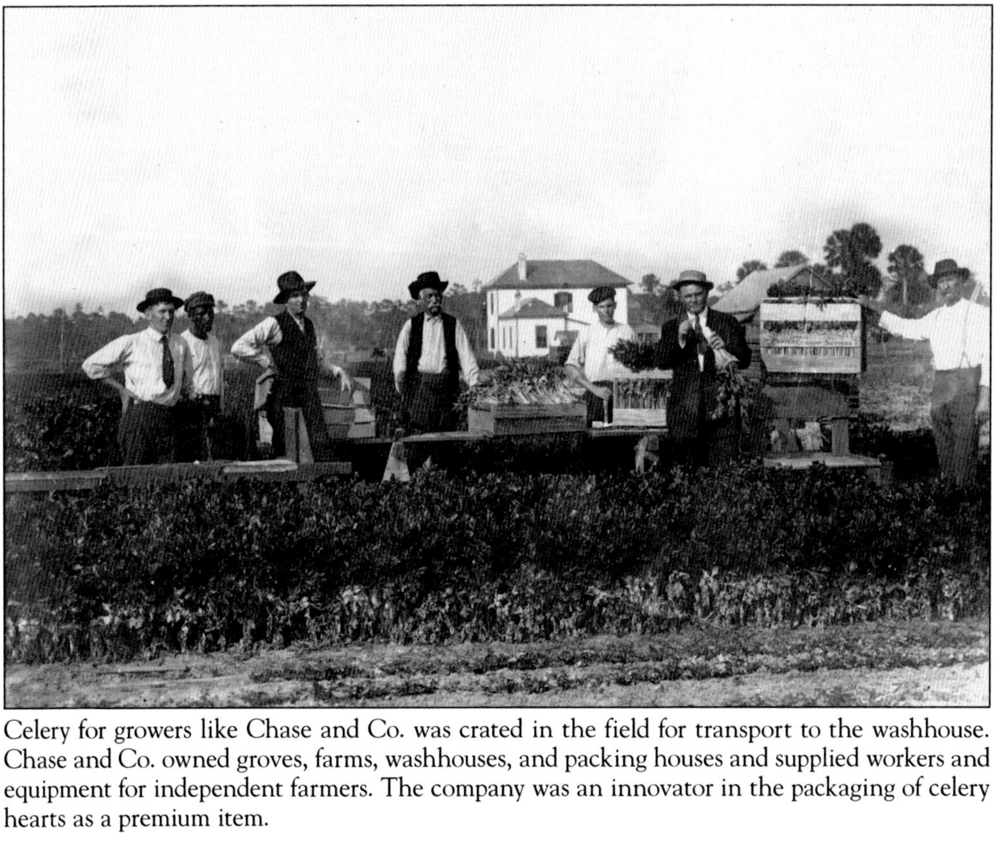

Celery for growers like Chase and Co. was crated in the field for transport to the washhouse. Chase and Co. owned groves, farms, washhouses, and packing houses and supplied workers and equipment for independent farmers. The company was an innovator in the packaging of celery hearts as a premium item.

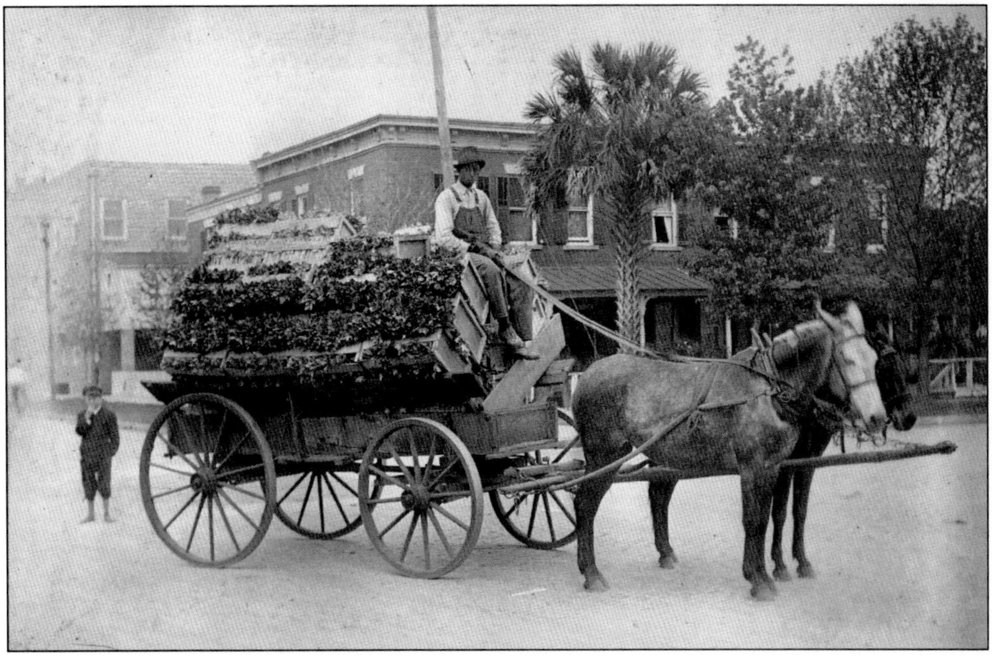

Celery crated for shipment was hauled to the railroad station in mule-drawn wagons like this one at the corner of Palmetto Avenue and Second Street.

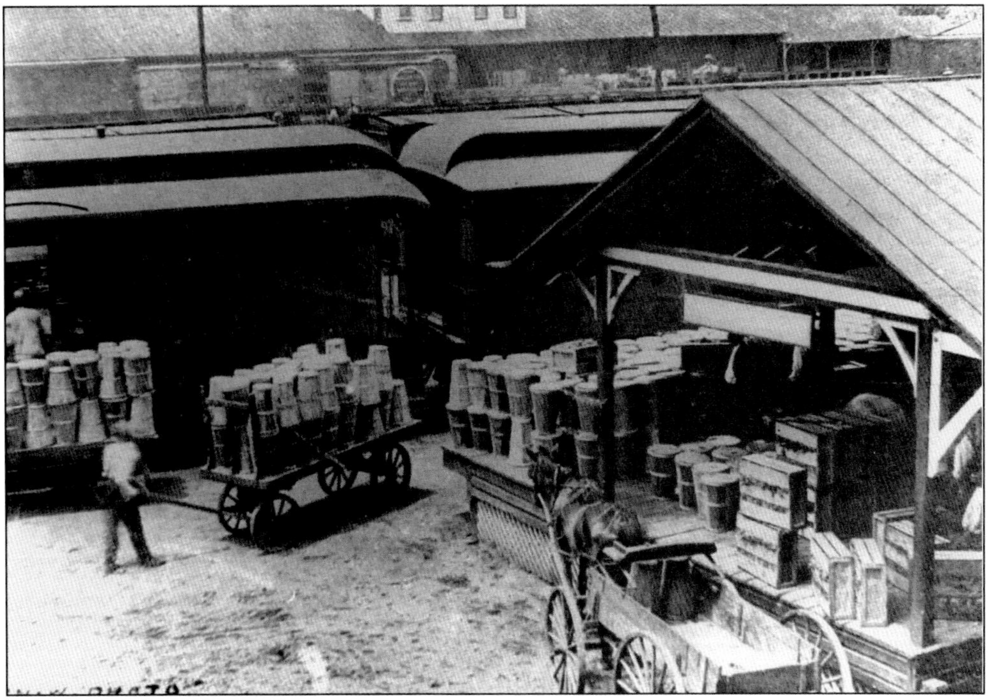

Vegetables were crated and shipped by rail. Box cars were cooled by compartments on each end that were filled with ice. The demand for ice eventually led to Sanford having the largest ice plant in the country.

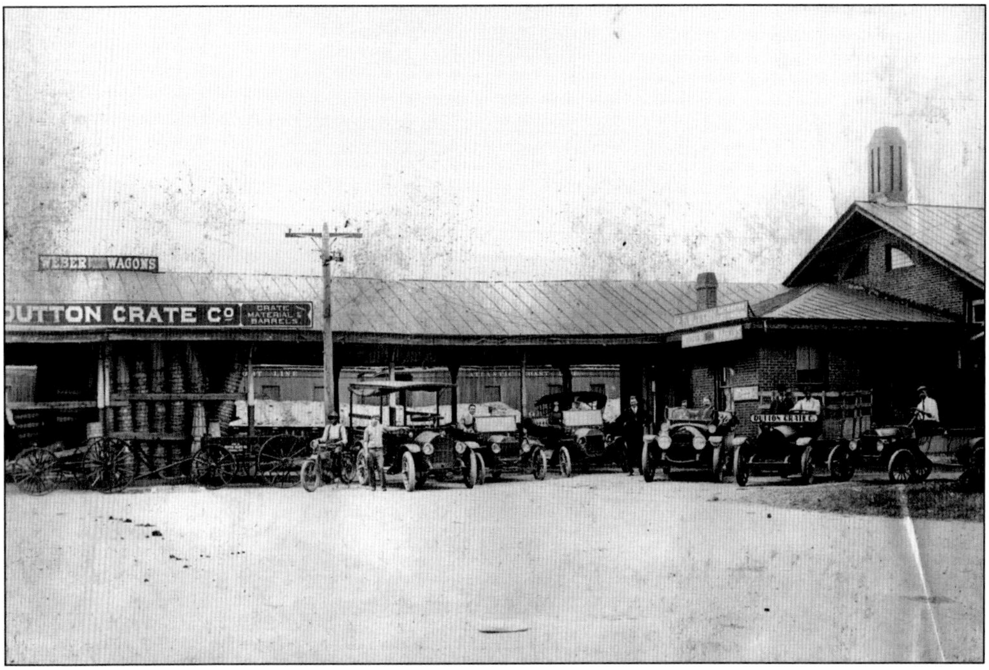

F.F. Dutton is credited with developing the pre-cooling system which contributed to Sanford's success with shipping celery.

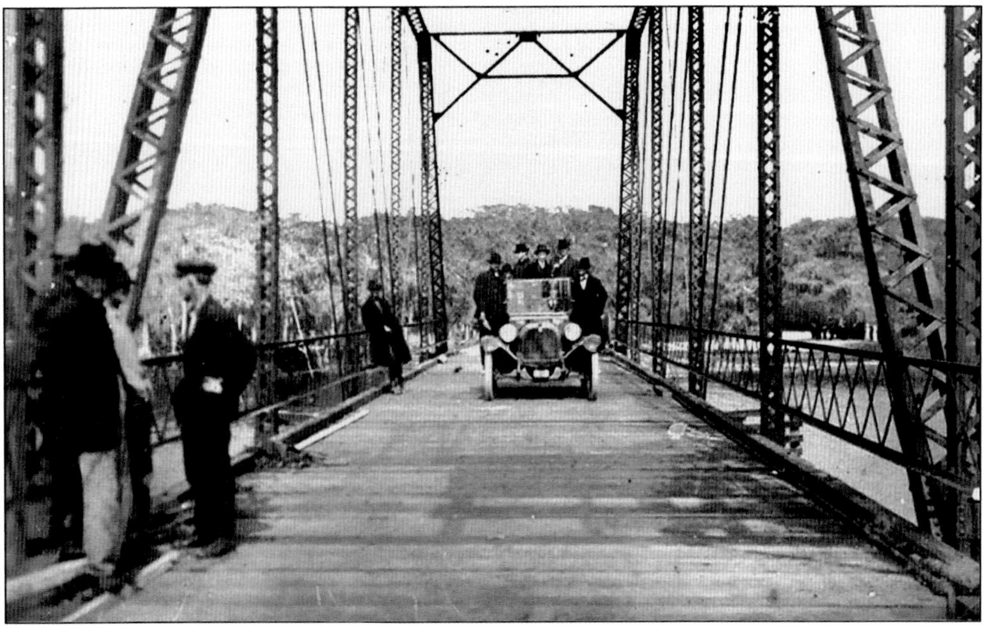

The first automobile bridge across the St. Johns River, between Volusia and Seminole counties, opened on February 16, 1916. Before the construction of this bridge, beginning in 1870, ferries provided the only way across the river. In 1934, a larger steel draw bridge was built just to the west. In 1961, the present bridge was built. (Courtesy of the Hawkins family.)

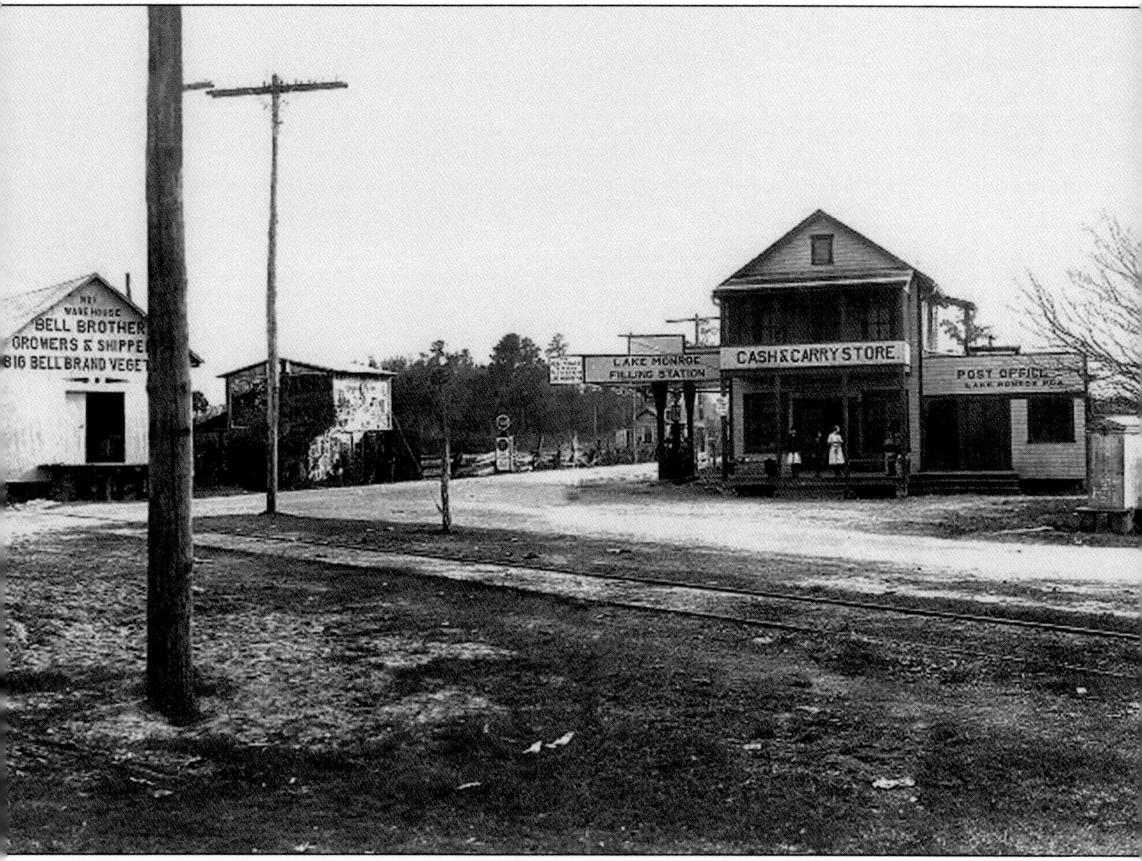

The town of Lake Monroe, pictured in this 1917 photograph, evolved out of an attempt in 1887 by Henry Sanford's Florida Land and Colonization Company to establish a Roman Catholic settlement called the St. Joseph's Colony. The colony was to be built around the Orange Belt Railroad's Monroe Station. When this venture was unsuccessful, the land was sold to anyone with money to buy it. Many of the first settlers were German immigrants that became prominent farmers. In 1916, the town name was changed to Ahearn, Florida, but six months later it was officially registered with the United States Post Office Department as Lake Monroe, Florida. (Courtesy of the Hawkins family.)

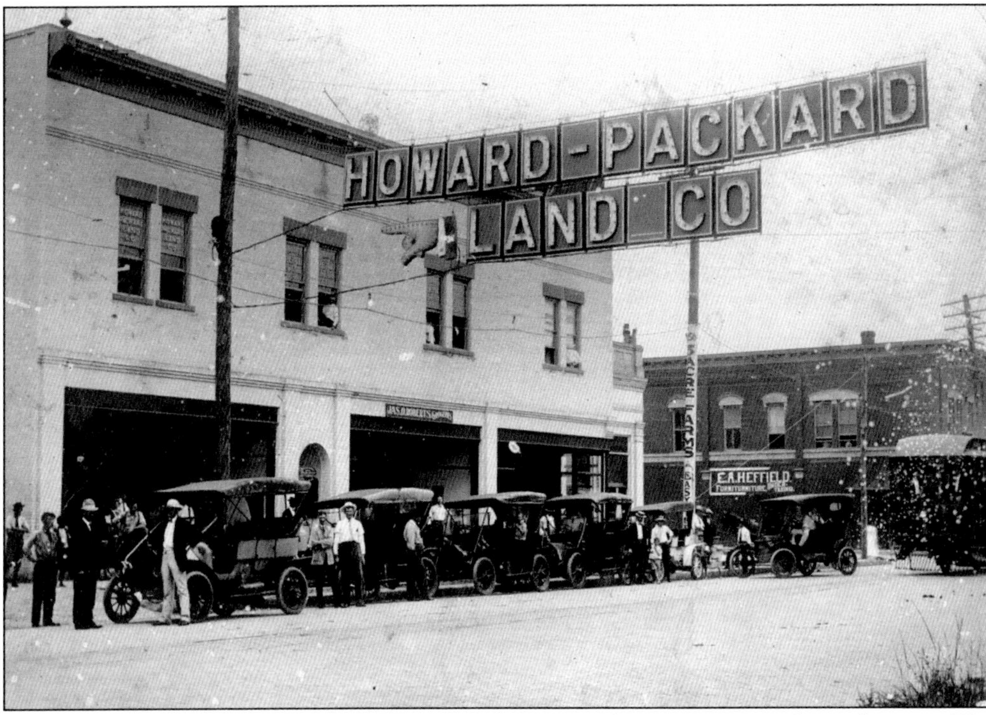

Sanford's success as a vegetable shipping center encouraged newcomers to take up farming. The Howard-Packard Land Co. sold farm land from an office in the Peoples Bank Block on East First Street.

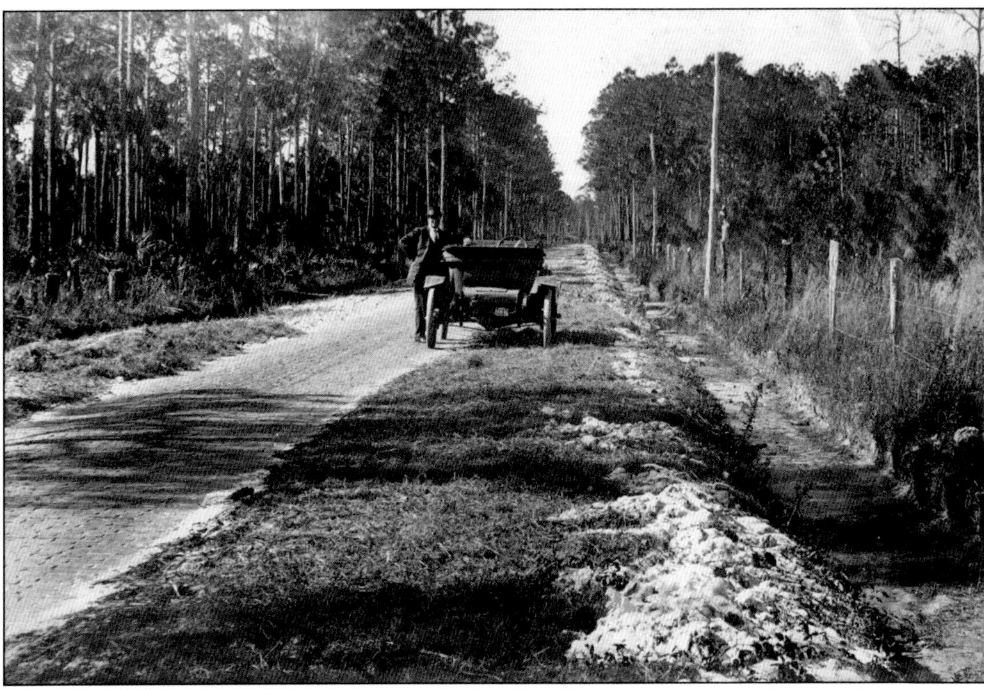

Many new roads were built as an increasing number of residents purchased cars. The road beds were filled with shell from ancient Indian mounds in the area.

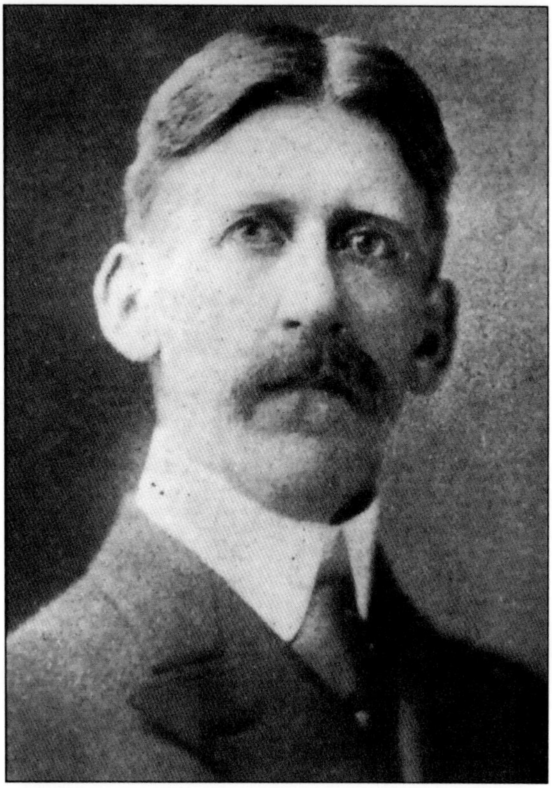

Forrest Lake, Sanford booster and mayor, had a large home on Park Avenue in what is Sanford's historic residential district today. Lake was the president of the Seminole County Bank and a promoter of the bulkhead construction. A banking scandal linked to the bulkhead ended his career in 1928.

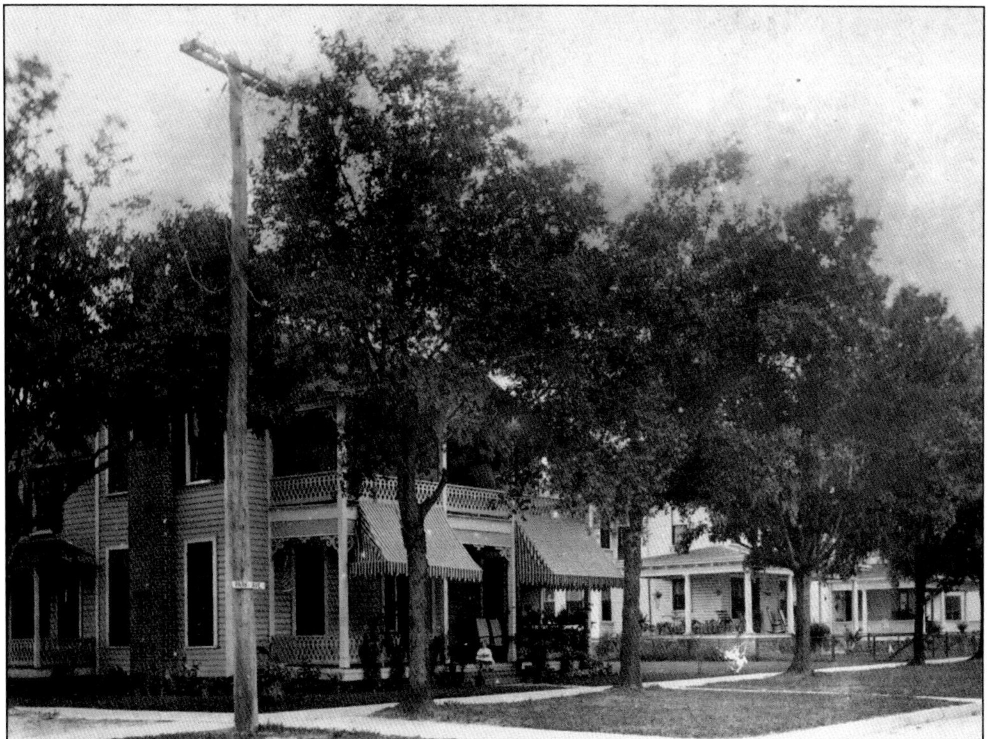

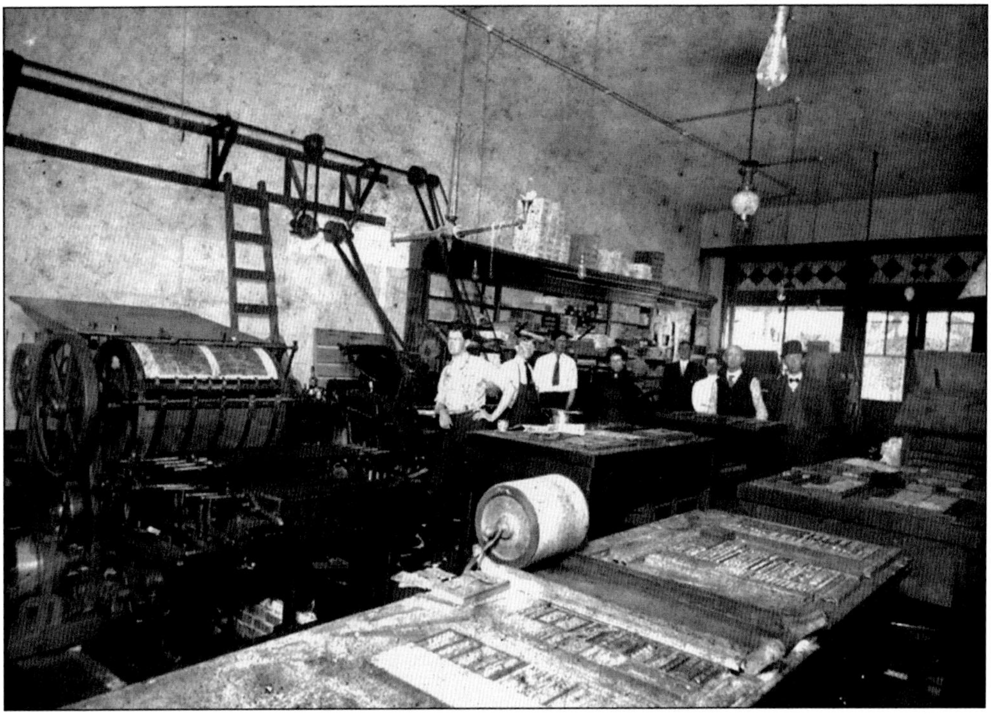

Thomas J. Appleyard began publishing the *Gate City Chronicle* in 1892. Sometime around 1908 the paper was sold to R.J. Holly and the name was changed to the *Sanford Chronicle*. By 1910 the name had changed again to the *Sanford Herald* and a new office was built at 107 South Magnolia Avenue. When the building was renovated in recent years, type from the presses, as shown in this photo, was found under the floorboards. The newspaper operates today as the *Seminole Herald*.

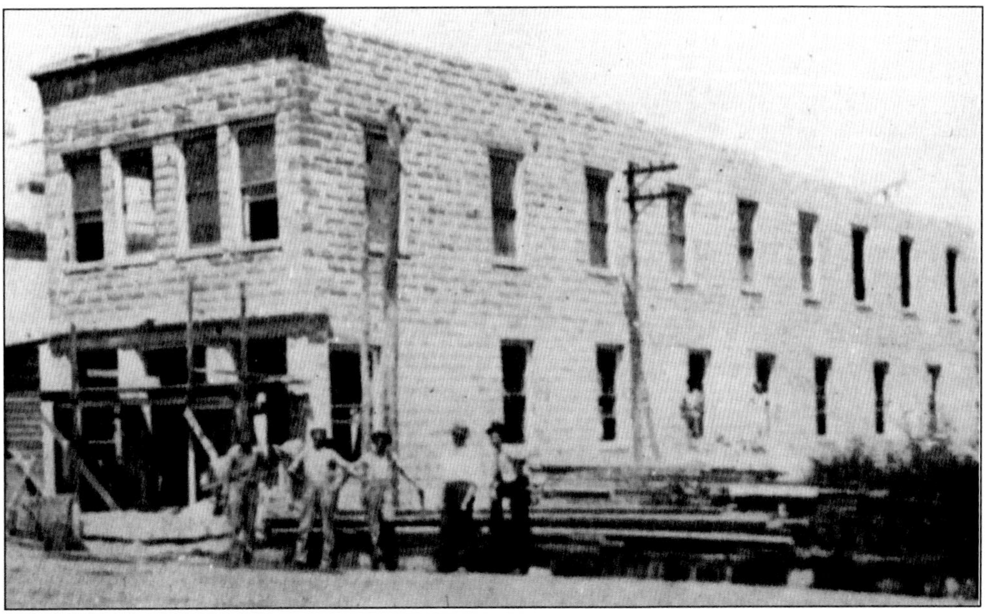

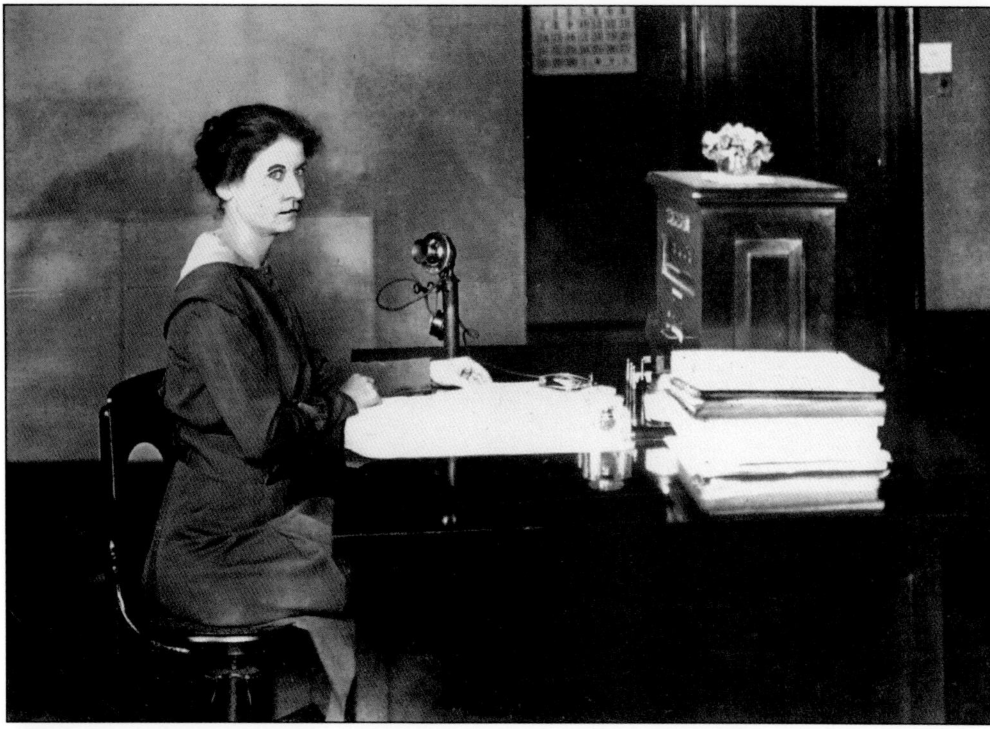

The first telephone exchange in Sanford was installed in December of 1884. In this 1912 photograph we see Versa Woodcock, chief operator for Sanford Telephone and Telegraph Co., at her station in 1912. (Courtesy of Christine Kinlaw Best.)

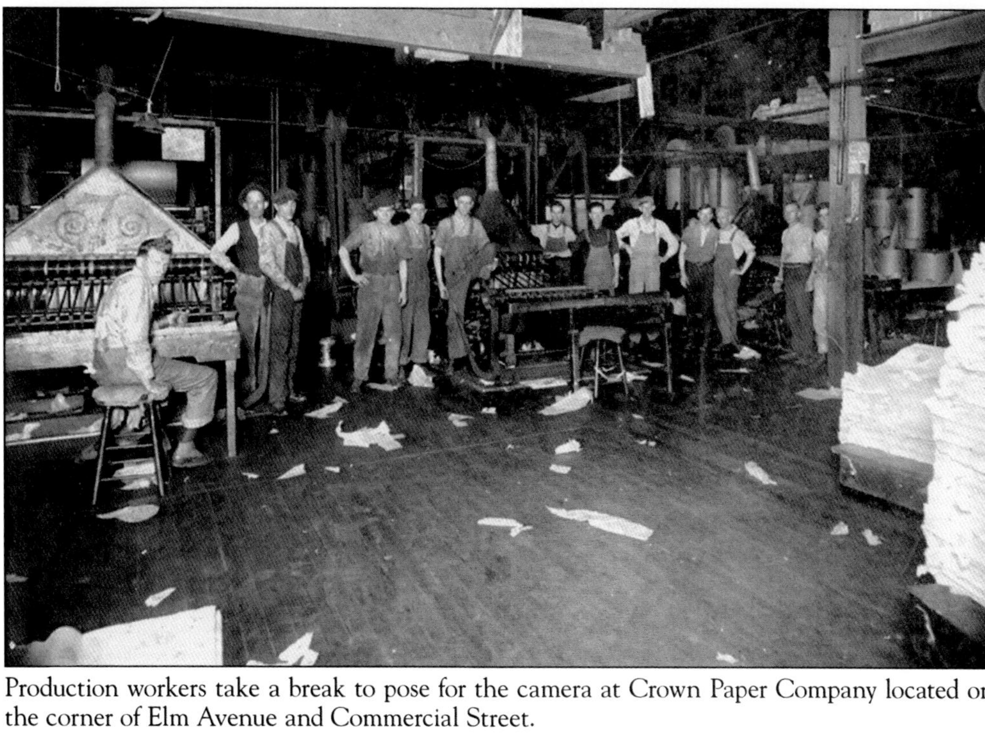

Production workers take a break to pose for the camera at Crown Paper Company located on the corner of Elm Avenue and Commercial Street.

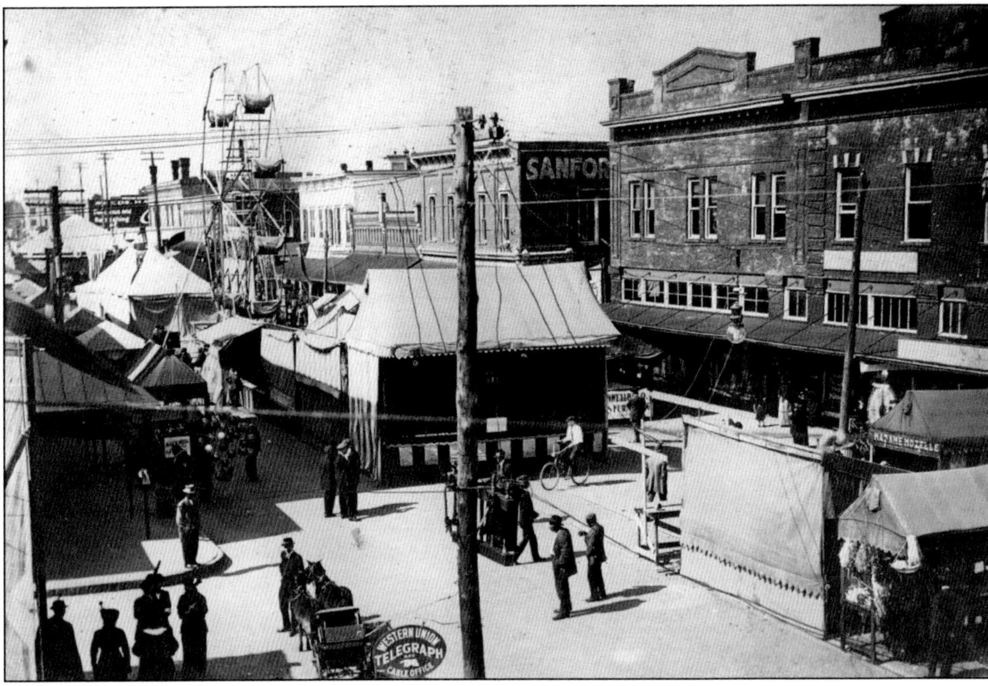

One of the first fairs in Sanford was the 1912 Street Fair, produced by the Moss and Marrs' Consolidated Shows. These photographs present views from opposite ends of First Street, showing the attractions that stretched from Park to Palmetto Avenue. The fair featured 15 tented shows, several free acts, and four amusement rides including a giant Eli Ferris Wheel and a Parker Carry-Us-All. The highlights of the event were C.H. Tompkin's Wild West Show and world famous high-diver, Professor Harry Six, who jumped from a 110-foot ladder into a pool 8 feet wide and only 36 inches deep.

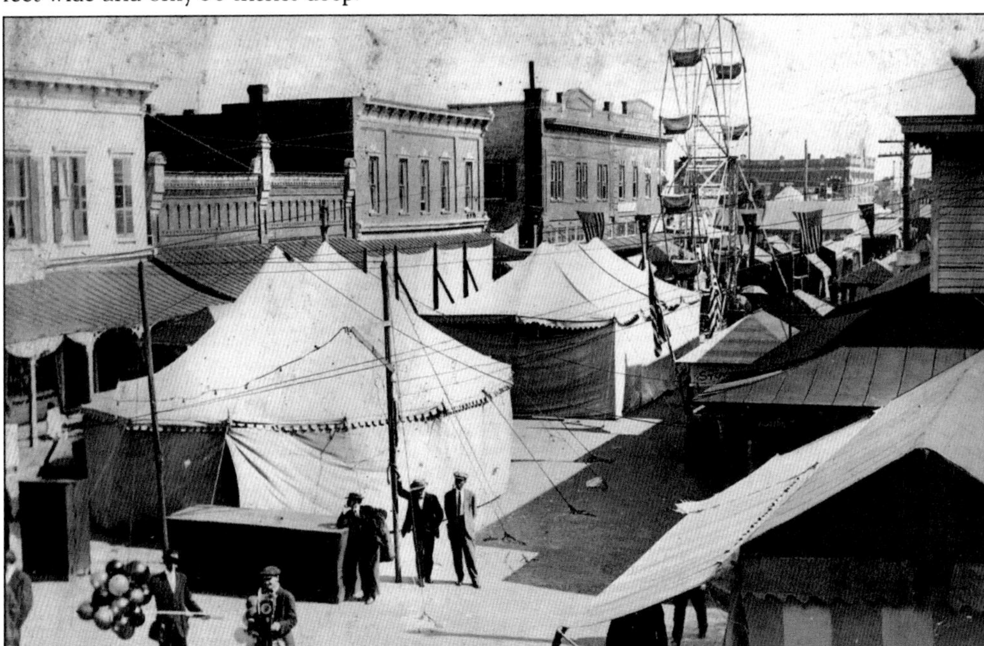

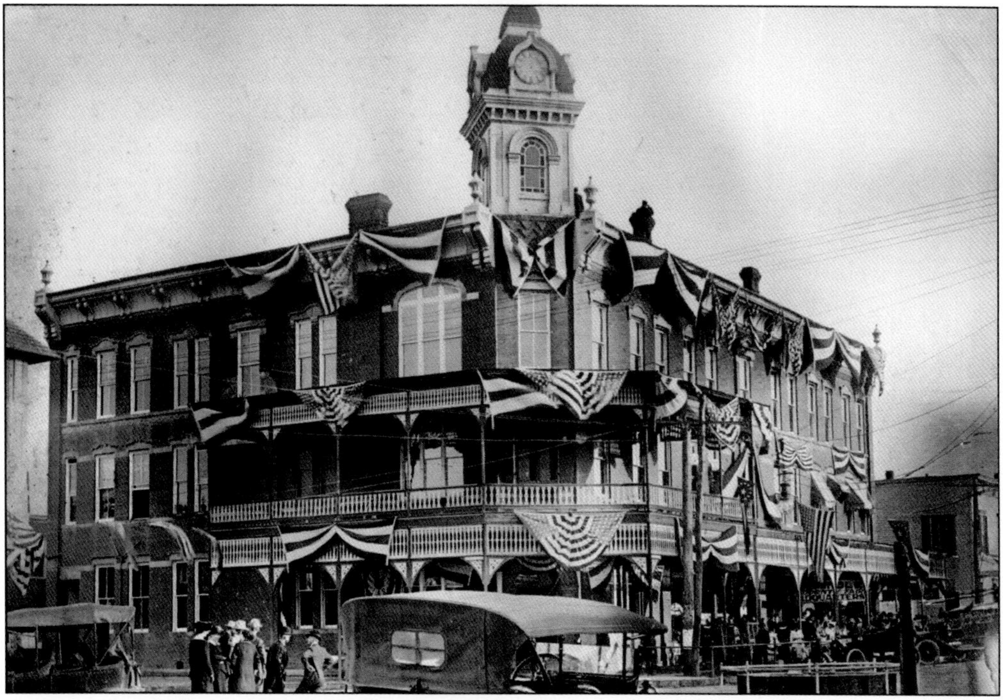

In 1913, the Welbourne Block on the southeast corner of Park Avenue and Commercial Street served as the first courthouse for the newly formed Seminole County. Built in 1887, it was remodeled in 1919 and opened as the Valdez Hotel.

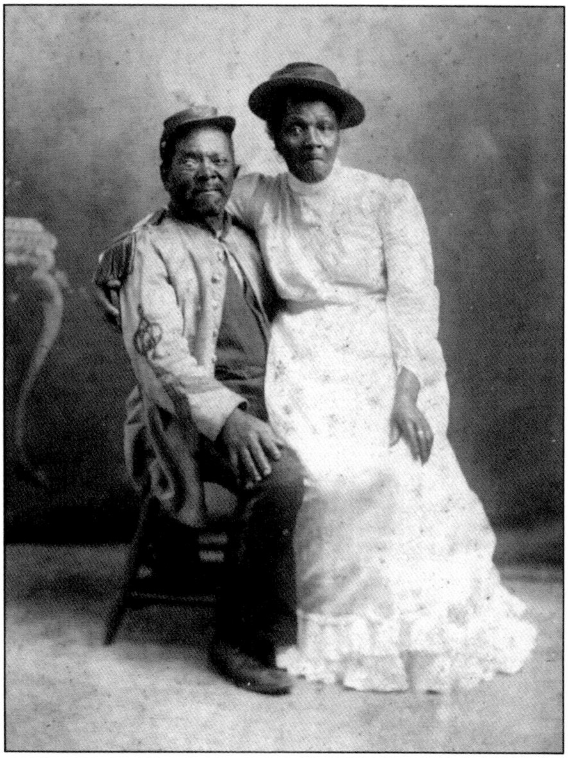

Adam and Rachel Shadrach are pictured in a photo taken c. 1910. "Old Shad" was a fisherman who served as Sanford's official gunner, firing the city cannon on special occasions. He was known for his unusual uniform with epaulets and blue trousers with a red stripe down the side. In 1913, during the celebration surrounding the forming of Seminole County, the cannon blew apart. A piece of the barrel was salvaged by Aaron Robbins and made into a fountain at his hotel. It was later donated to the Sanford Chamber of Commerce and today serves as the base of a flagpole.

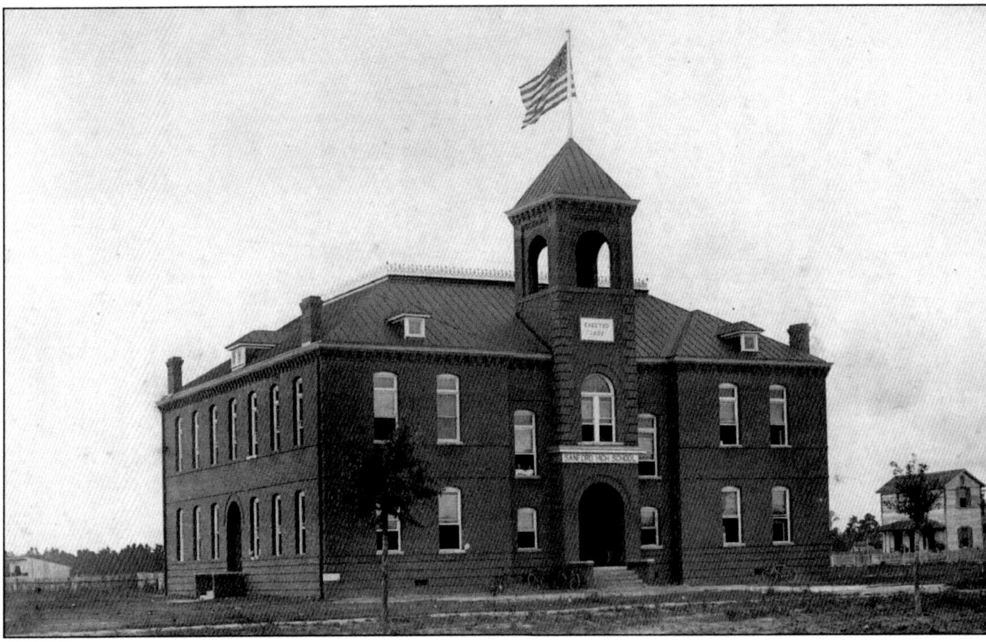

Sanford High School on Seventh Street was built in 1902. It became Sanford Grammar School when a new high school was built in 1911.

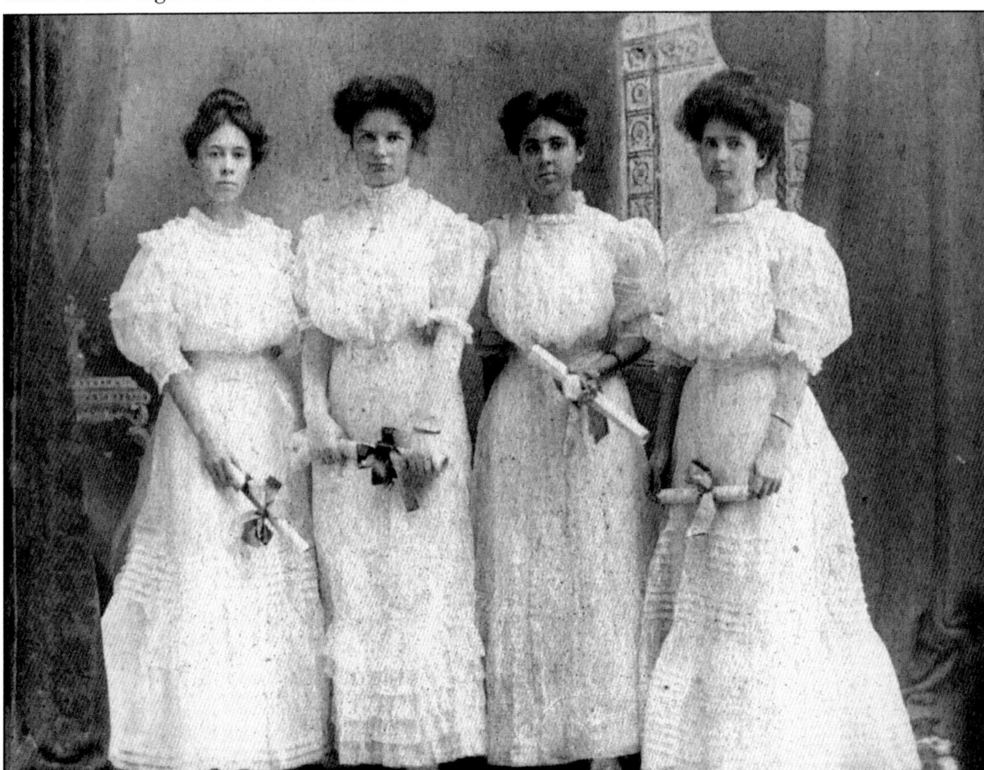

The first graduating class of Sanford High School in 1907 included only four girls. From left to right they are Alberta Hill, Peacha Leffler, Clara Miller, and Mabel Bowler.

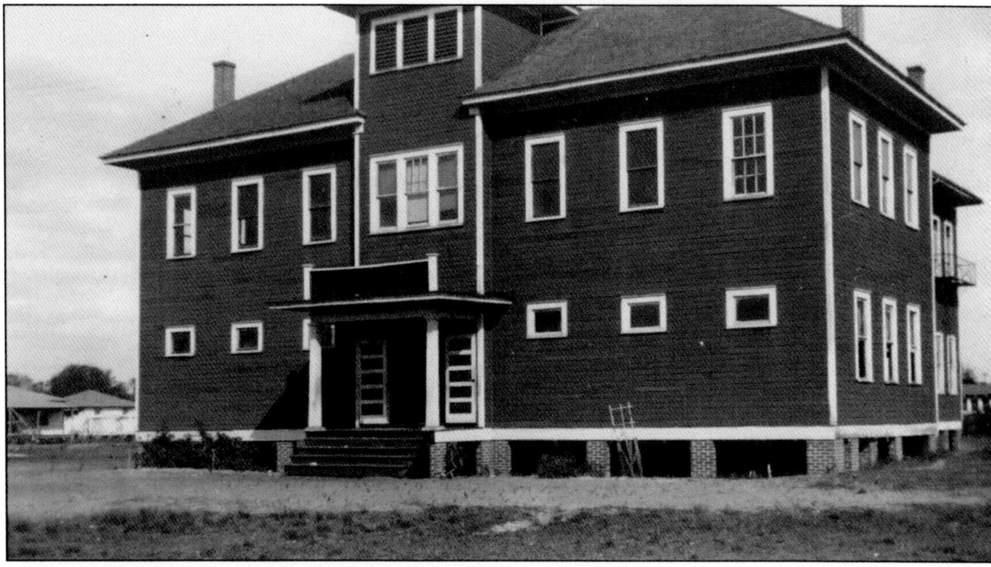
Hopper Academy at 1111 South Pine Avenue was built before 1910. The principal was J.N. Crooms, for whom Crooms Academy would later be named.

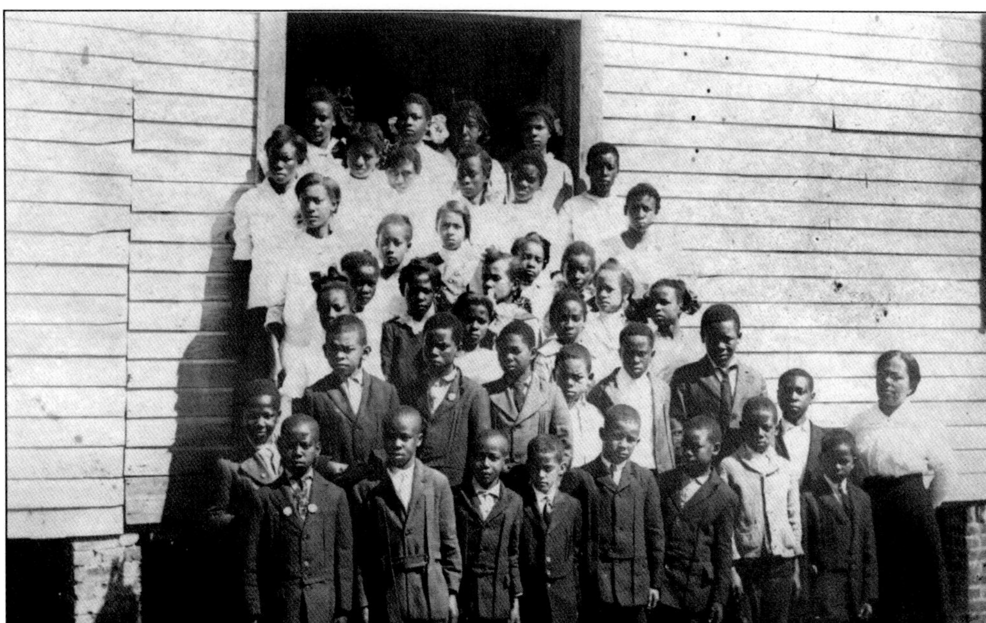
Montez Harris and her third grade students stand on the steps of the elementary school at Seventh Street and Cypress Avenue.

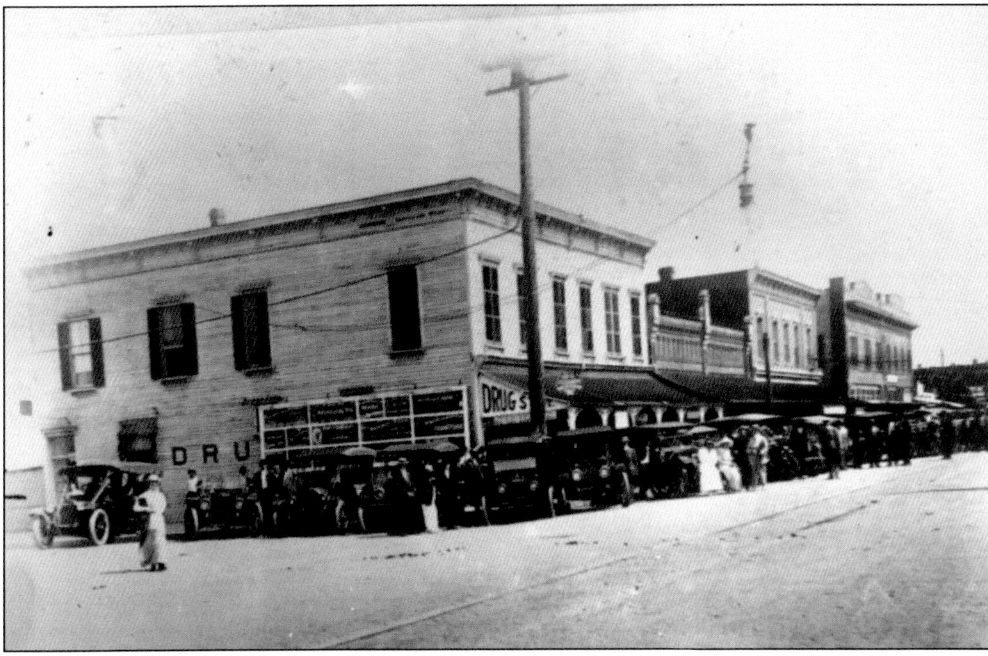

L.R. Philips' drugstore stood on the northeast corner of First Street and Park Avenue. It was replaced by the Brumley-Puleston Building, a high rise, in 1922.

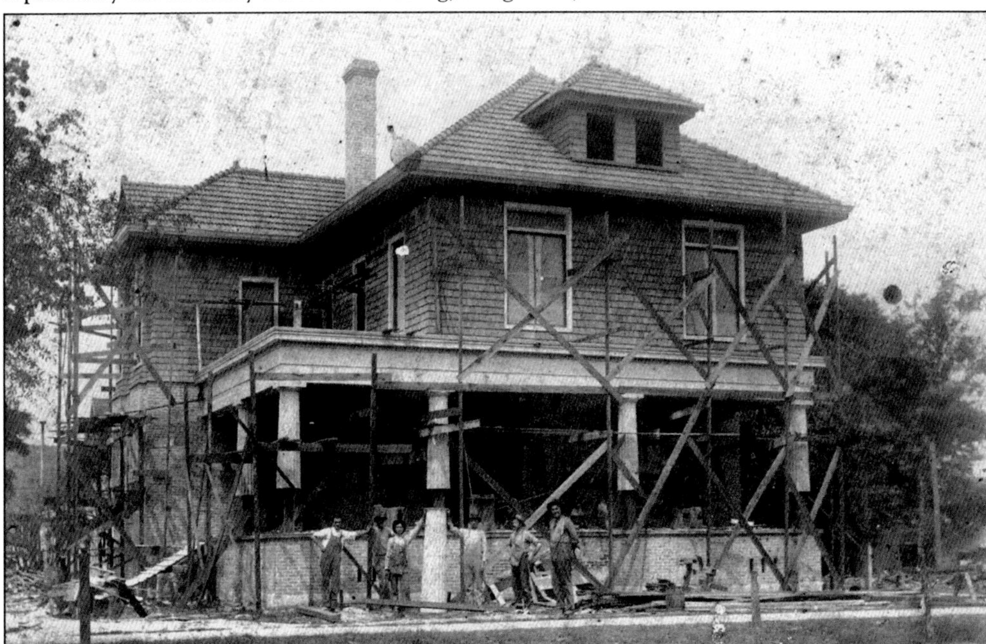

Fernald-Laughton Memorial Hospital, 500 South Oak Avenue, was built in 1910 as the home of George and Mabel Fernald. Mr. Fernald owned a hardware company in Sanford. On her husband's death in 1916, Mrs. Fernald donated the house to the county for use as a hospital. Named in memory of Mrs. Fernald's husband and mother, it served as the county hospital from 1919 to 1947 and from 1951 to 1956. In the late 1940s the clinic at the temporarily closed Navy base was used. A new hospital was built on East First Street in 1955.

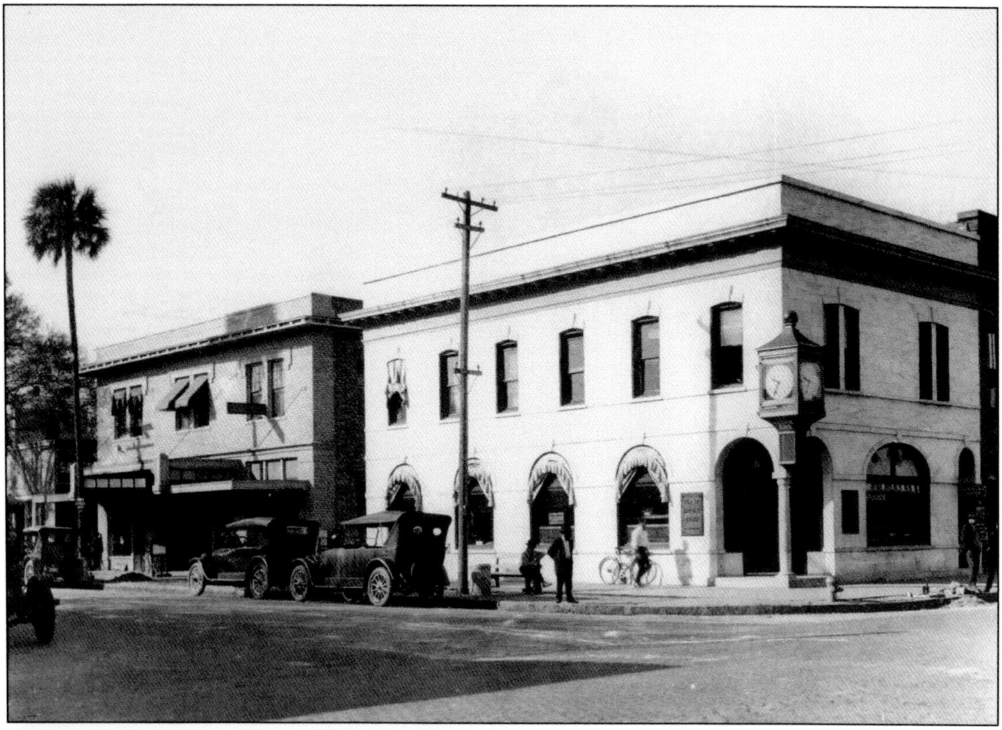

The Lyman Bank was built in 1883. In 1885 Rollins College was chartered here during a meeting of the college's founders. In 1887 the Lyman Bank became the First National Bank. The old building was extensively altered; a marble façade was added and the door was moved from Park Avenue to the corner. The town clock was purchased and hung on the building during these renovations. The bank remained here until 1923 when the high rise across Park Avenue was constructed. The building today has a stucco façade and the door faces First Street.

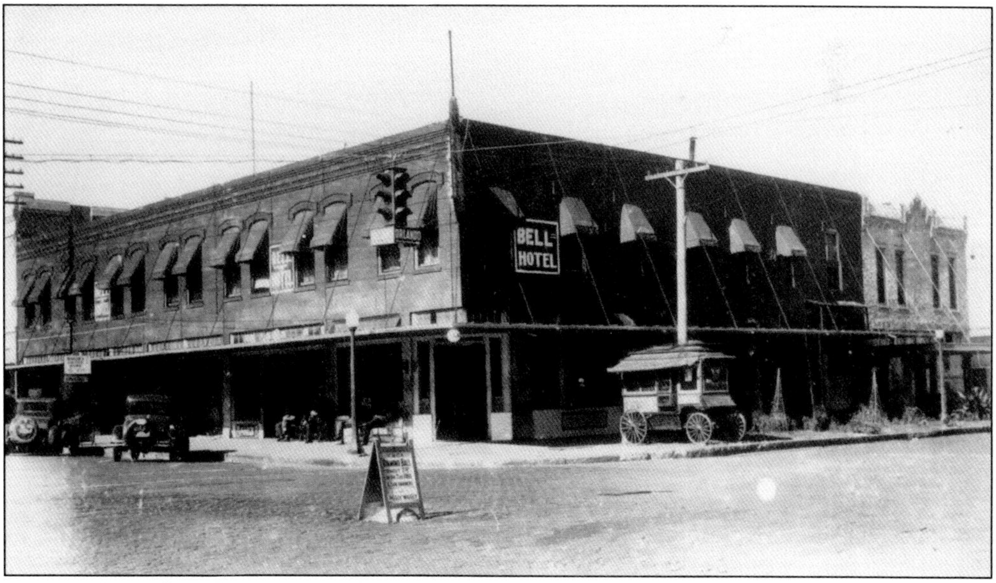

In 1917, the Bell Café was owned by Manuel Dandelake, a Greek immigrant. The Bell Hotel is remembered for Joe's Smokehouse and Silas Biggers's peanut wagon which sat out front.

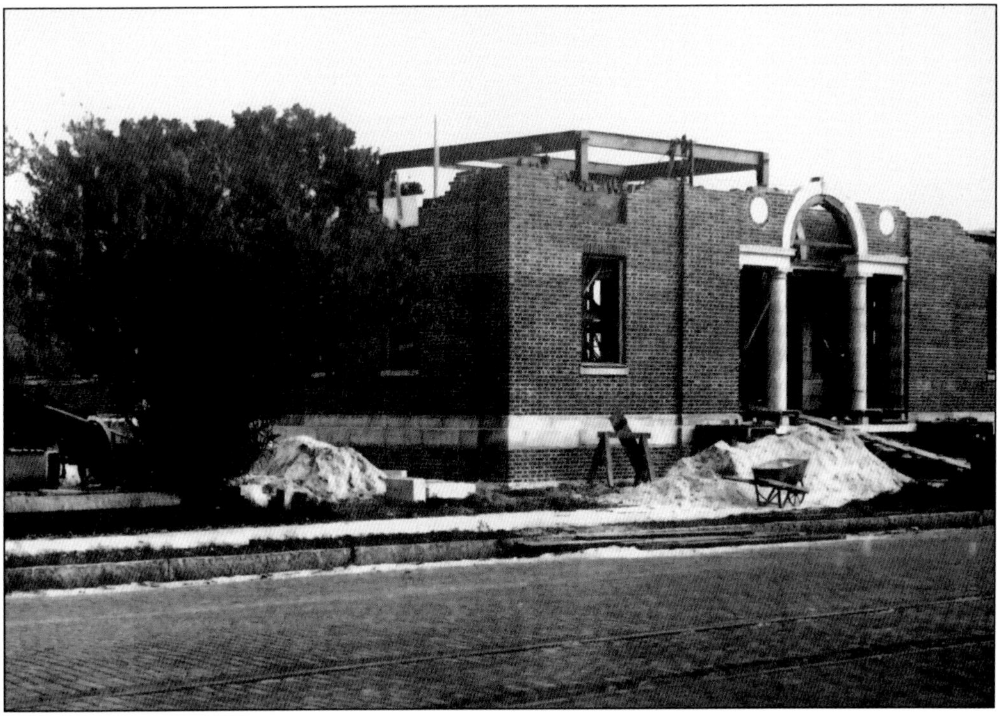

The post office at 230 East First Street was built in November 1917. The building became the Sanford Public Library in 1963 and part of the Seminole County Library system in 1975. Today it serves as a police substation.

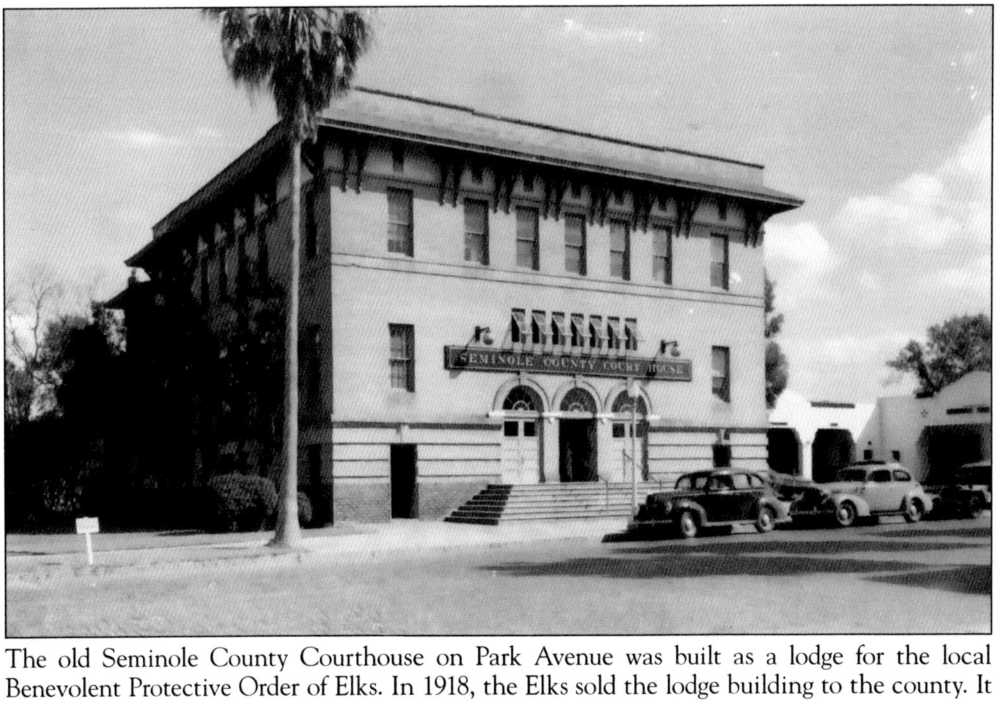

The old Seminole County Courthouse on Park Avenue was built as a lodge for the local Benevolent Protective Order of Elks. In 1918, the Elks sold the lodge building to the county. It was demolished in 1972 to make room for the present courthouse.

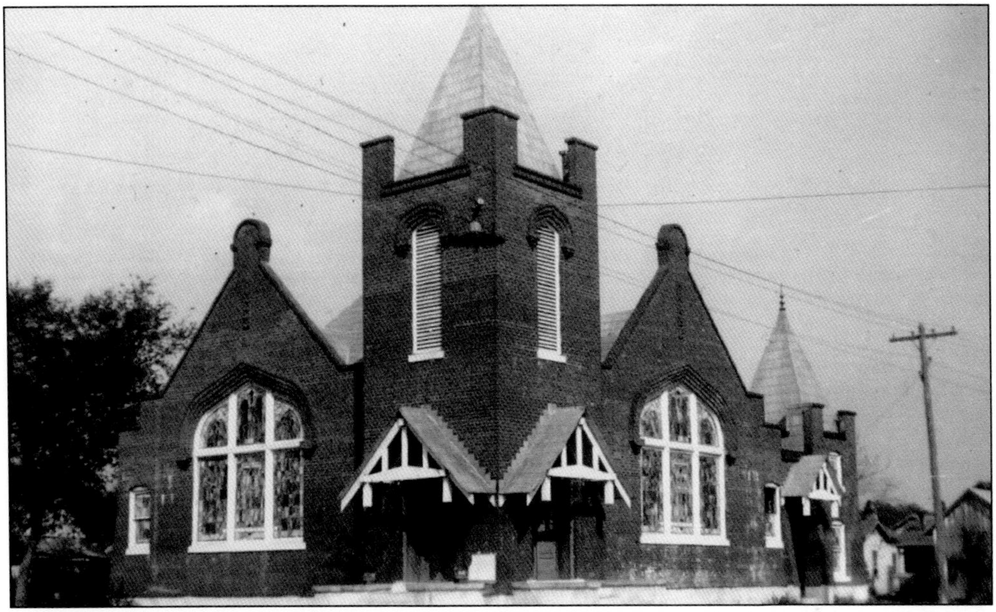

Prince W. Spears designed homes and churches in Sanford at the beginning of the 20th century. This self-taught African-American architect was born in Georgia in 1879 and began as a mason. The finest surviving example of his work is St. James AME Church, located at 819 Cypress Avenue, which was built in 1913 for a congregation organized in 1867. The church was designated a local landmark in 1990.

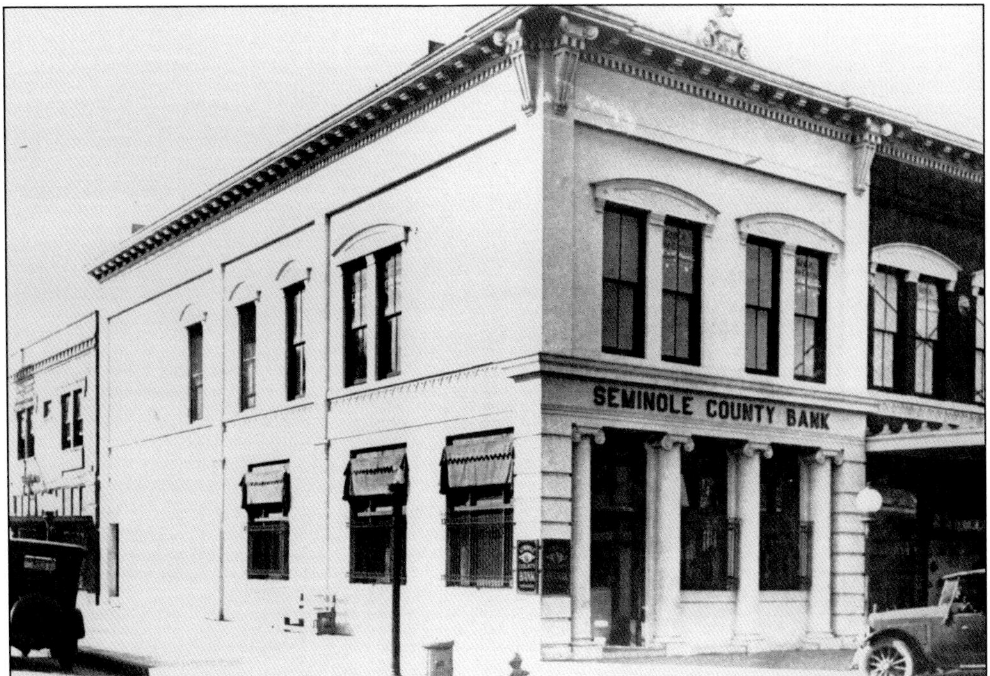

The Seminole County Bank was located in the eastern half of the Henry DeForest block at the corner of Magnolia Avenue and First Street. The Victorian façade was altered in 1917 to the appearance in this photo. B.L. Perkins men's wear store filled the west half of the building.

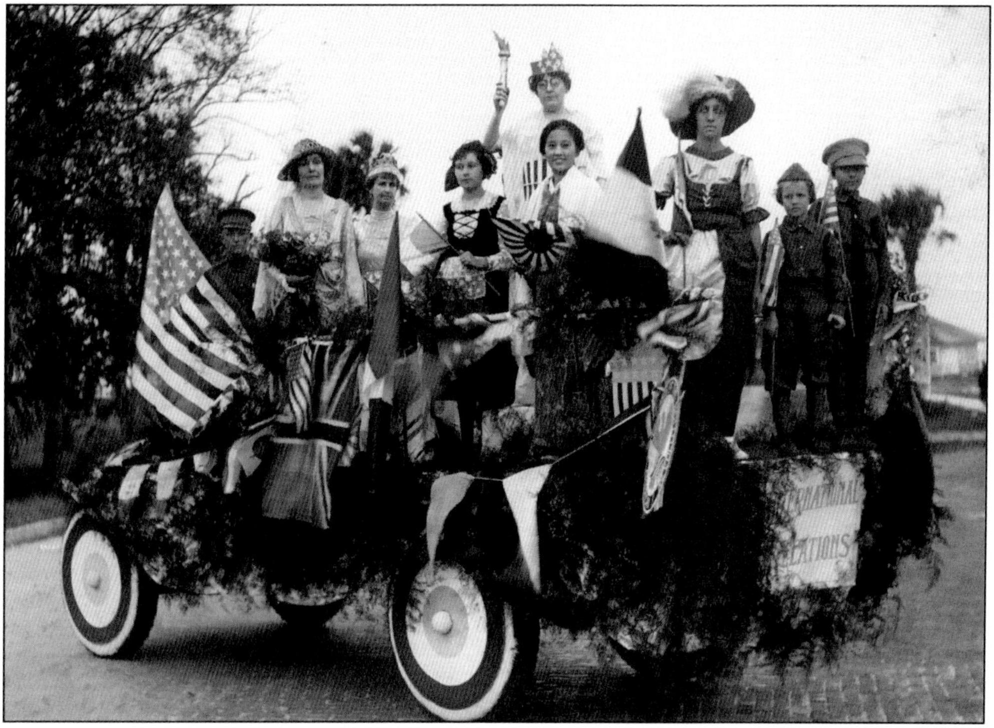

Heberta Leonardy, Sanford's first female attorney, stands atop the DAR float in the 1920 Armistice Day parade. Women had just won the right to vote.

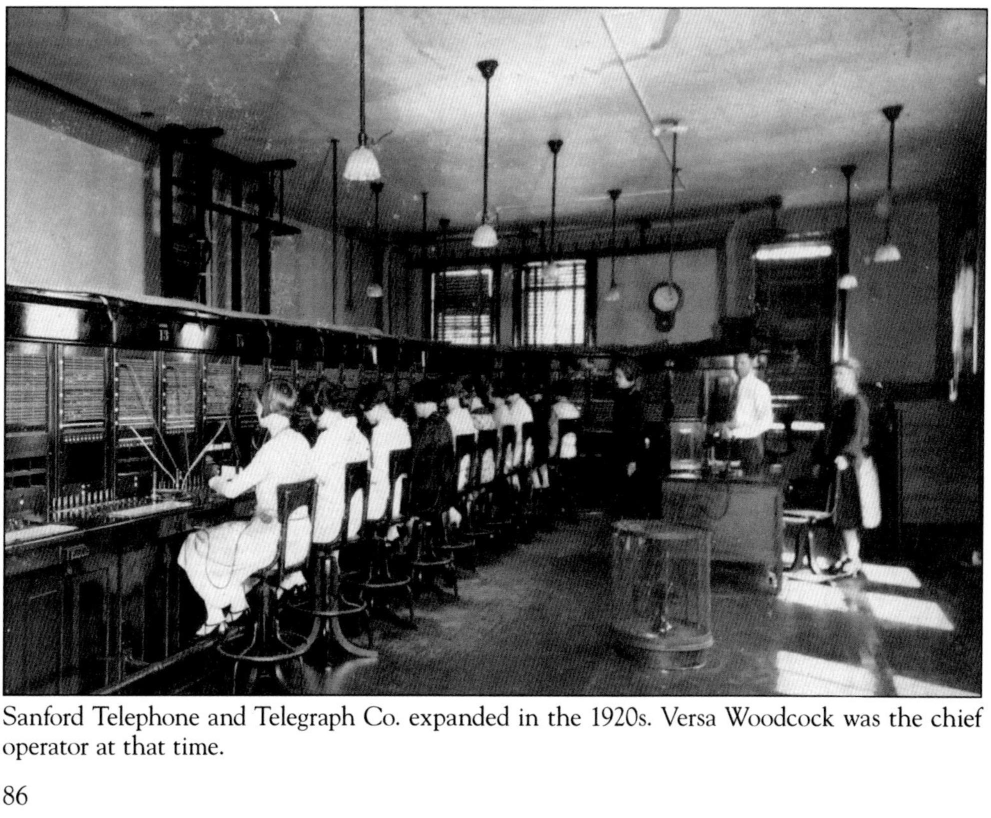

Sanford Telephone and Telegraph Co. expanded in the 1920s. Versa Woodcock was the chief operator at that time.

Four

THE CITY SUBSTANTIAL

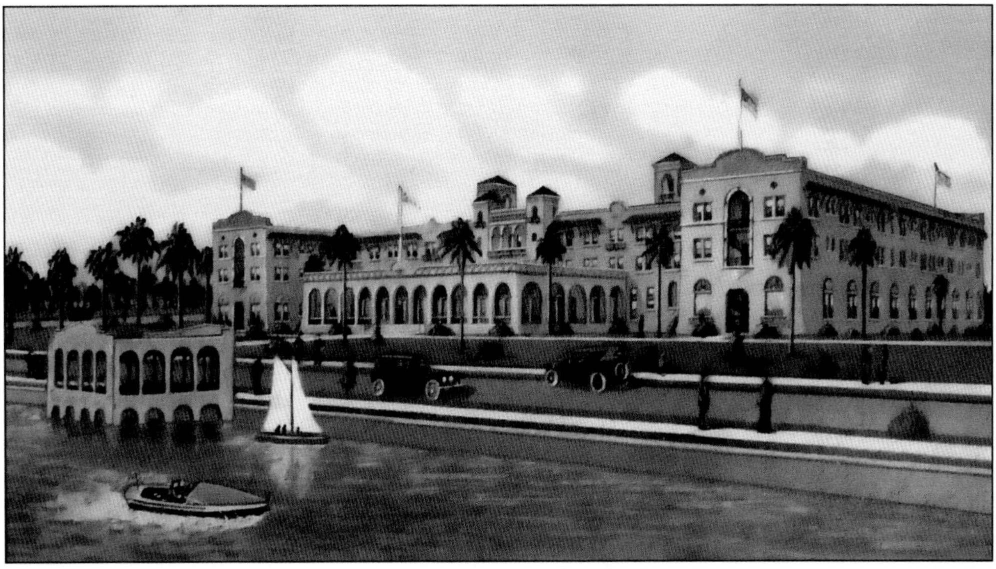

The Hotel Forrest Lake opened in January 1926 just after the First Street extension opened. The building was purchased by the city in 1930 and the name was changed to the Mayfair Hotel. In 1947, the hotel was bought by the New York Giants and renamed the Mayfair Inn. In 1963, it became the Sanford Naval Academy and was run as a school until it was sold to the New Tribes Mission in 1976. The hotel was designed by Elton J. Moughton.

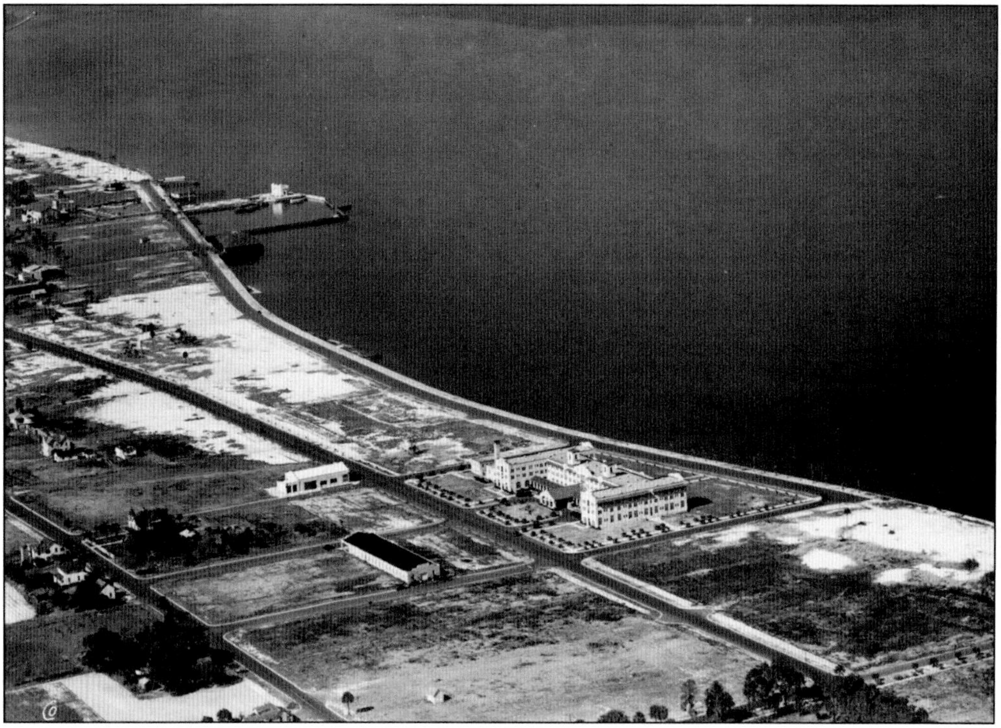

In 1911, the Sanford City Commission decided to appropriate funds to create desirable lake front property by the construction of a bulkhead. Automobiles were becoming popular, a lakeside boulevard was desired, and with the land boom on, it seemed a good time to reclaim land from the lake. In December 1916, construction began.

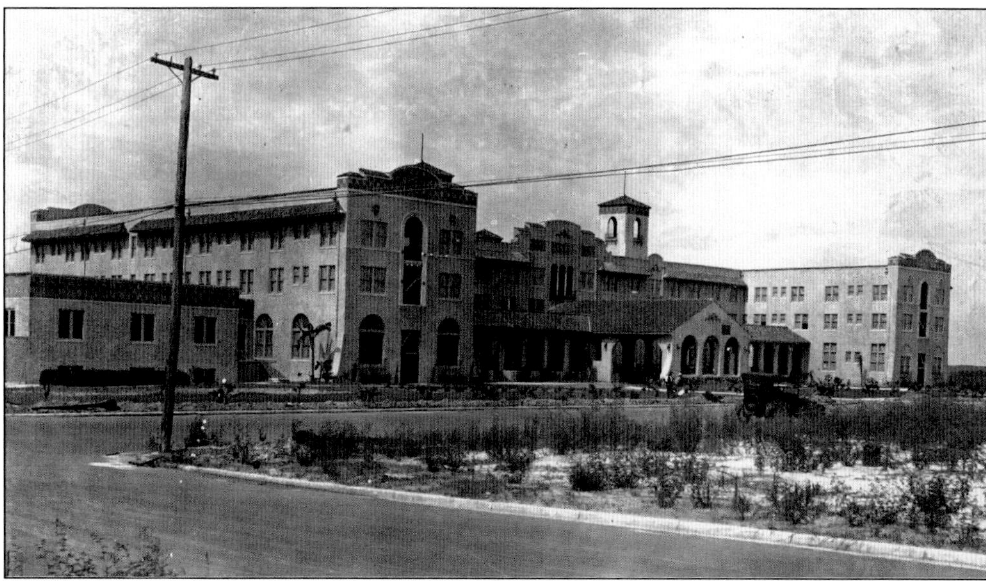

The Hotel Forrest Lake was part of a political/financial scandal in 1928. Mayor Forrest Lake, who was also president of the Seminole County Bank, was accused of issuing unauthorized city securities to keep his bank open. The investigation led to the closing of the Seminole County Bank in 1927. Forrest Lake was sent to prison, but was later pardoned.

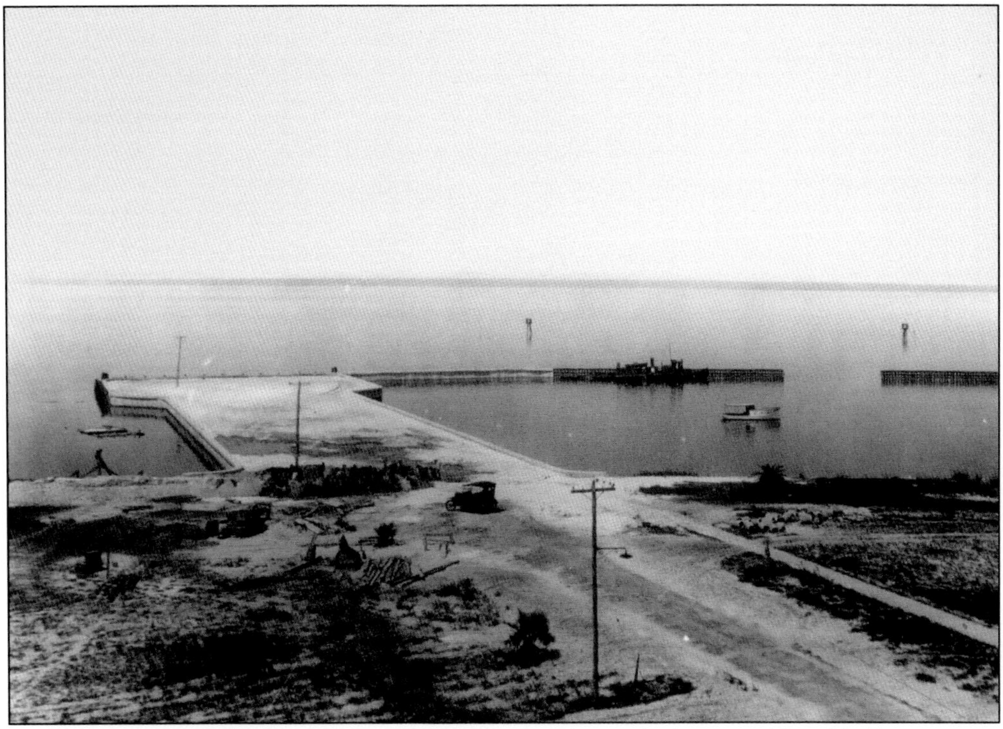

Sanford's Memorial Park was built as the city pier with a yacht basin and bandshell in 1924. In 1927, a flagpole and fountain were dedicated in memory of the war dead of World War I. The park was renamed Memorial Park in 1973 when it was rededicated to all veterans. In 2003, the original flagpole was demolished as part of the Riverwalk Project.

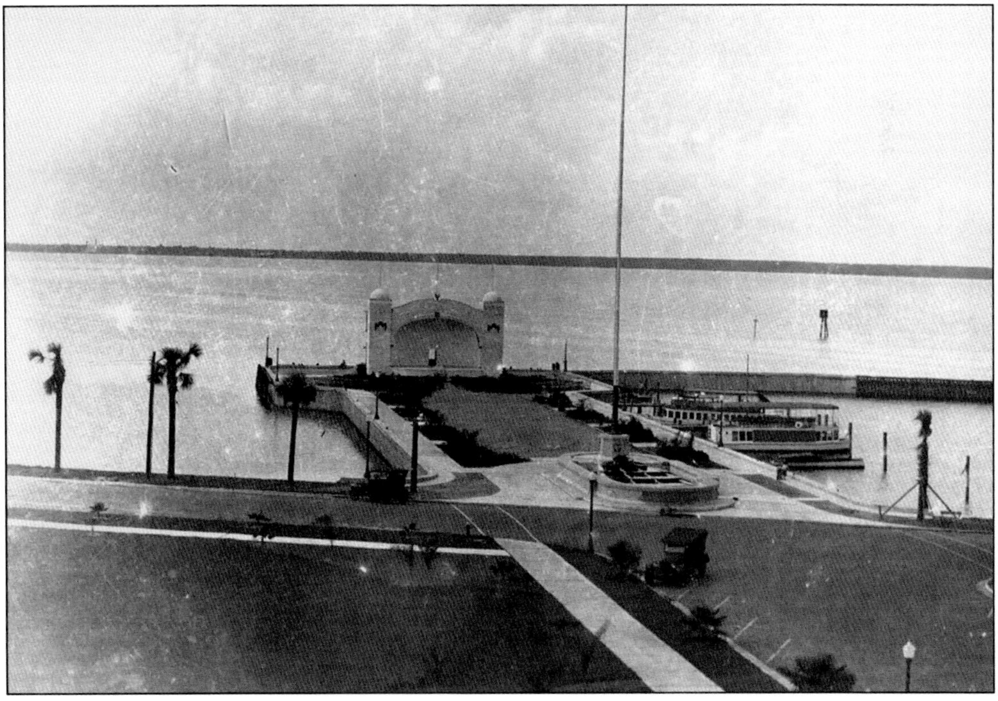

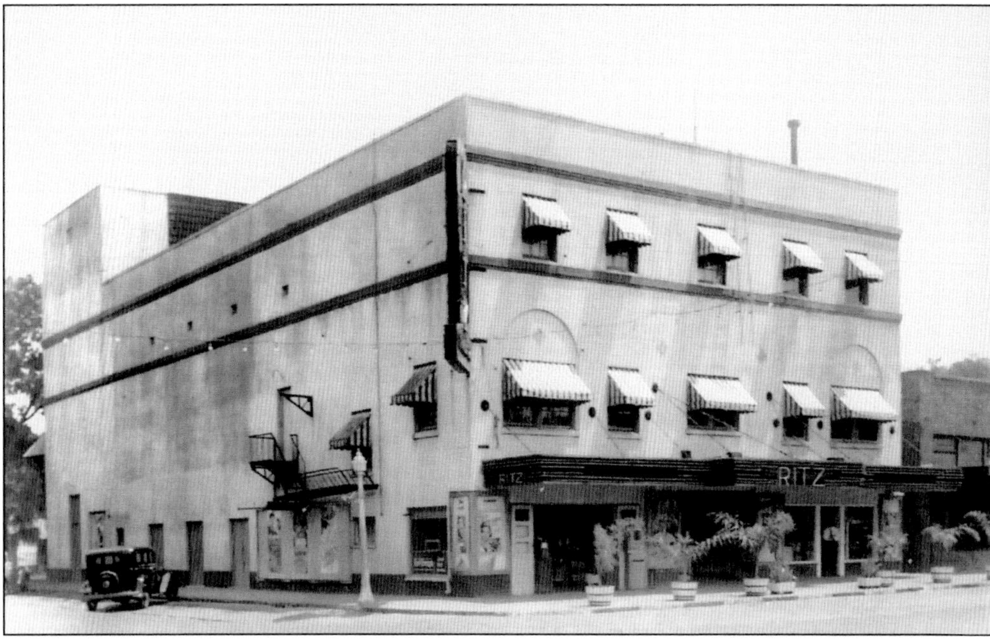

The Milane Theatre, a silent movie house, opened on August 2, 1923. The theater at 201 South Magnolia Avenue was built by the Milane Amusement Co. and was named for owners Frank Miller and Ed Lane. The theater was a center of activity in town. There were vaudeville and Chautauqua programs. Election returns and World Series results were announced here. The theater was known as the Ritz from 1941 to 1977. Renovated in the late 1990s and renamed the Helen Stairs Theatre on May 6, 2000, the building now serves as a cultural center for Sanford.

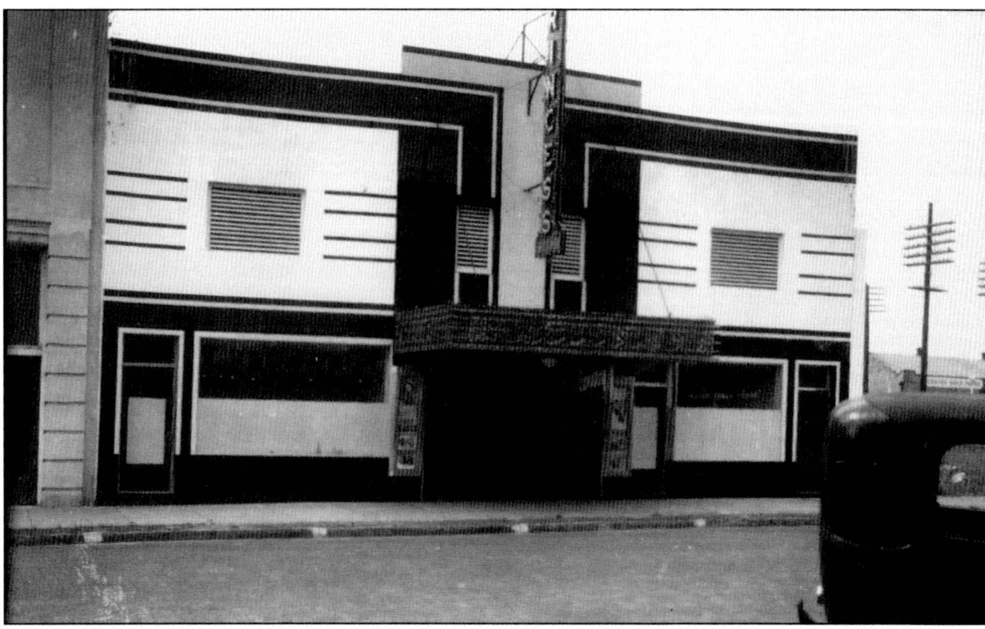

The Princess Theater, at 113 West First Street, was built in 1915 as the Allen Theater, a silent movie house. For many years, beginning in 1952, the building housed Sanford Auto Parts.

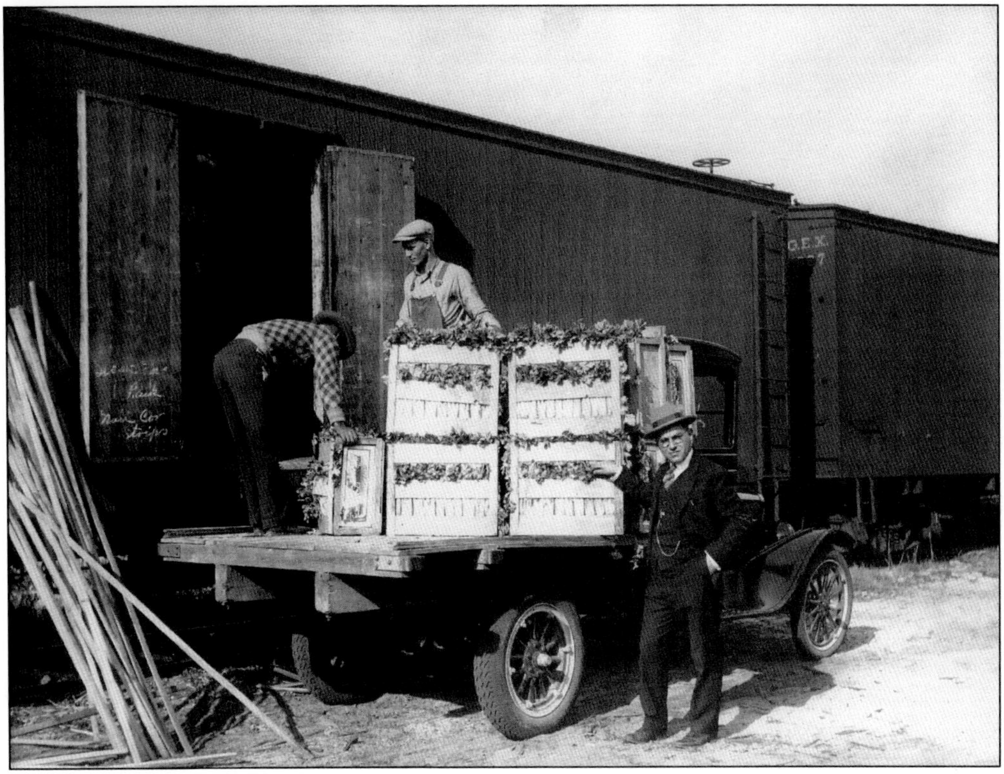

Morris Moses supervises the loading of a shipment of Sanford celery in this photograph taken February 16, 1926. Moses was a partner with his father in the firm of A.H. Moses and Son. A.H. Moses built Sanford's Jewish Community Center and donated the town clock to the city.

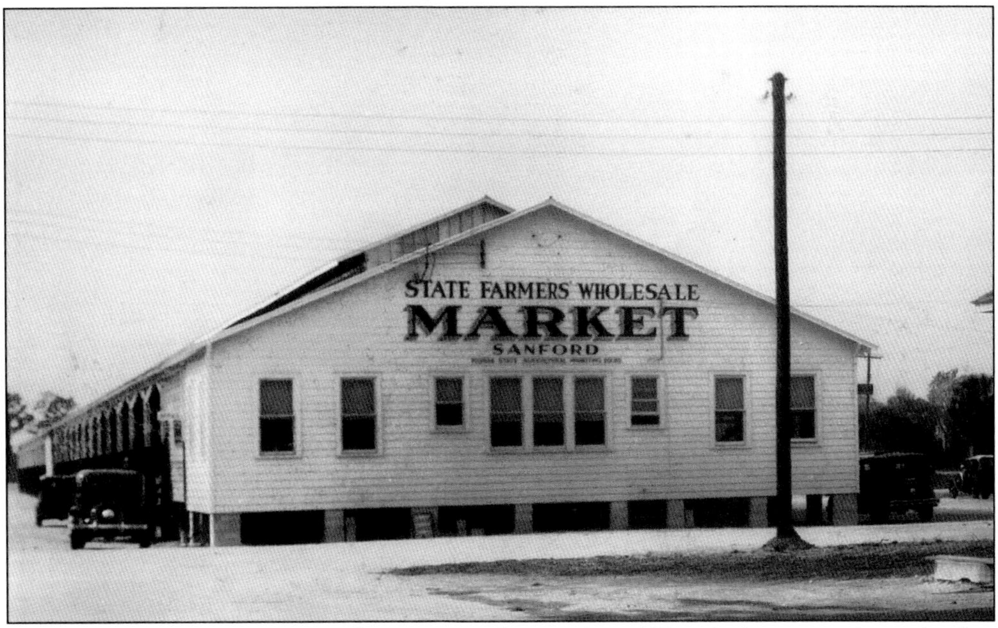

Sanford's Farmer's Market opened in 1934 at Thirteenth and French Avenue and was the first such operation in the state of Florida. The building was destroyed by fire in 1957.

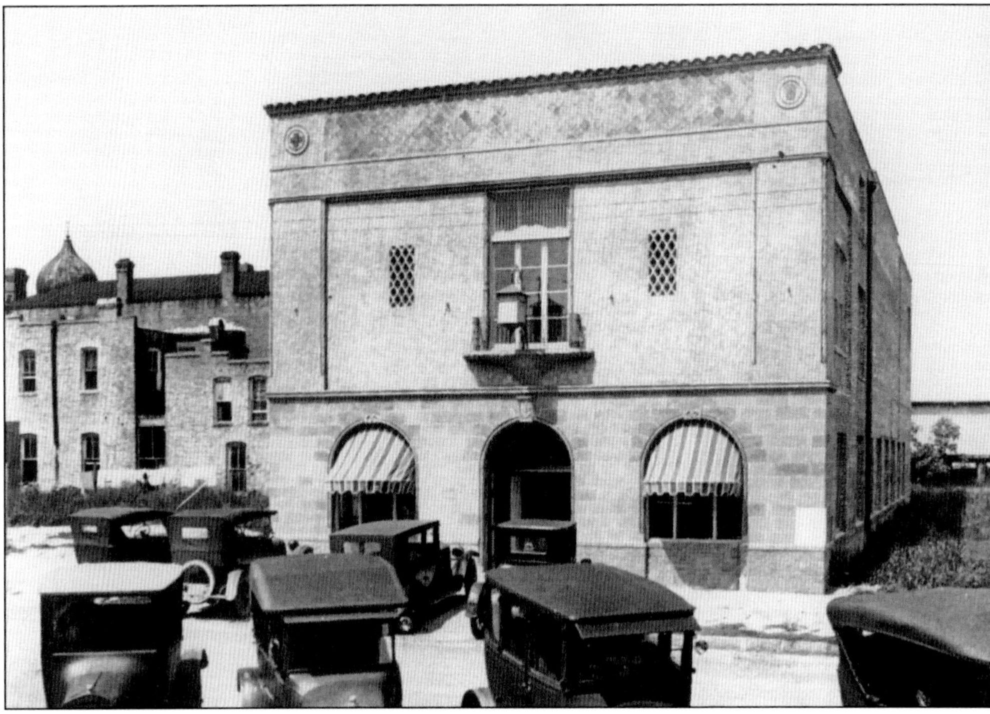

This is Masonic Lodge #62 at 212 North Park Avenue. Built in 1924, it was designed by Sanford architect Elton J. Moughton. This photograph was taken immediately after construction was completed.

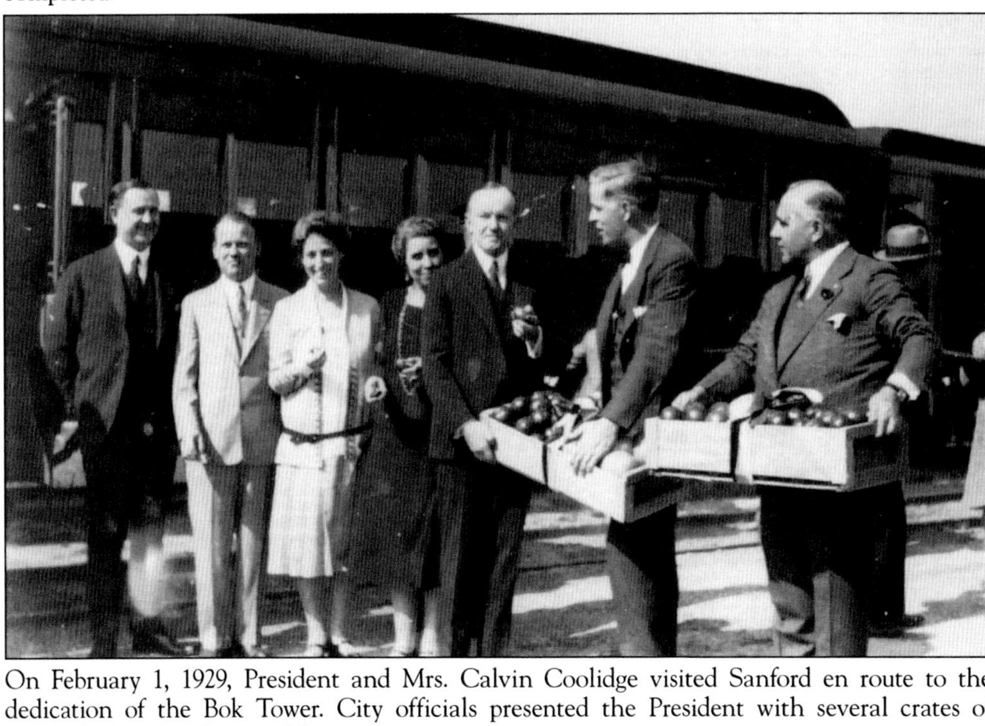

On February 1, 1929, President and Mrs. Calvin Coolidge visited Sanford en route to the dedication of the Bok Tower. City officials presented the President with several crates of Sanford grown produce and fruits.

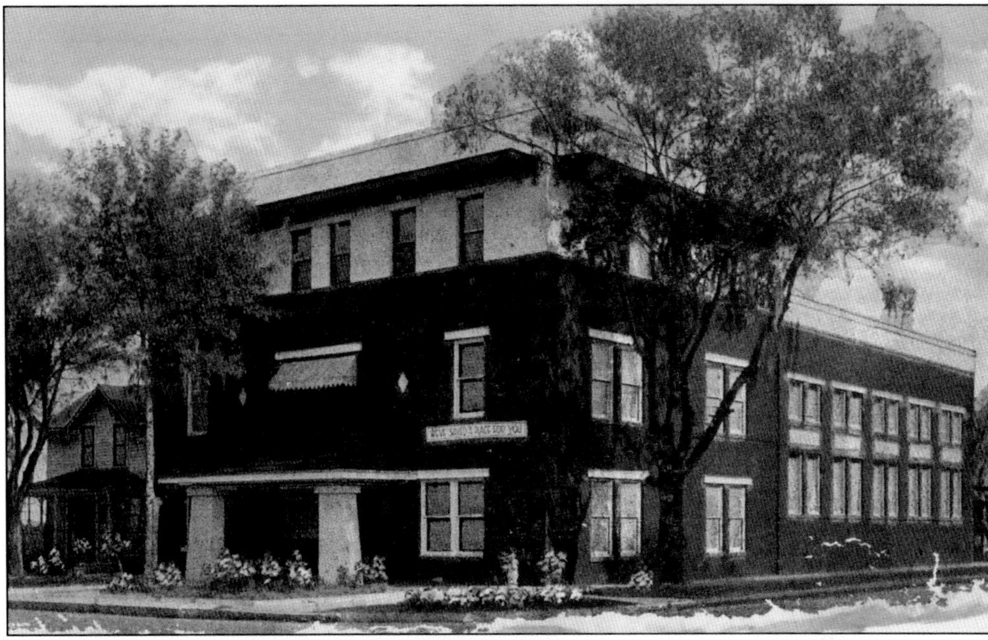

First Baptist Church was organized in 1884. The first service in the building shown here was on December 26, 1920.

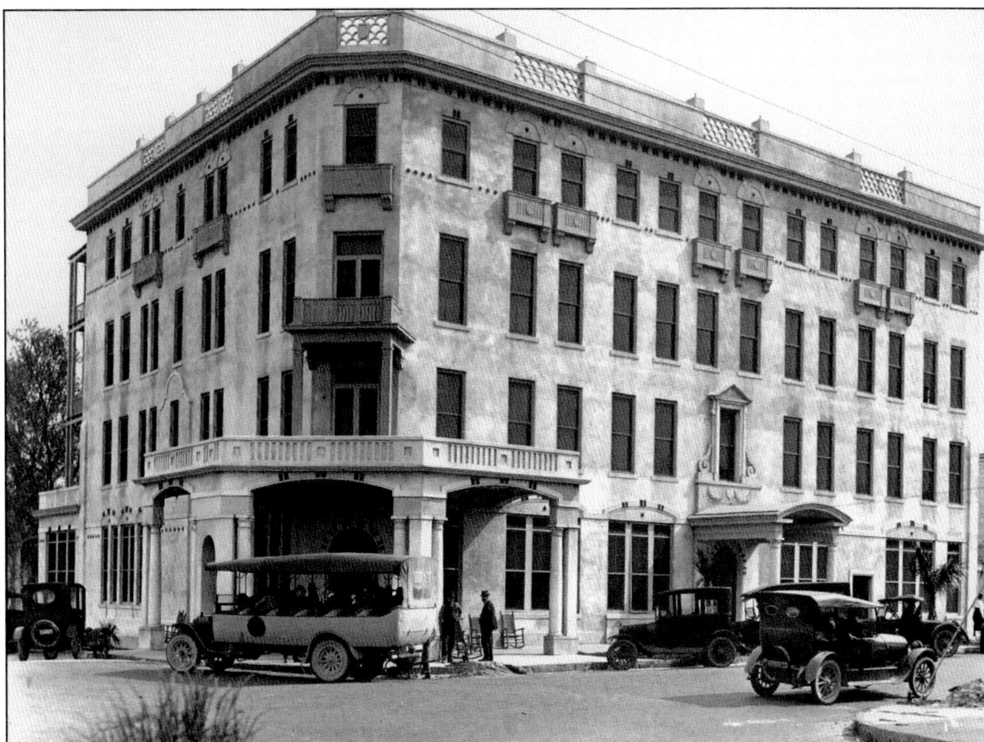

Pictured here is the Valdez Hotel, located at the corner of Commercial and Park Avenue, *c.* 1920. The hotel was originally built in the 1890s as the Welborne Block. In 1913 it served as the Seminole County Courthouse.

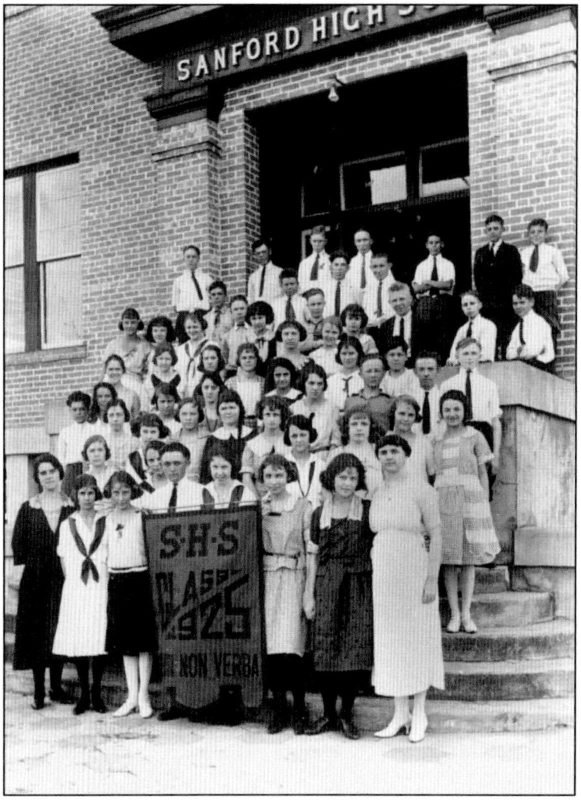

Sanford High School became Sanford Junior High School in 1927. The building was last used as a school in 1961.

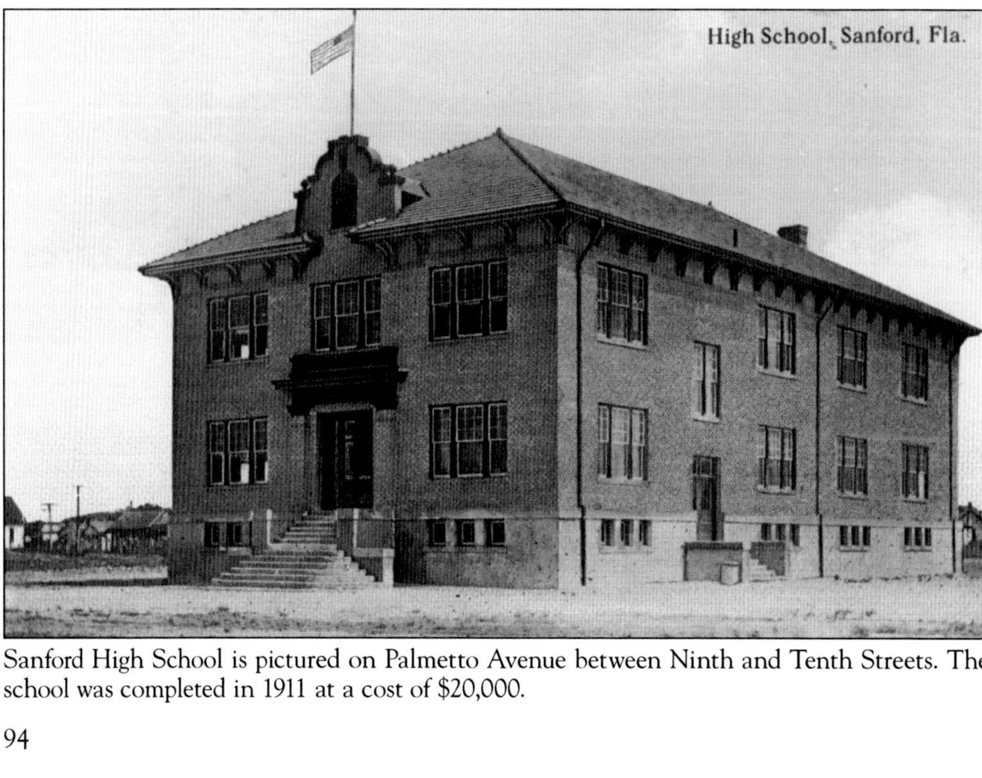

Sanford High School is pictured on Palmetto Avenue between Ninth and Tenth Streets. The school was completed in 1911 at a cost of $20,000.

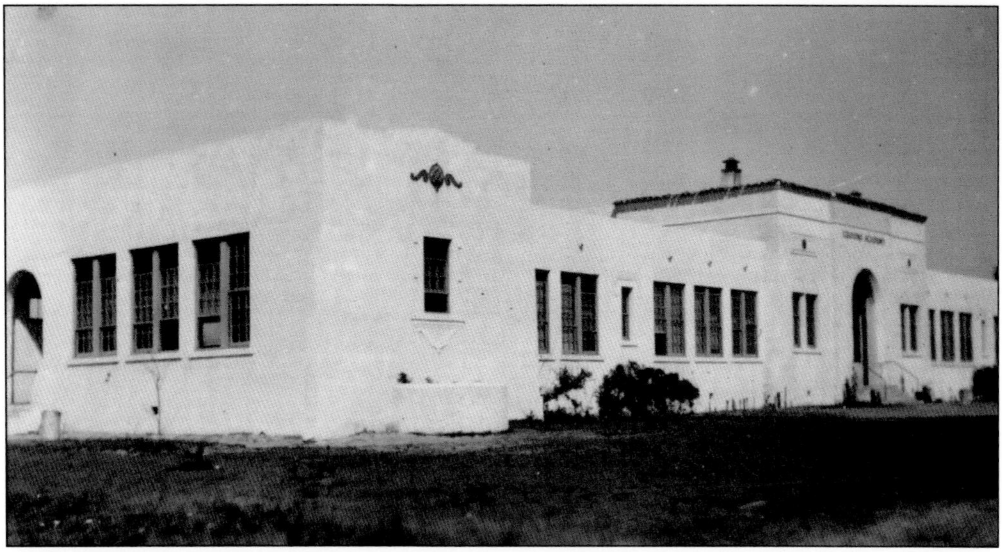

Crooms Academy opened in 1926 during the years of school segregation. The school was named for J.N. Crooms, a respected educator and former principal of Hopper Academy. Professor Crooms wife, Wealthy, was also a teacher.

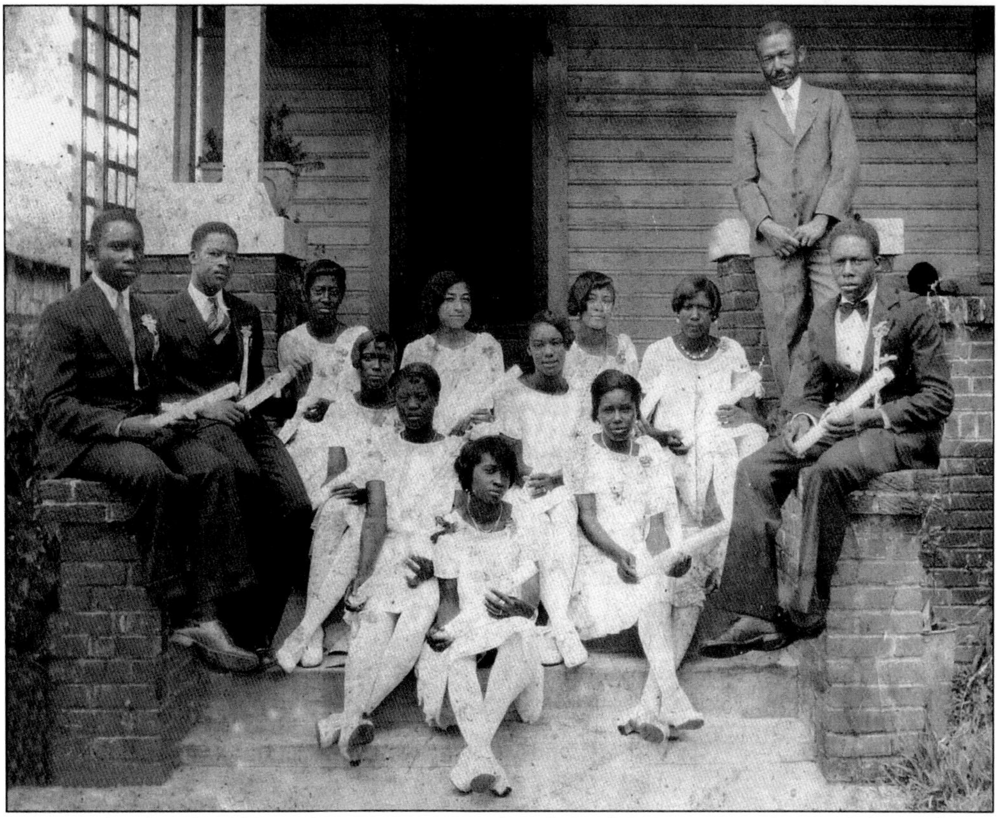

Crooms Academy's 1929 graduates are pictured with Prof. J.N. Crooms (top right). Graduates are seated on the front steps of the Crooms home at 812 South Sanford Avenue. (Courtesy of Altermese Bentley.)

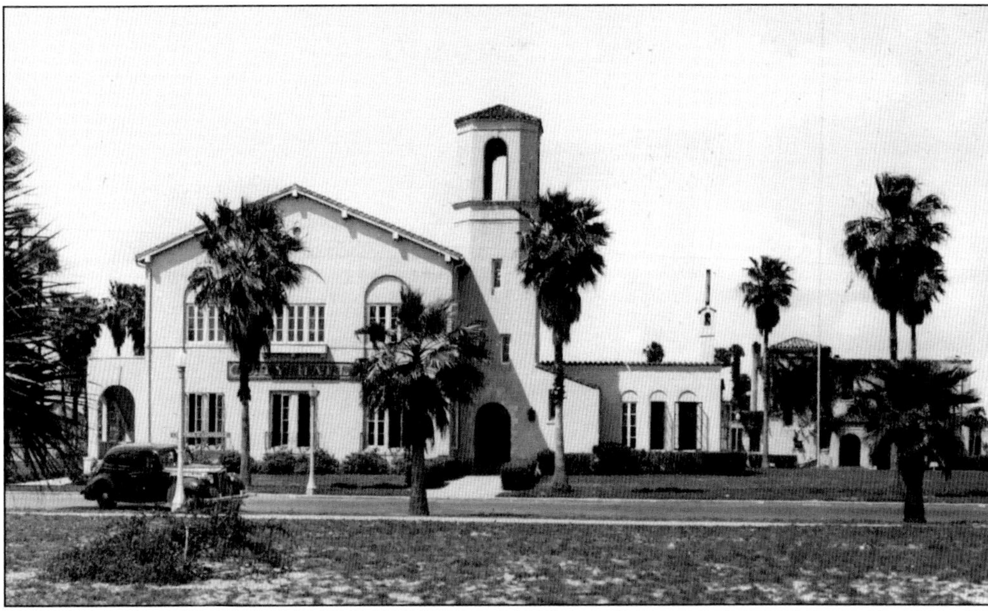

Sanford City Hall on North Park Avenue was built in the 1920s from a design by Elton J. Moughton. The assembly room on the second floor, nicknamed the "Celery Crate" was used for dances by the students from Seminole High. The building was demolished in 1976 to become the parking lot of the present city hall.

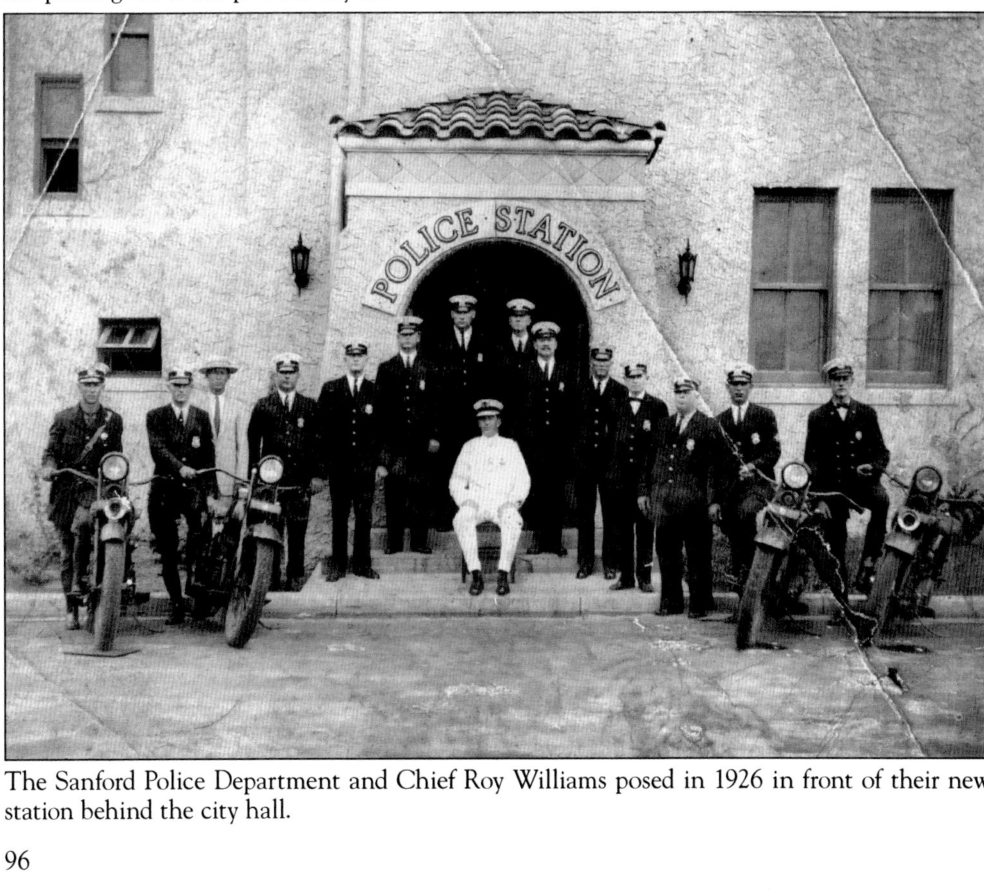

The Sanford Police Department and Chief Roy Williams posed in 1926 in front of their new station behind the city hall.

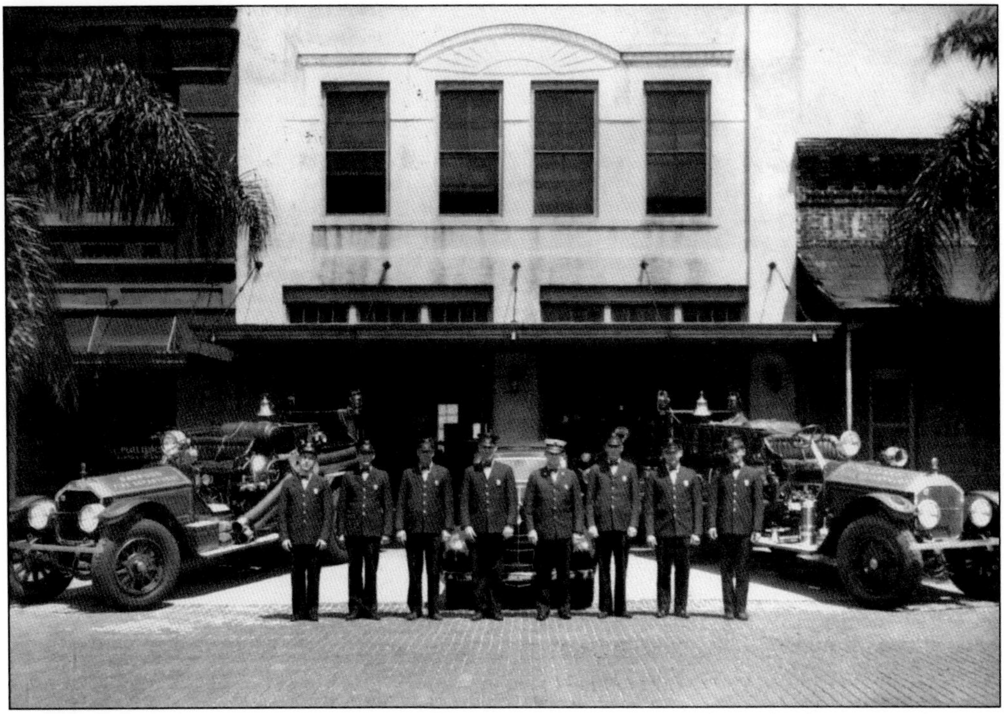

In 1923, Sy Smith, a custodian at the Elks Club, was given a monkey which, in turn, he gave to the fire department. The firemen built a cage and soon acquired a second monkey. Within a year, the department had a collection of animals, including possums, stray cats, geese, alligators, and even a porcupine. When city officials ordered the department to get rid of the animals, Police Chief Roy Williams offered to build cages at the jail. The Jaycees became involved and soon the animals were relocated to their own spot near the jailhouse. This was the beginning of Sanford's Municipal Zoo.

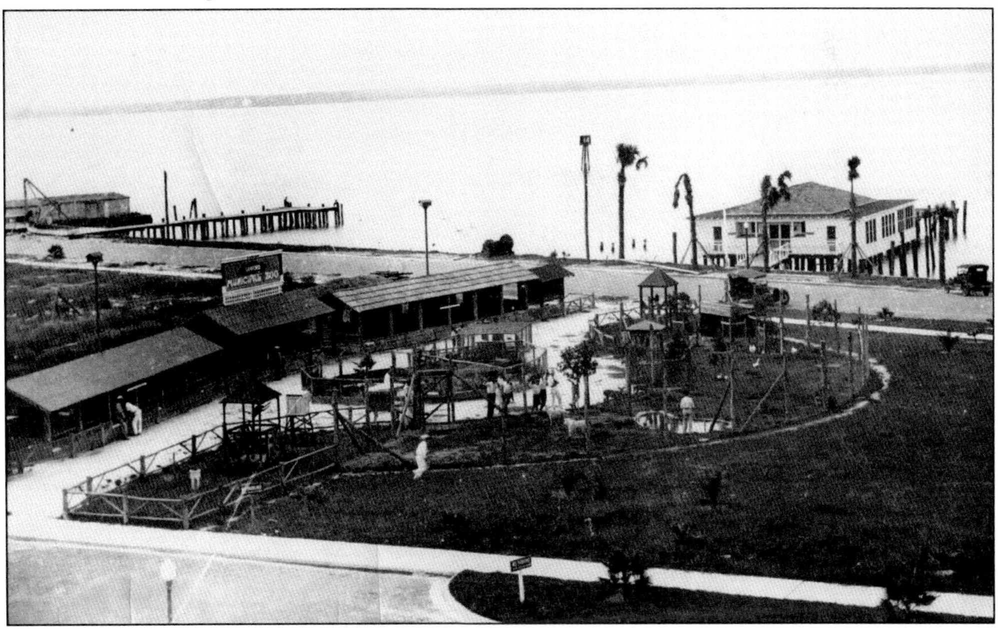

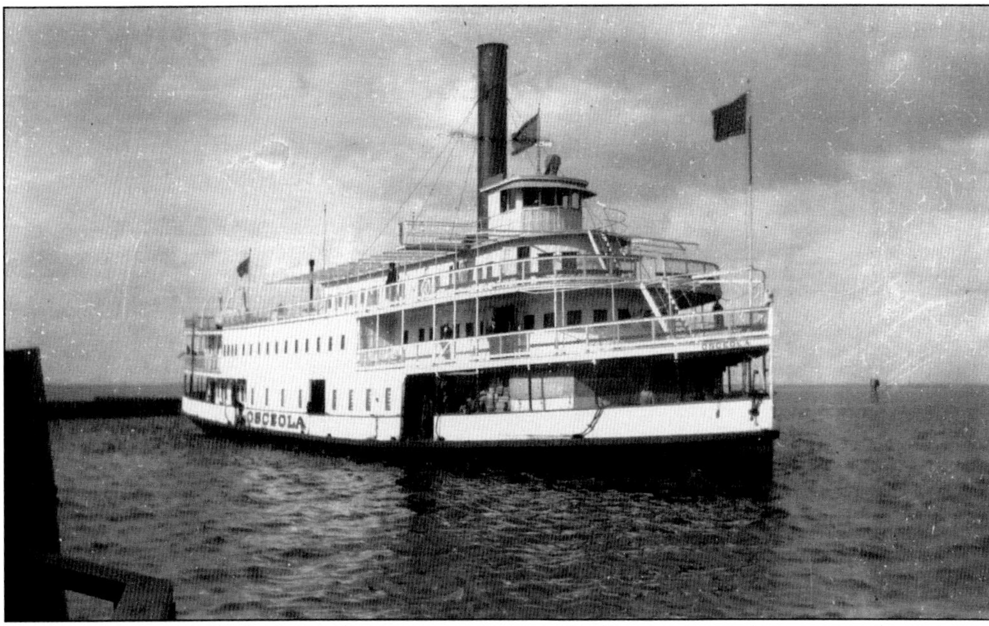

The *Osceola* was a Clyde Steamship Company stern wheeler riverboat that operated on the St. Johns River from 1913 to 1937.

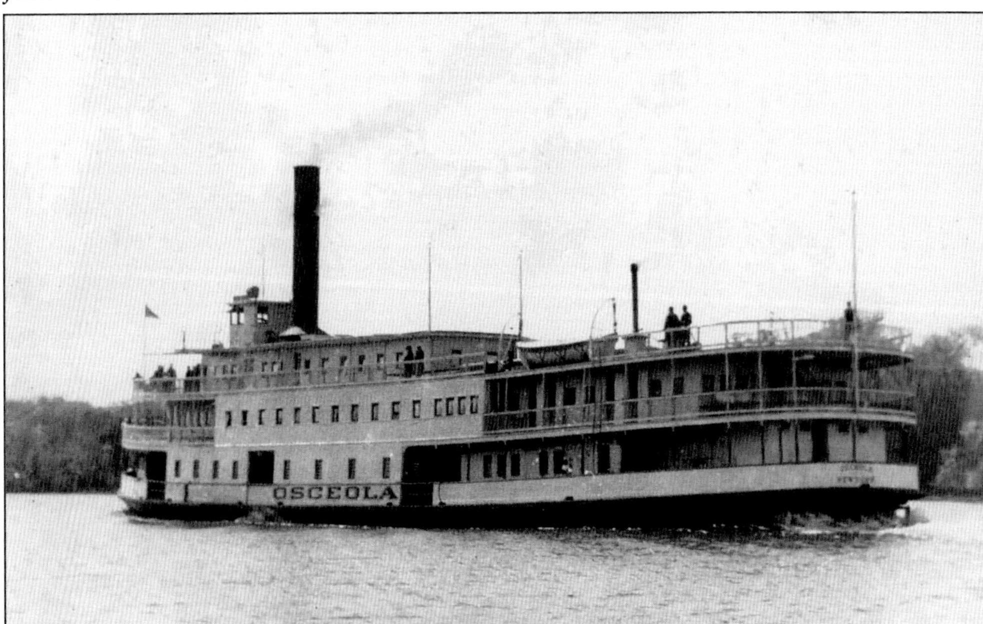

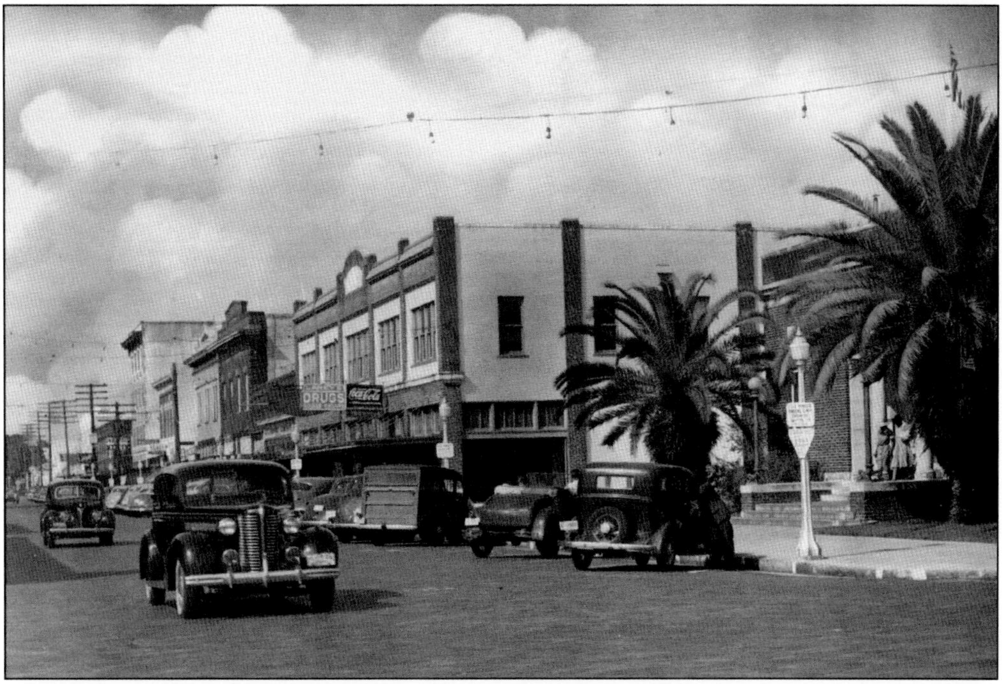

The Meisch Building was built on First Street in 1922 and 1923 for John Meisch of the Sanford Investment Co. The Piggly Wiggly and Sanford's Lu-Beth cafeteria were located here.

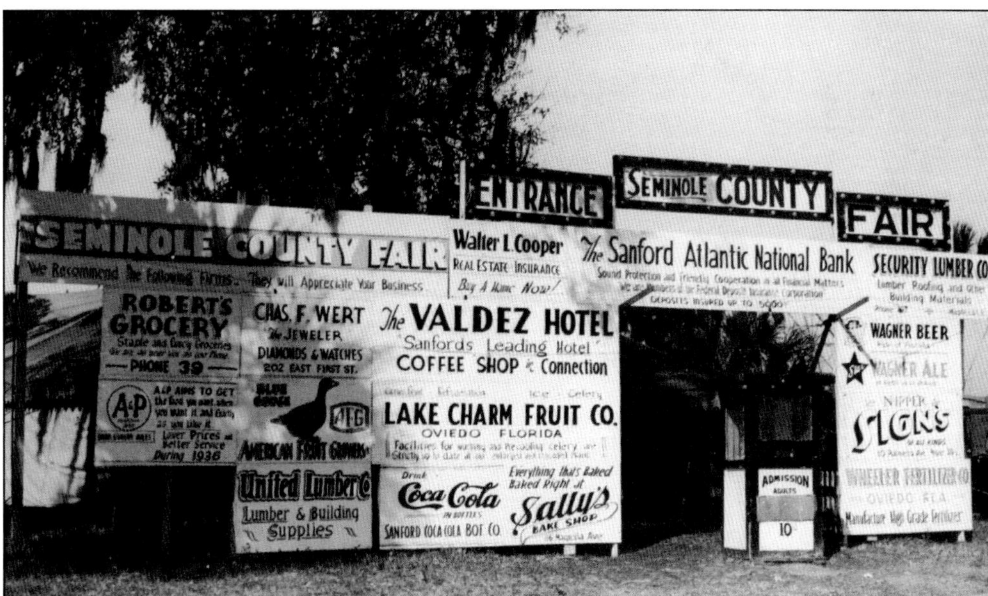

The Seminole County Fair in 1936 was a chance to show off the continued success of Sanford's truck farms and citrus groves.

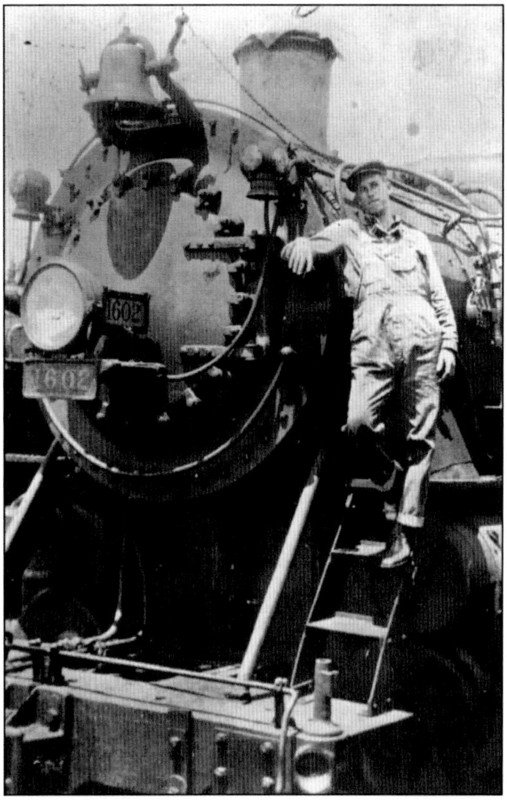

Joe Jarrell and Atlantic Coast Line (ACL) steam engine #1602 are pictured in 1928. Jarrell went to work for the ACL in 1925 as a fireman. He fired the train for the next 17 years and always said he loved it with a passion until the automatic stoker came into use. He then spent 33 as an engineer for the ACL and its successors, retiring with 50 years of service.

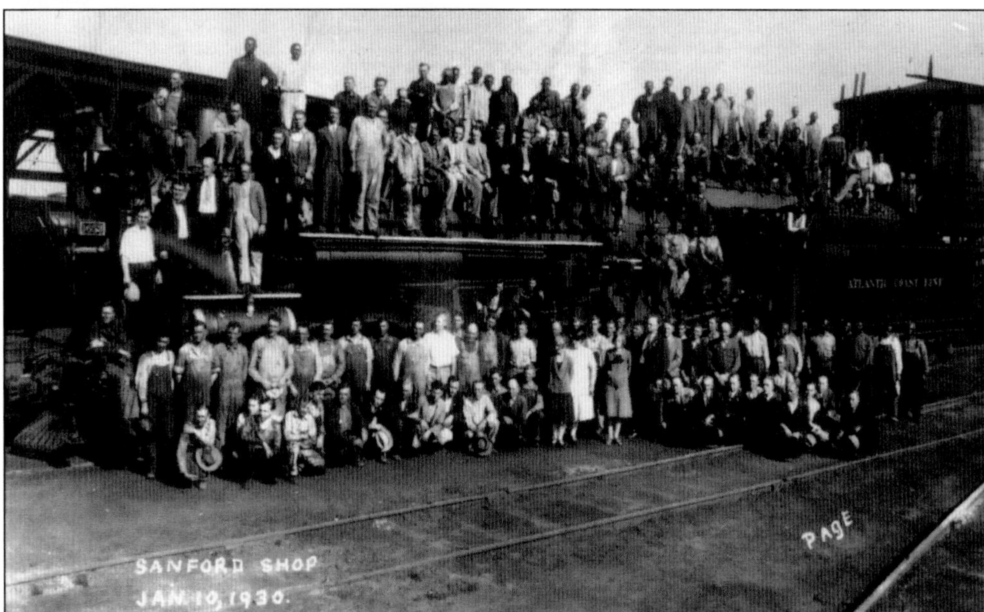

The Atlantic Coast Line System absorbed the Plant System in 1902. As a railroad city, Sanford was the base for train crews and repair shops. In 1967 the ACL merged with the Seaboard Air Line to form the Seaboard Coast Line. In 1980, the present CSX Corporation resulted from the merger of the Chessie System and the Seaboard Coast Line.

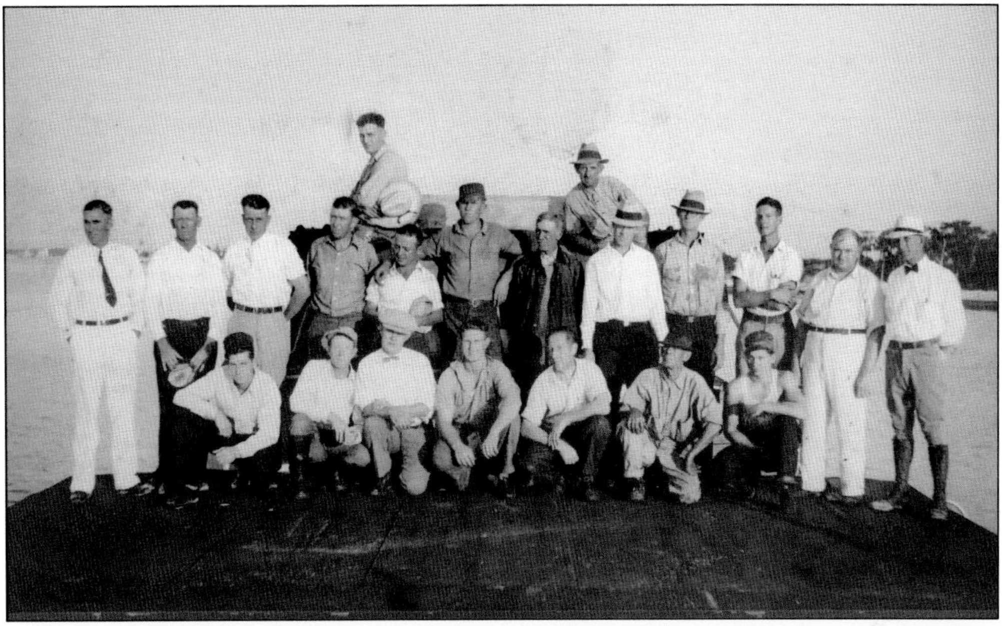

This crew of the dredge boat *Tennessee* dredged the fill for Highway 17-92 along the waterfront from the Lake Monroe Bridge in 1933. This photograph was taken by Wieboldt Studios of Sanford. (Courtesy of the Carlson family.)

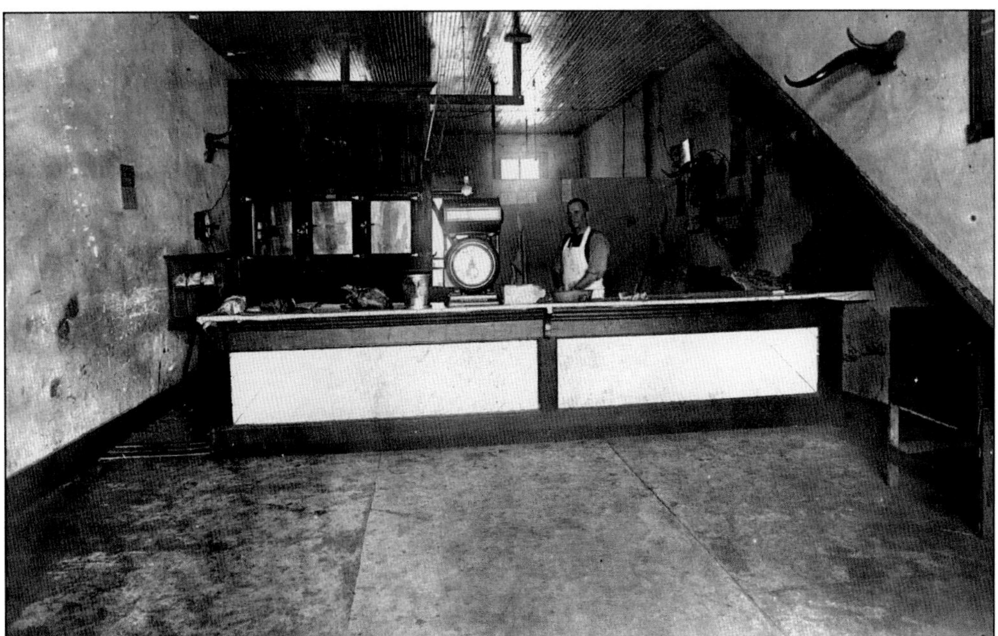

Albert Hawkins stands behind the counter at his meat market at 303 Sanford Avenue. This was the second store Hawkins had at this address. The first opened in the 1920s and this store opened in 1934. (Courtesy of the Carlson family.)

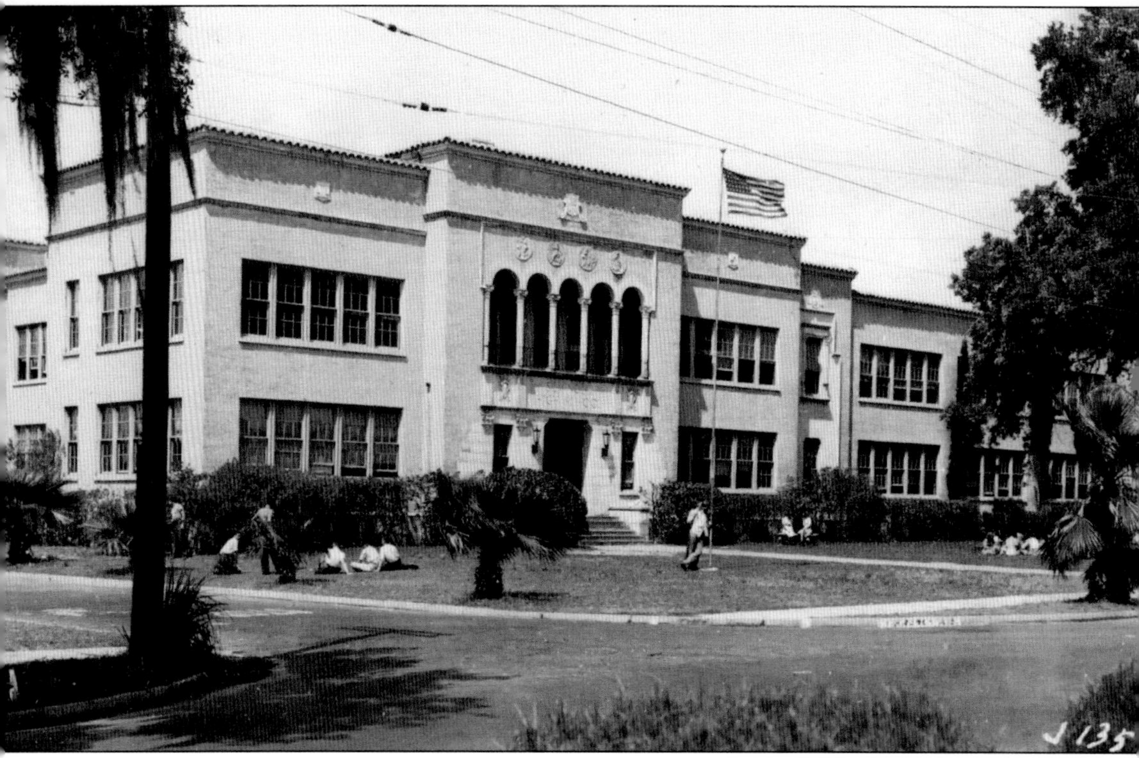

Seminole High School at 1700 French Avenue was designed by Elton J. Moughton and was built in 1927. When the present Seminole High School opened, this building became Sanford Middle School. When the building was demolished in 1991, parts of the façade were incorporated into the new school.

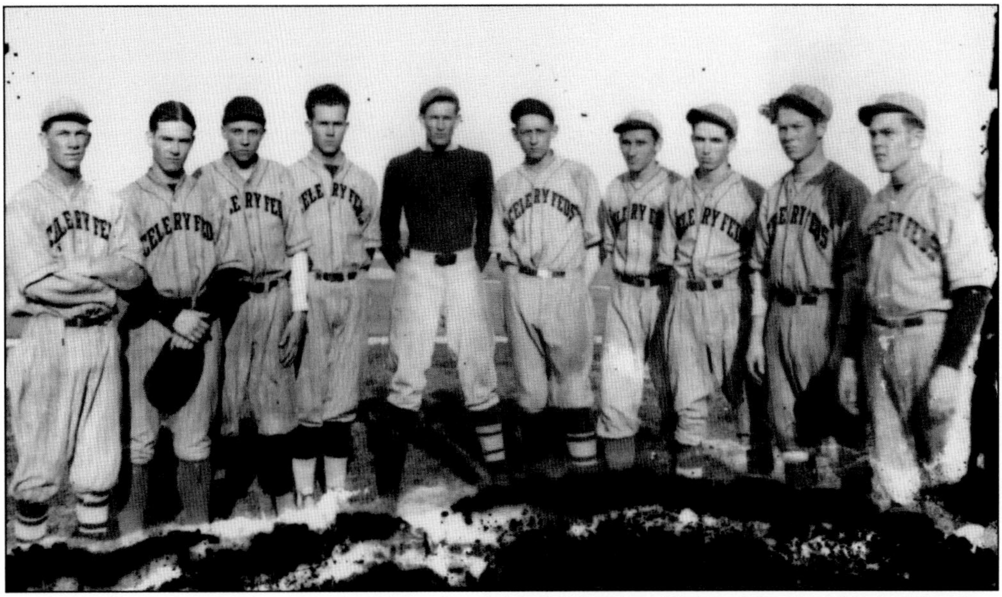

Renowned radio sportscaster Red Barber played for the "Celery Feds" of Sanford High School in 1926. He is second from the right in this photograph from his high school annual, the *Salmagundi*.

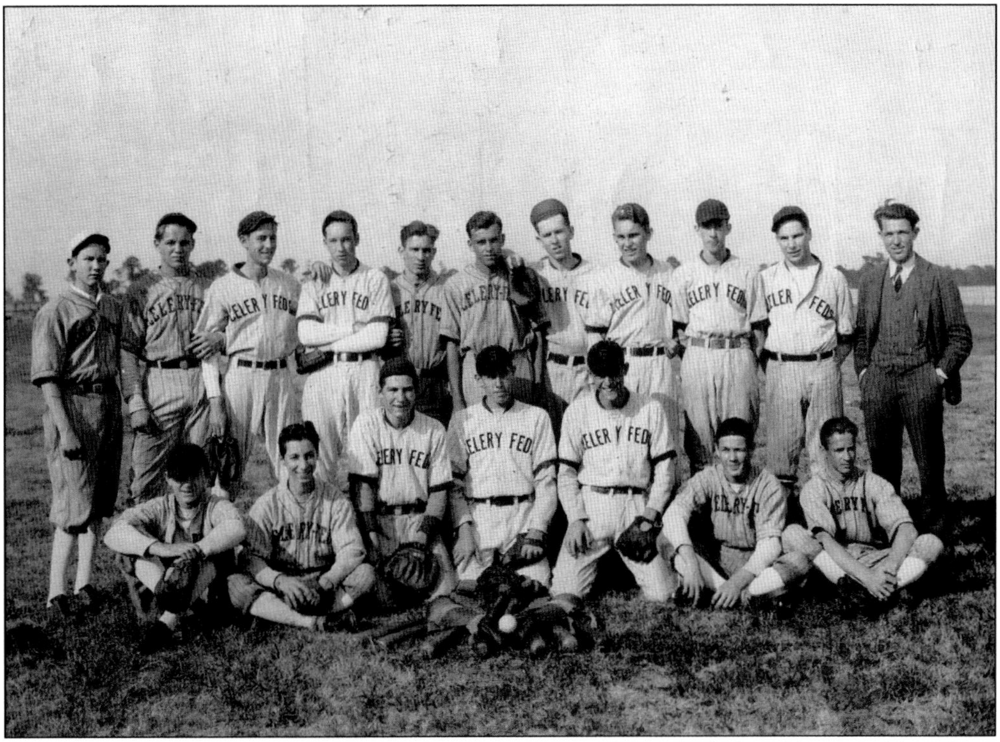

These are the 1930 "Celery Feds" of Sanford High School. Sanford's local hero Buddy Lake is on the front row in the middle. Bernard "Buddy" D. Lake pitched the first perfect game in the Florida State League during an outstanding professional career. He is remembered for pitching a shut-out 19-inning game in 1947 in which he hit the only home run.

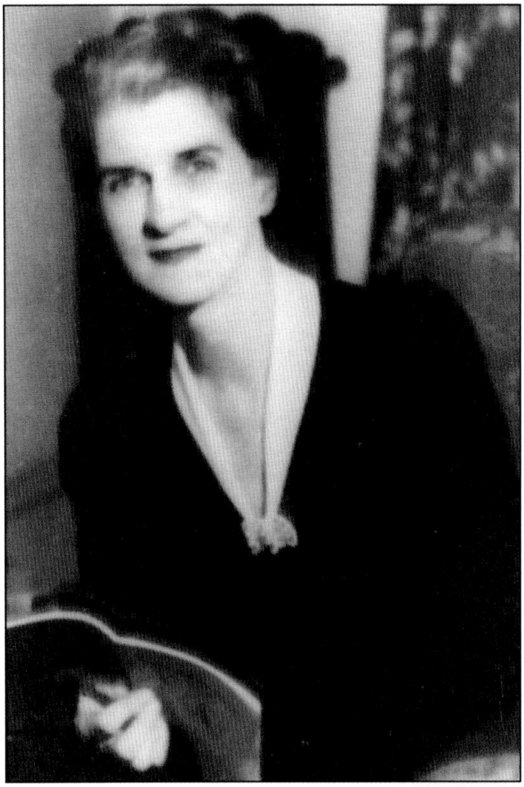

Childrens book author and illustrator Elvira Garner came to Sanford from Tennessee. Her best known book is *Ezekiel* in which every chapter begins "Way down in Sanford, Florida…" This photo was taken in 1956.

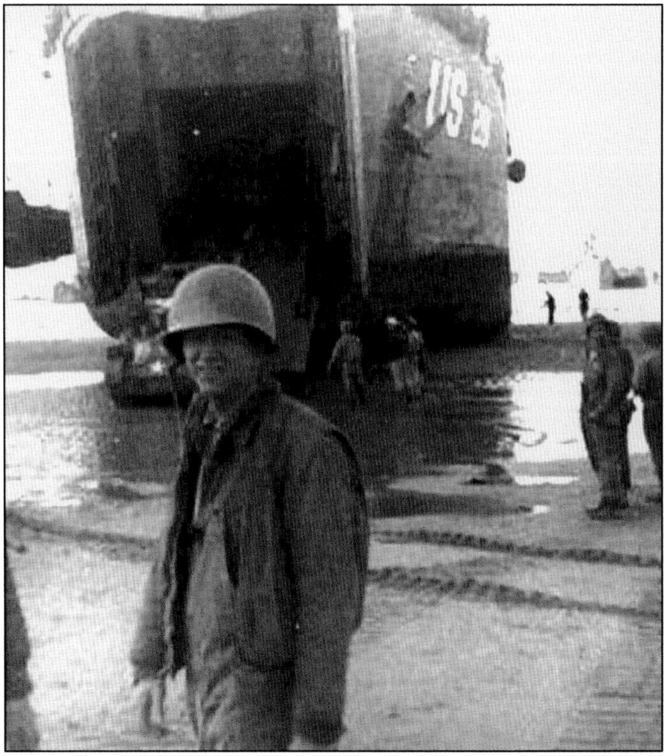

Sam Byrd stands in front of an LST landing craft on Omaha Beach following the D-Day invasion. Byrd graduated from Sanford High School in 1925 and went straight into a Broadway career, starring in the original productions of *Tobacco Road* and *Of Mice and Men*. In 1942 he wrote *Small Town South*, a fictionalized account of the Forrest Lake scandal. During World War II he served as a lieutenant in the United States Navy and was Beachmaster on Omaha Beach. (Courtesy of Julius Shoulars.)

Five

THE FRIENDLY CITY

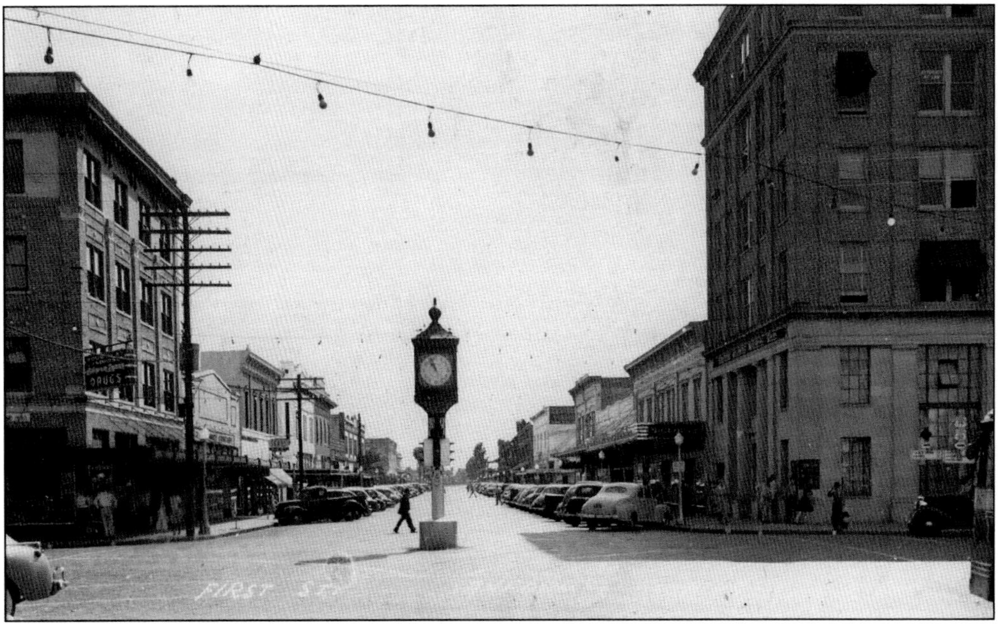

For many years the tallest building in Sanford was the First National Bank (right), built in 1922. The town clock came from this building when the bank closed in the 1920s.

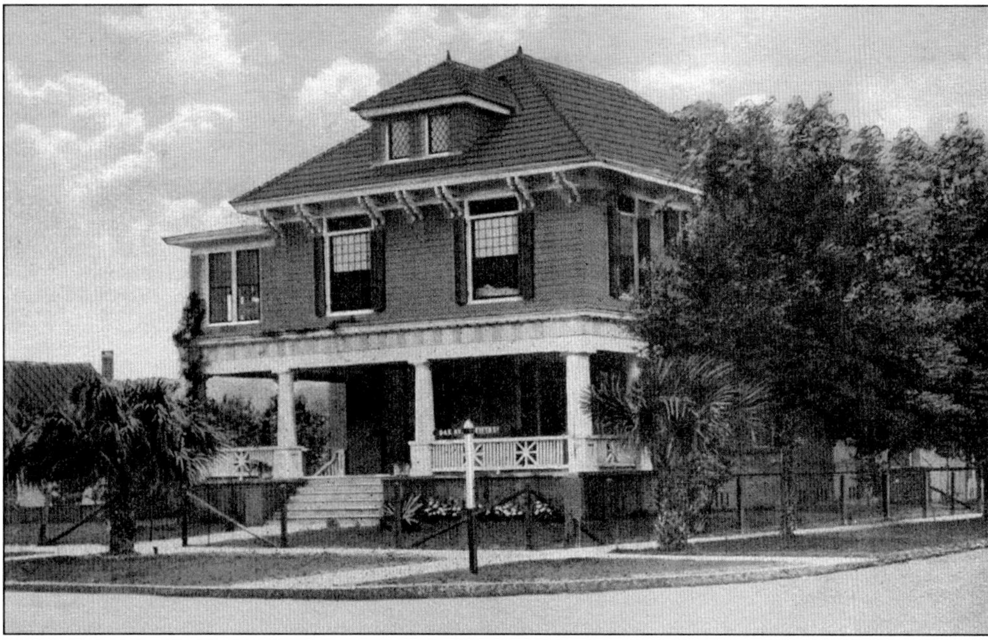

Fernald-Laughton Hospital, once a private residence, served Seminole County until 1956.

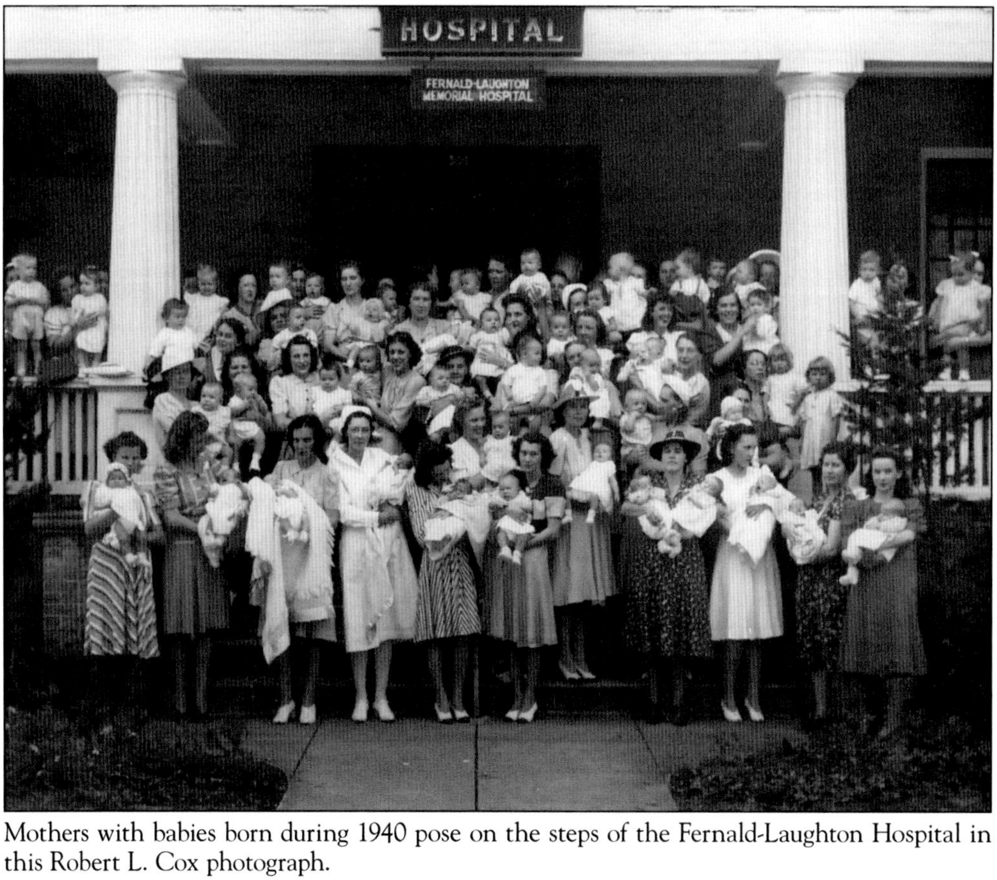

Mothers with babies born during 1940 pose on the steps of the Fernald-Laughton Hospital in this Robert L. Cox photograph.

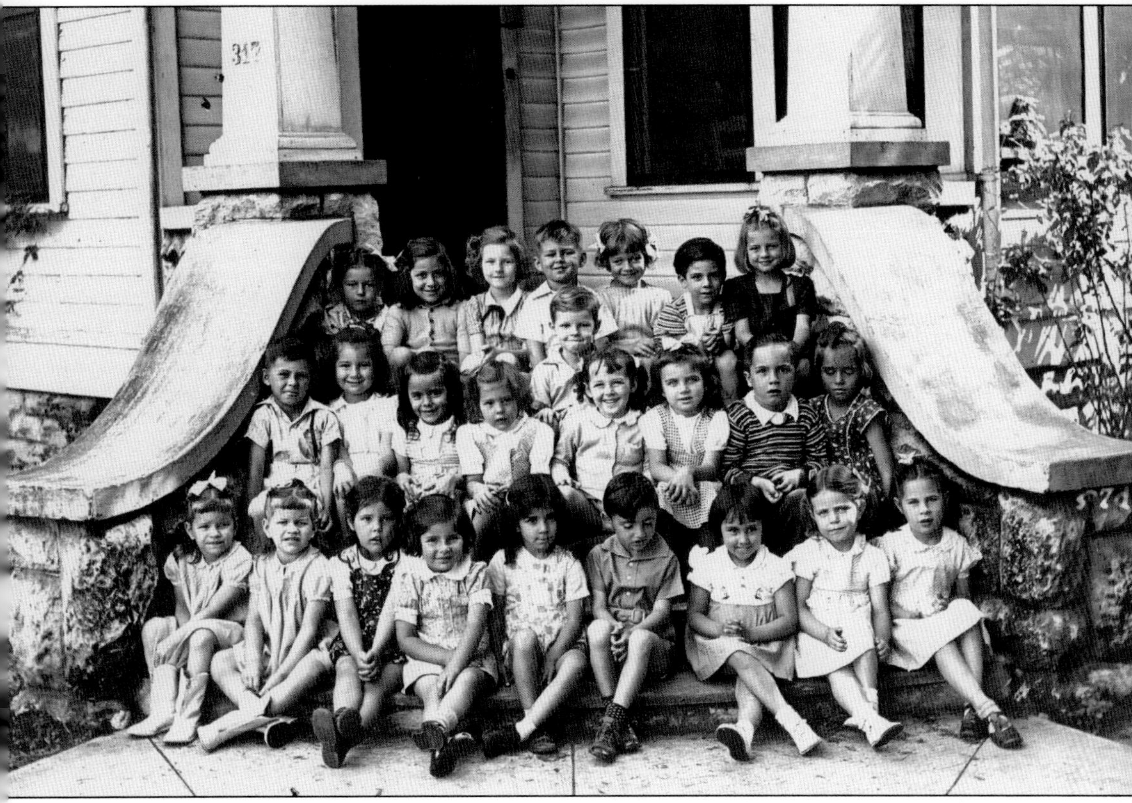

Ruth Gordon Wright had her students pose on the corner of Oak Avenue and Fourth Street during the 1941–1942 school year. (Courtesy of Grace Marie Stinecipher.)

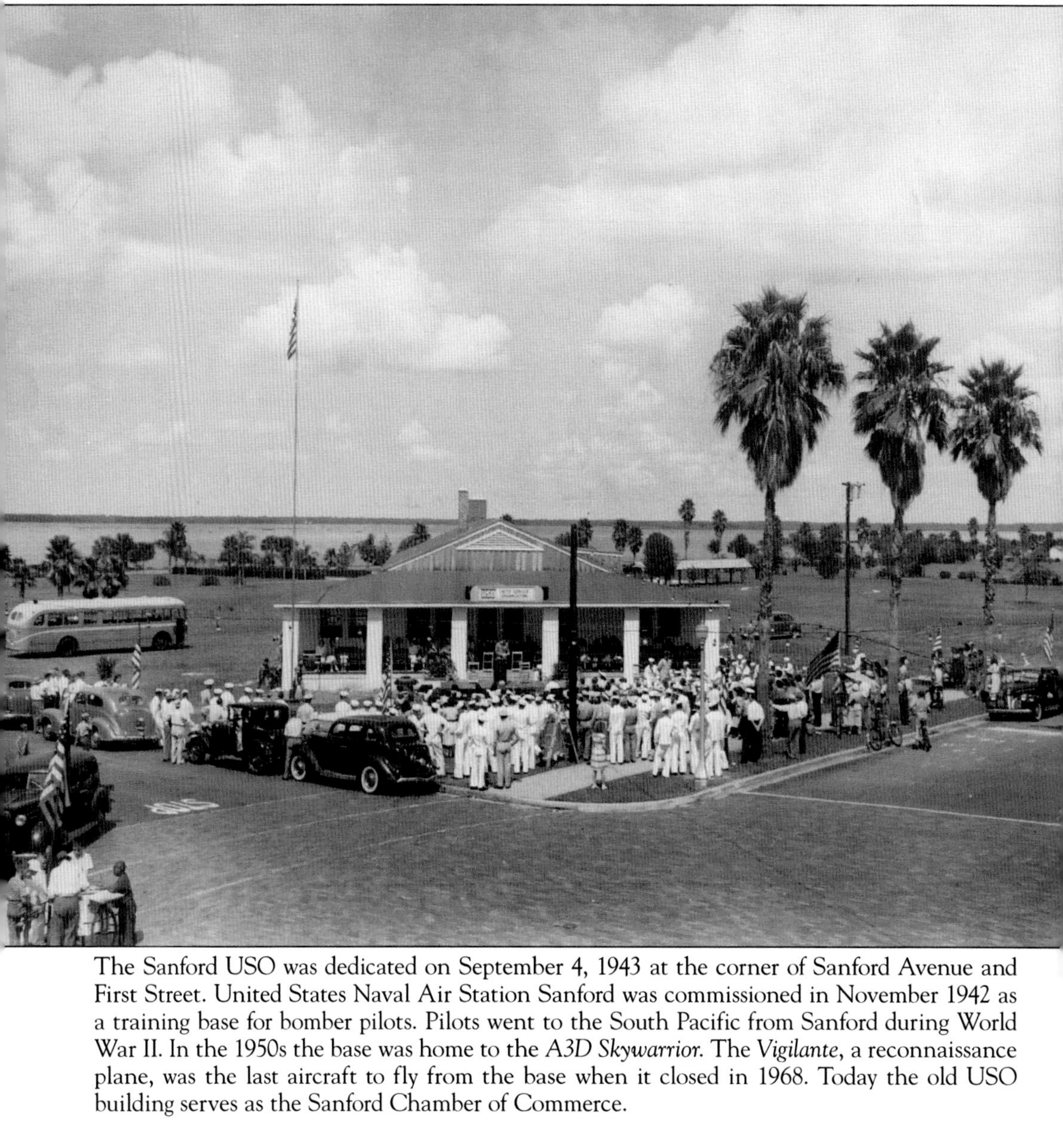

The Sanford USO was dedicated on September 4, 1943 at the corner of Sanford Avenue and First Street. United States Naval Air Station Sanford was commissioned in November 1942 as a training base for bomber pilots. Pilots went to the South Pacific from Sanford during World War II. In the 1950s the base was home to the *A3D Skywarrior*. The *Vigilante*, a reconnaissance plane, was the last aircraft to fly from the base when it closed in 1968. Today the old USO building serves as the Sanford Chamber of Commerce.

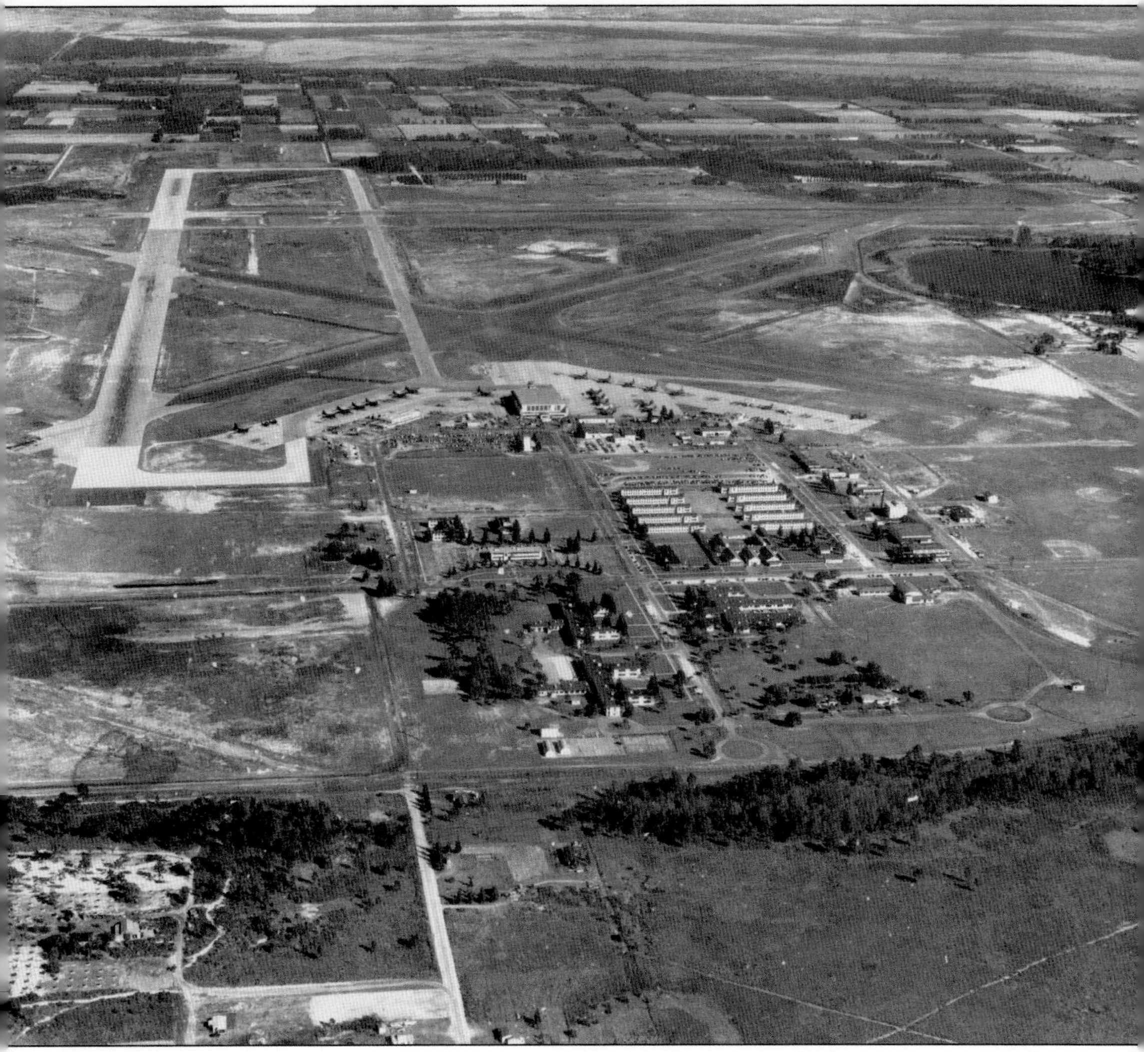

The Sanford Naval Air Station, also known as Naval Air Station Sanford, was commissioned on November 3, 1942 as a naval aviation training facility. The field at the station was named in 1958 in memory of Robert W. Ramey, an A3D pilot, who went down with his plane to save the lives of civilians on the ground. The station closed in 1968. This 1956 aerial view of Naval Air Station Sanford shows the long runways which are still used today at the Orlando-Sanford International Airport. (Courtesy of Bill Shepard.)

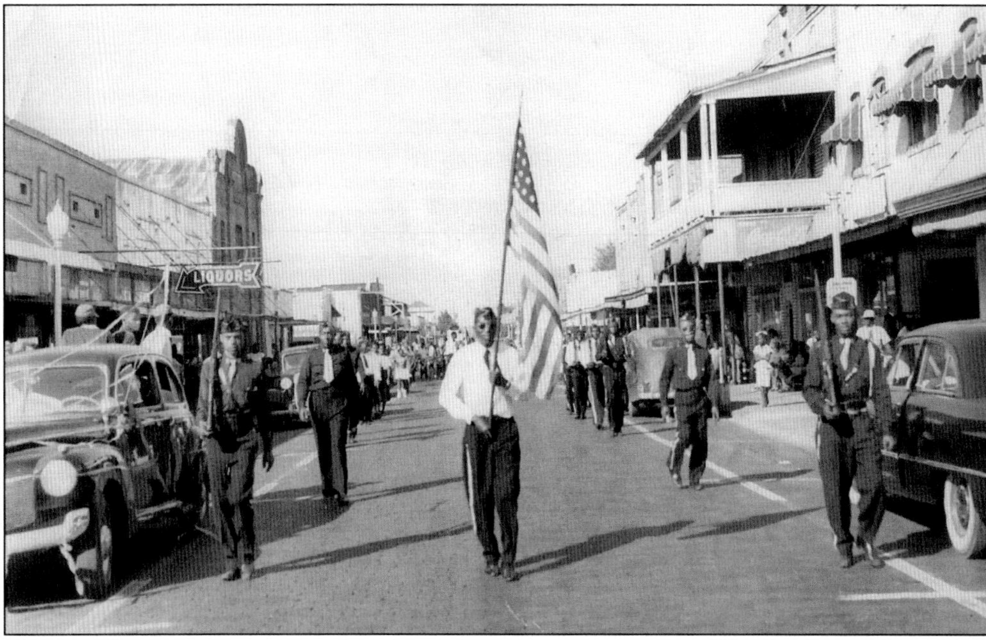

This photograph of David N. Roberts Sr. leading a military parade south on Sanford Avenue shows what Sanford Avenue looked like in the 1940s. They are just passing Jerry's Arcade and Dr. George Starke's office on the right. The buildings shown here are all gone in 2003. (Courtesy of Roberta Terry.)

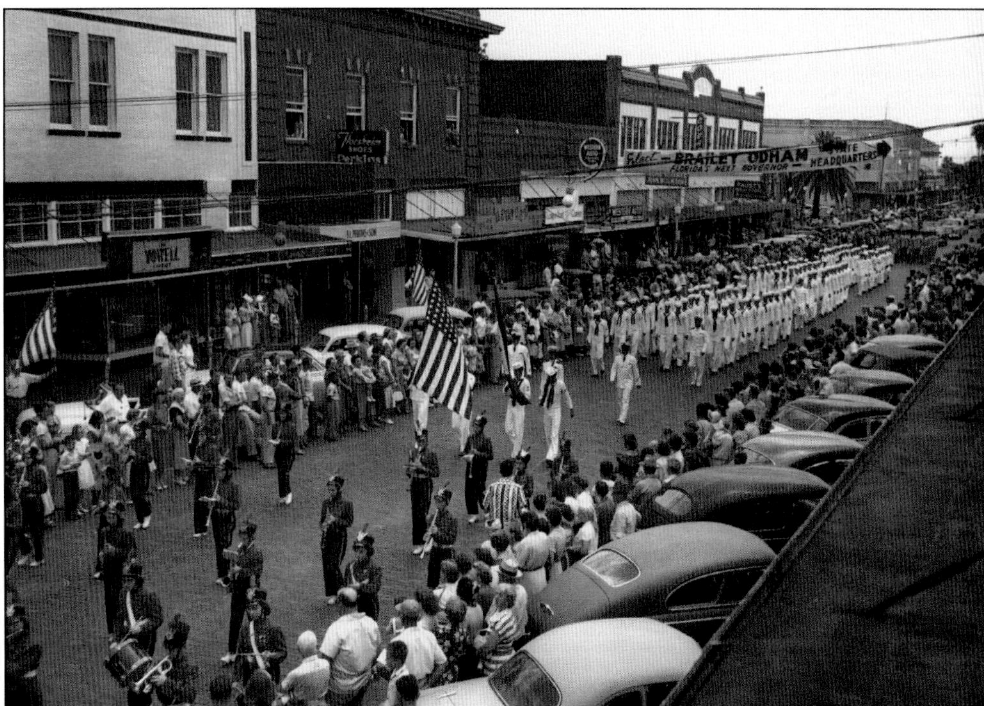

Seminole High School Band in an Armed Forces Day parade on First Street, May 17, 1952. This photograph is by Raymond Studios.

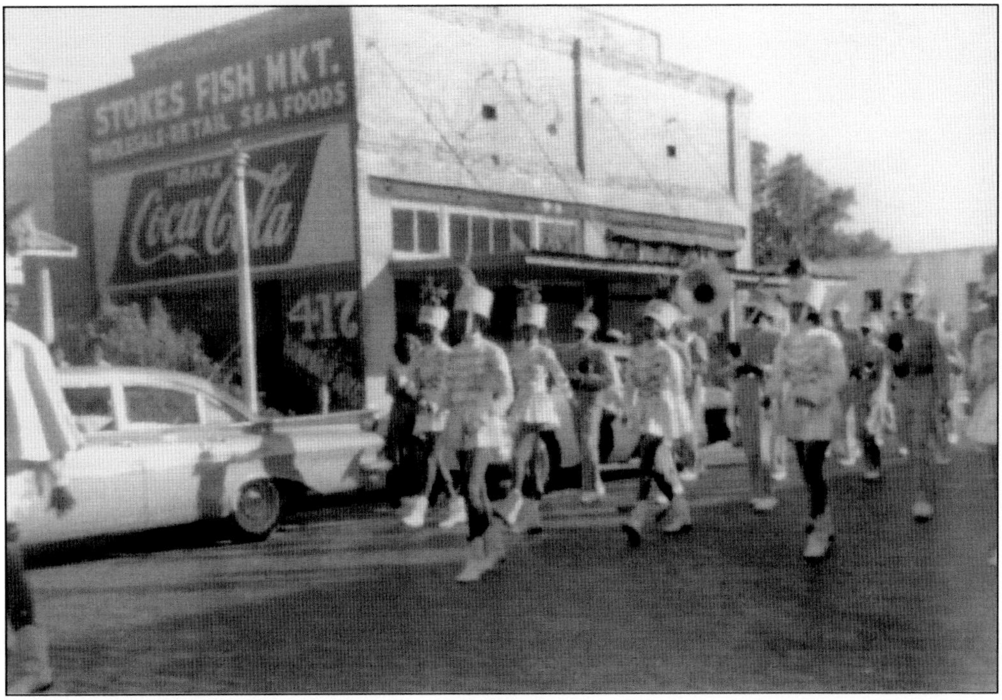

The Crooms Academy Mighty Panthers marched down Sanford Avenue for their Homecoming parade in 1949. (Courtesy of Victoria Brown-Smith.)

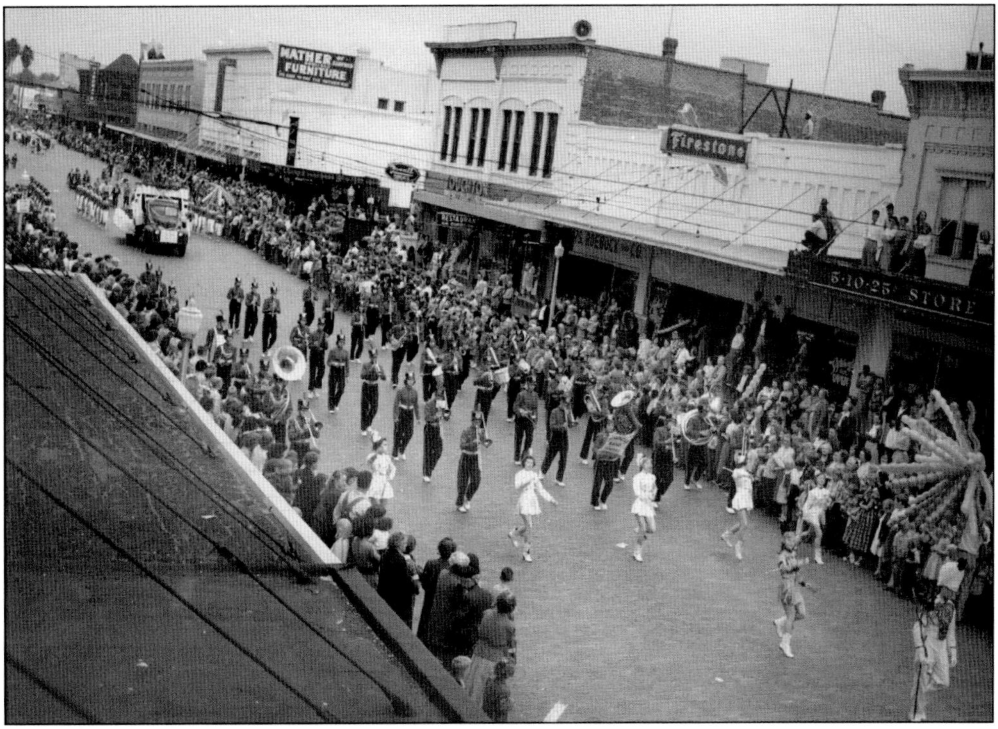

In the 1950s, Sanford was known for its Christmas parades down First Street. In 1952, this parade was sponsored by the Jaycees and the Sanford merchants.

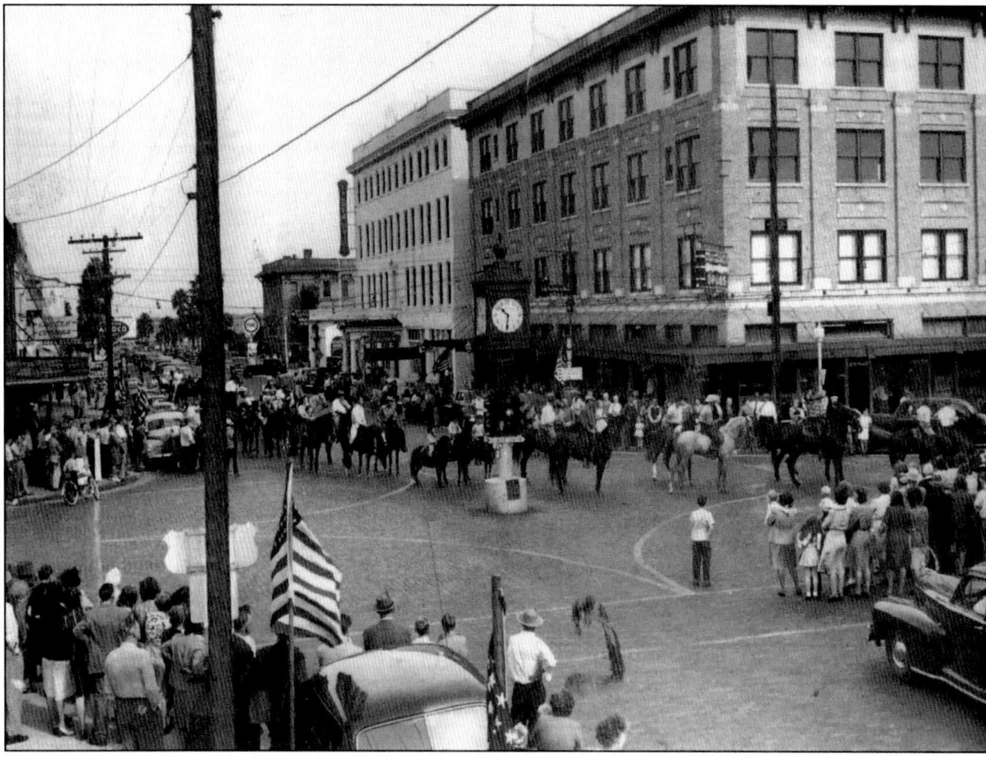

Dusty Boots Riding Club members bring up the rear of the parade as they cross the intersection of Park Avenue and First Street. (Courtesy of Margaret Duggar.)

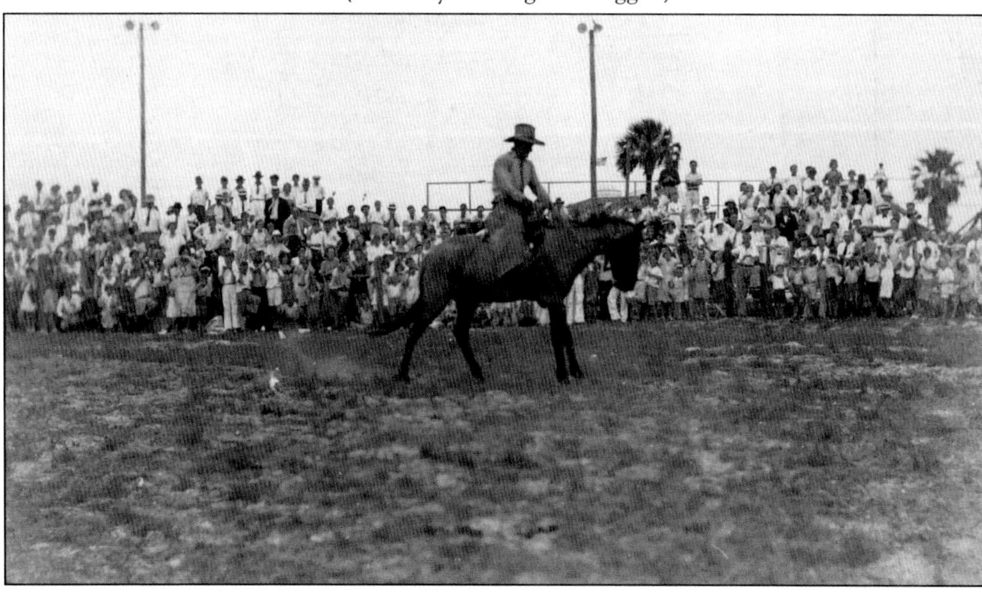

In February 1949, Milt Hinkle, sponsored by the Kiwanis Club, brought Col. Zack T. Miller's 101 Ranch and Wild West Show to Sanford. This was an attempt by Hinkle and Miller to revive the original Oklahoma show that had shut down in 1933. It featured Sanford's own Dusty Boots Riding Club and was held on the football field behind Seminole High on French Avenue. It was the last great wild west show to play in Central Florida.

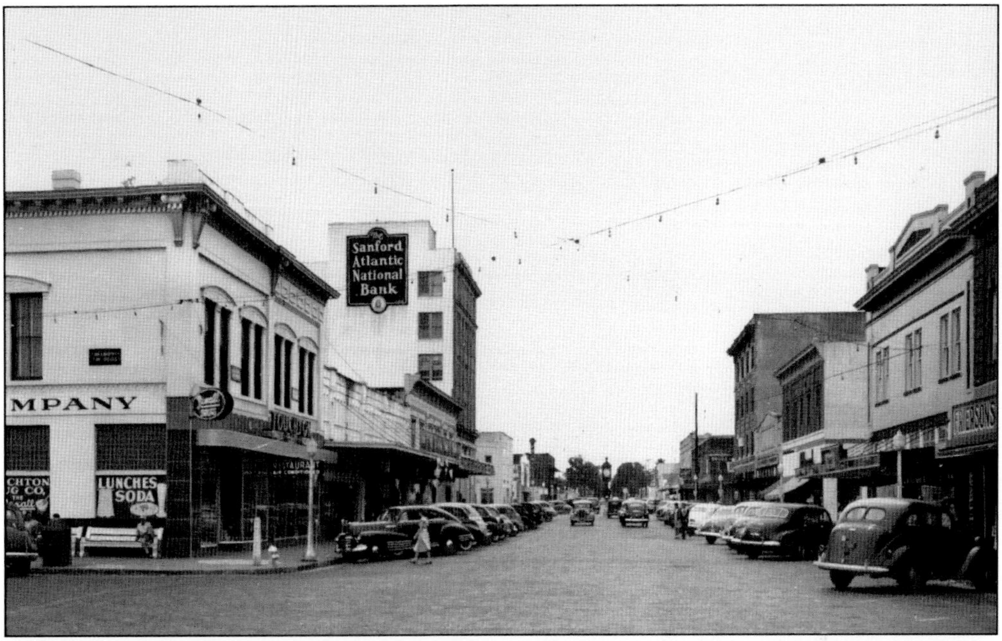

This photograph was taken at the intersection of Magnolia Avenue and First Street, looking west. In the 1970s Magnolia Avenue was closed to traffic and a pedestrian mall was created.

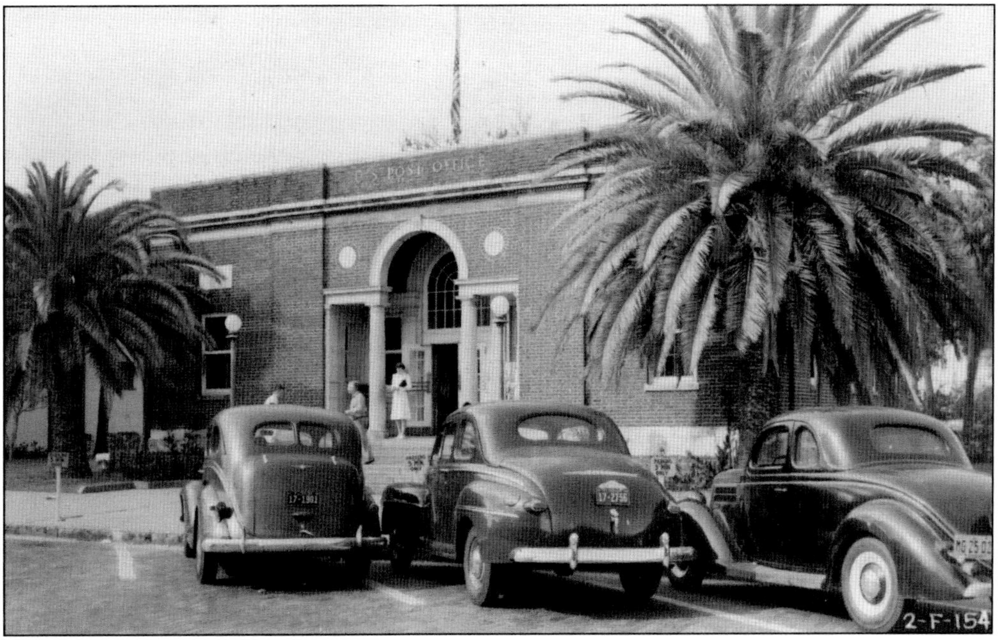

This classical revival style building served as the public library from 1963 to 1975. It was originally built as a post office in 1917.

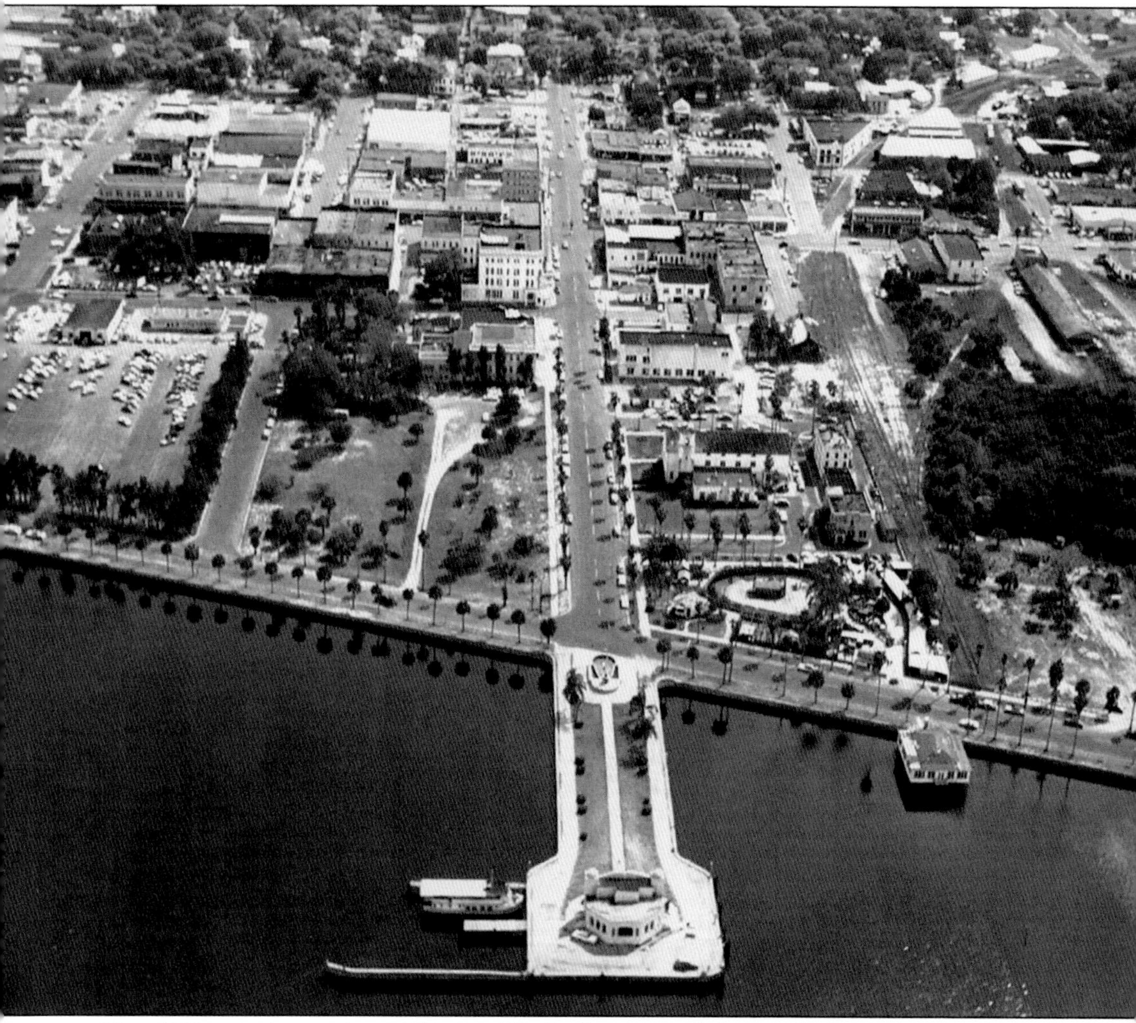

This 1950s aerial view shows Memorial Park, the zoo, and the city hall on the waterfront.

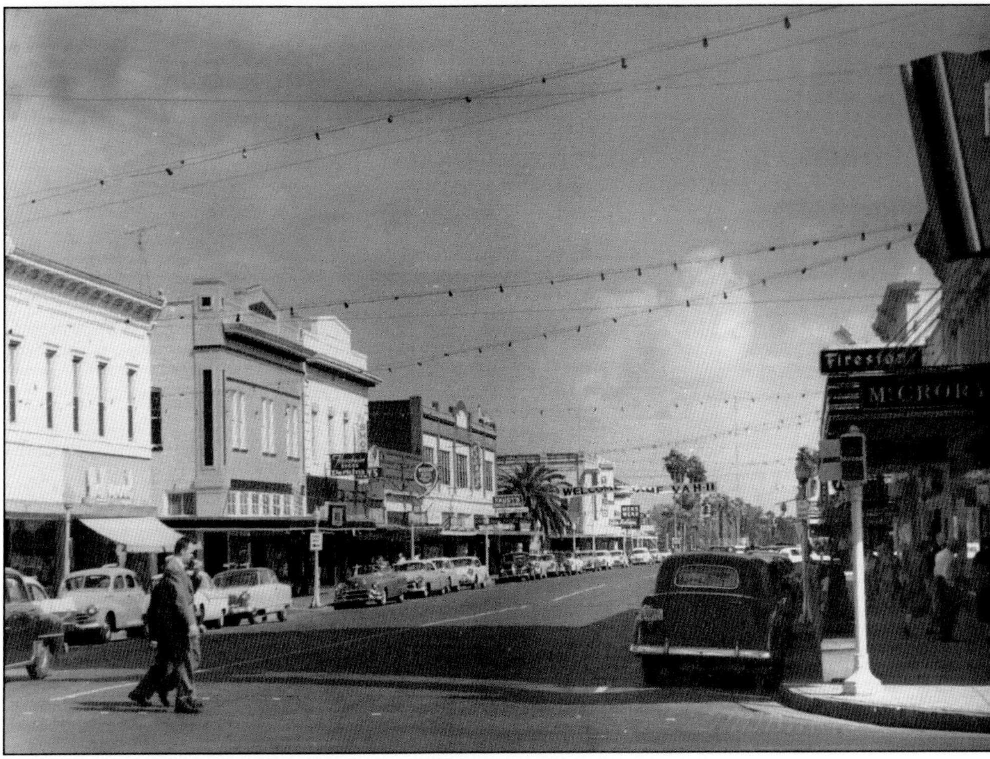

This photograph shows First Street in 1955, looking east from Park Avenue.

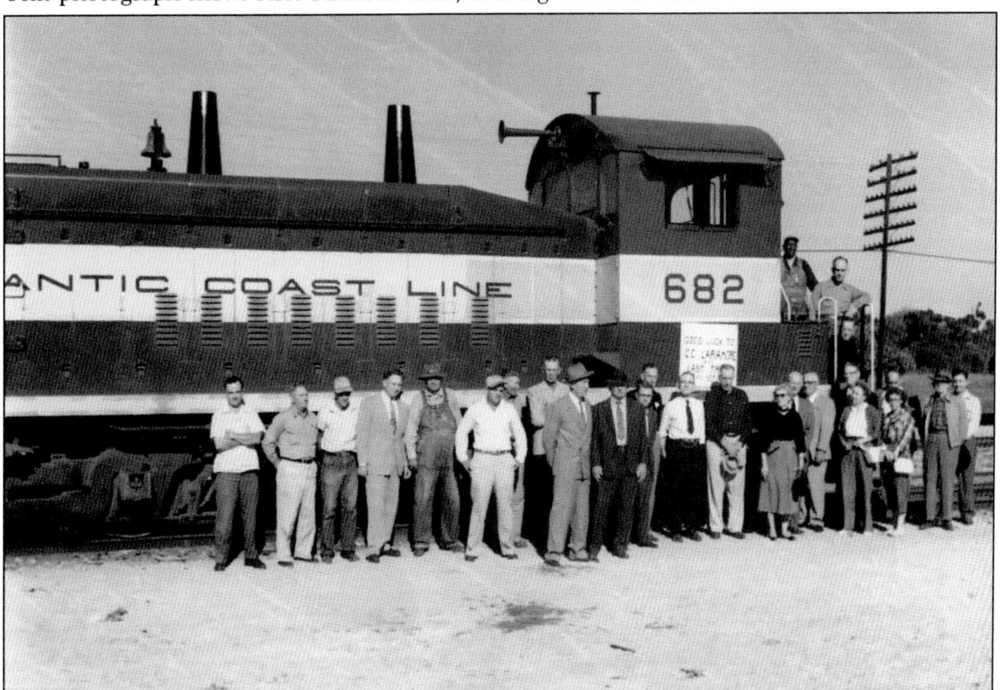

The Atlantic Coast Line was one of the South's largest railroad systems with a main terminal and roundhouse in Sanford. The equipment, such as this switch engine, was purple and white.

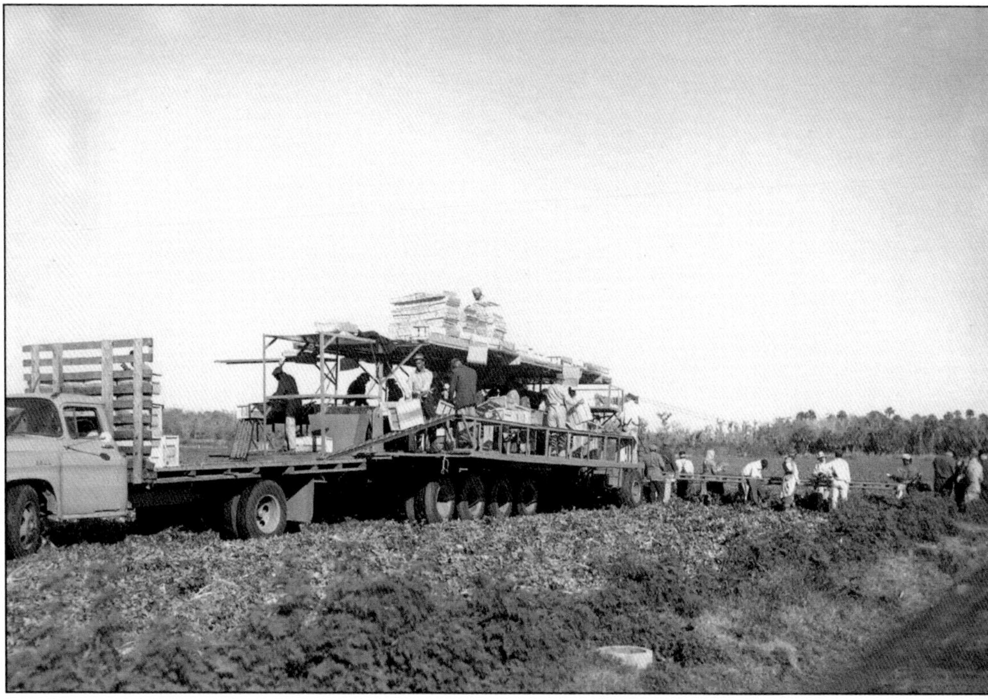

Mechanical harvesters called "mule trains" made it possible to cut and pack celery faster than ever before. Since these machines could cover more acreage, celery growing began moving to the larger muck farms of South Florida. This marked the beginning of the end of Sanford's celery era.

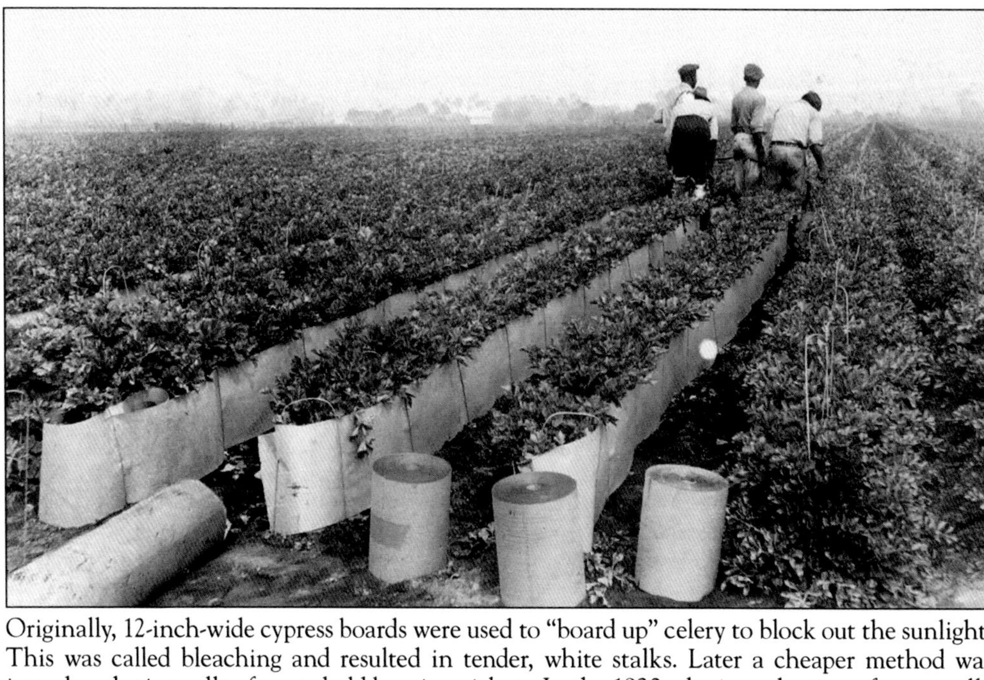

Originally, 12-inch-wide cypress boards were used to "board up" celery to block out the sunlight. This was called bleaching and resulted in tender, white stalks. Later a cheaper method was introduced using rolls of paper held by wire wickets. In the 1920s the introduction of a naturally white celery, called Pascal, reduced the need for bleaching.

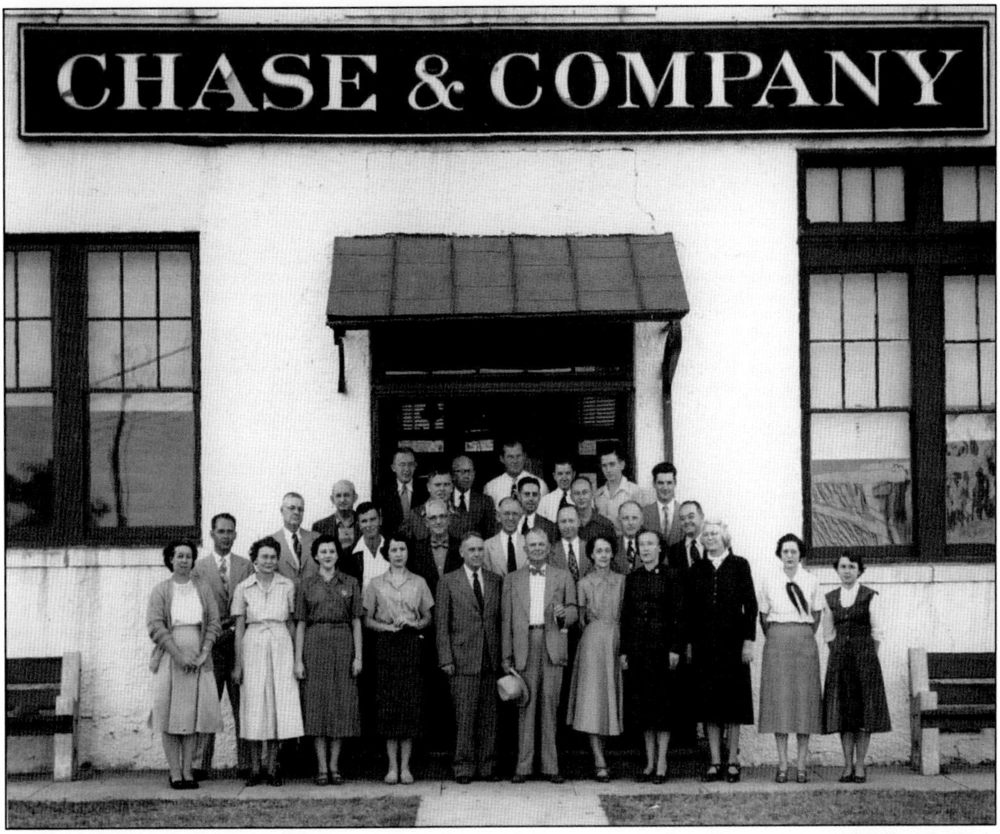

The employees of Chase and Co. pose in front of the company headquarters at 200 South Oak Avenue, c. 1952.

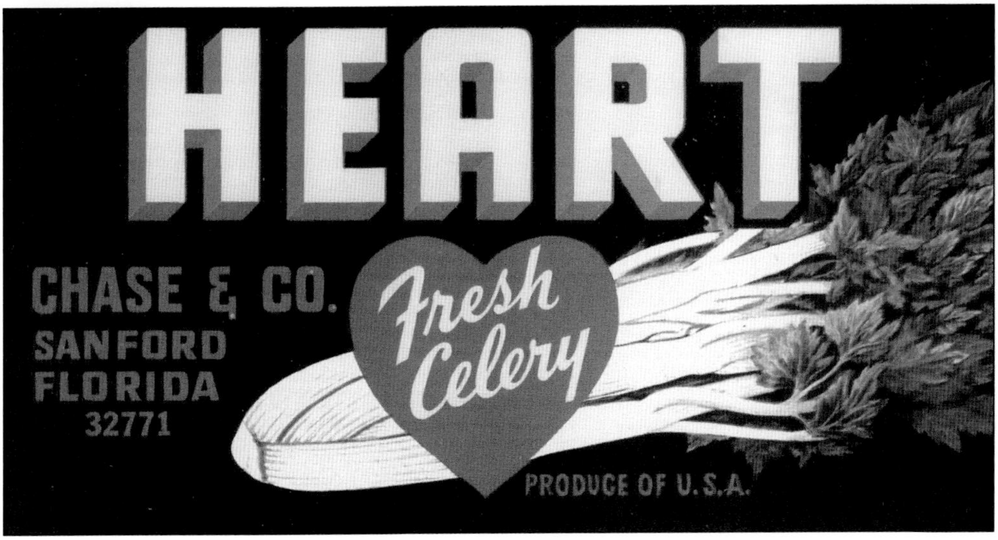

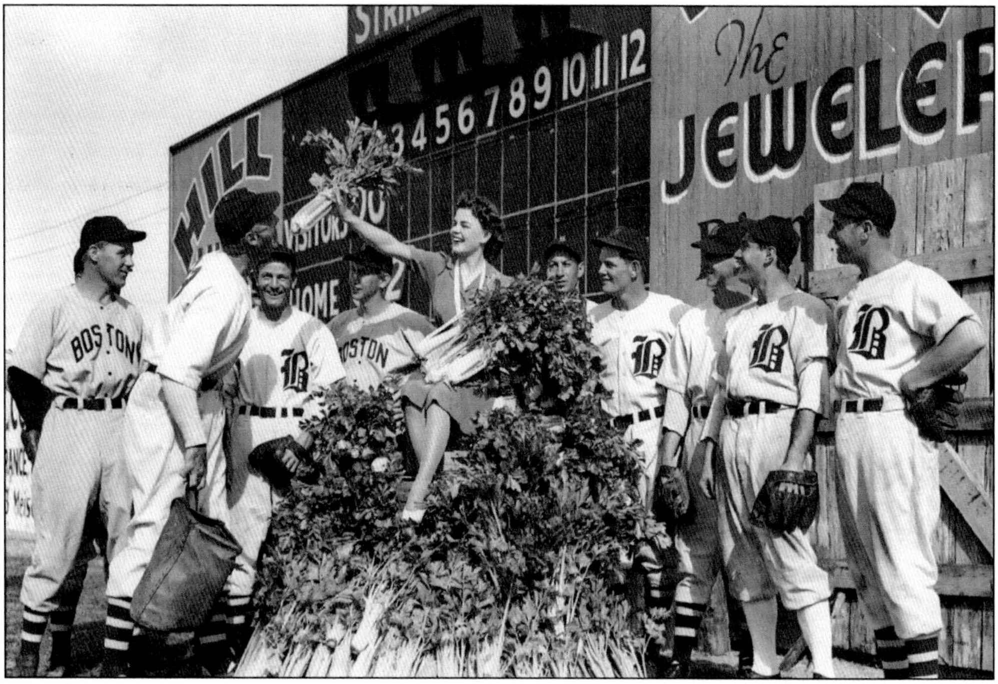

Dorothy Sanford Gatchel sits on a throne of celery and offers a delicious stalk to one of the admiring Boston Braves. This photo was taken at the old ballpark in 1942, the only year the Braves trained in Sanford

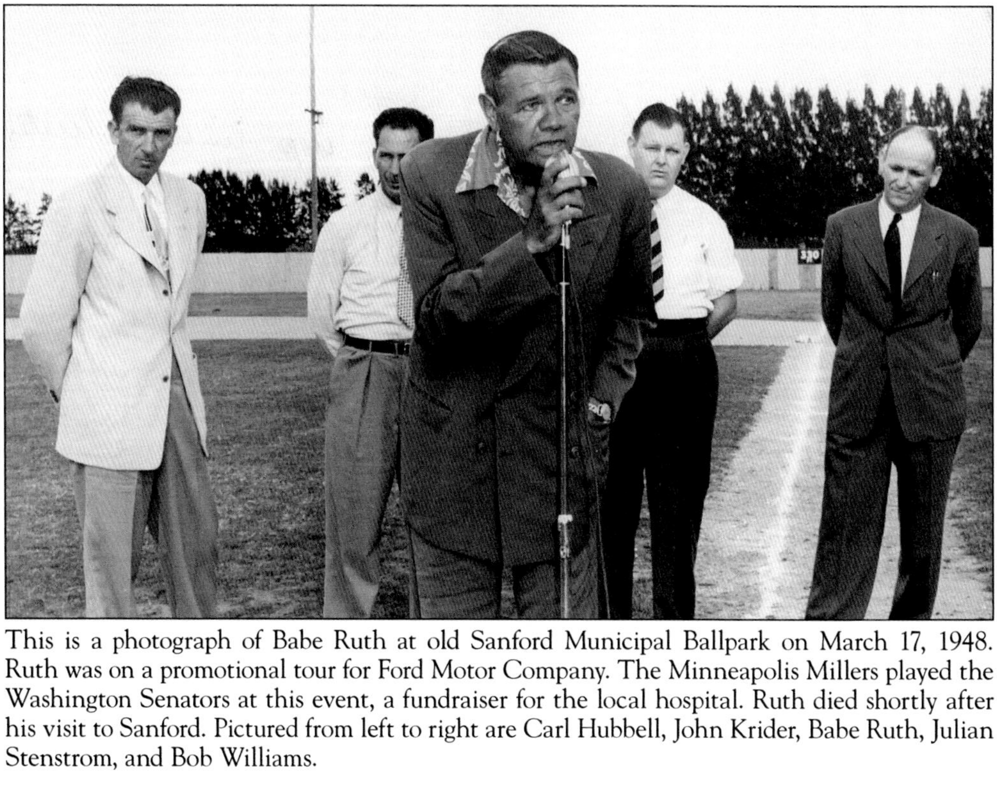

This is a photograph of Babe Ruth at old Sanford Municipal Ballpark on March 17, 1948. Ruth was on a promotional tour for Ford Motor Company. The Minneapolis Millers played the Washington Senators at this event, a fundraiser for the local hospital. Ruth died shortly after his visit to Sanford. Pictured from left to right are Carl Hubbell, John Krider, Babe Ruth, Julian Stenstrom, and Bob Williams.

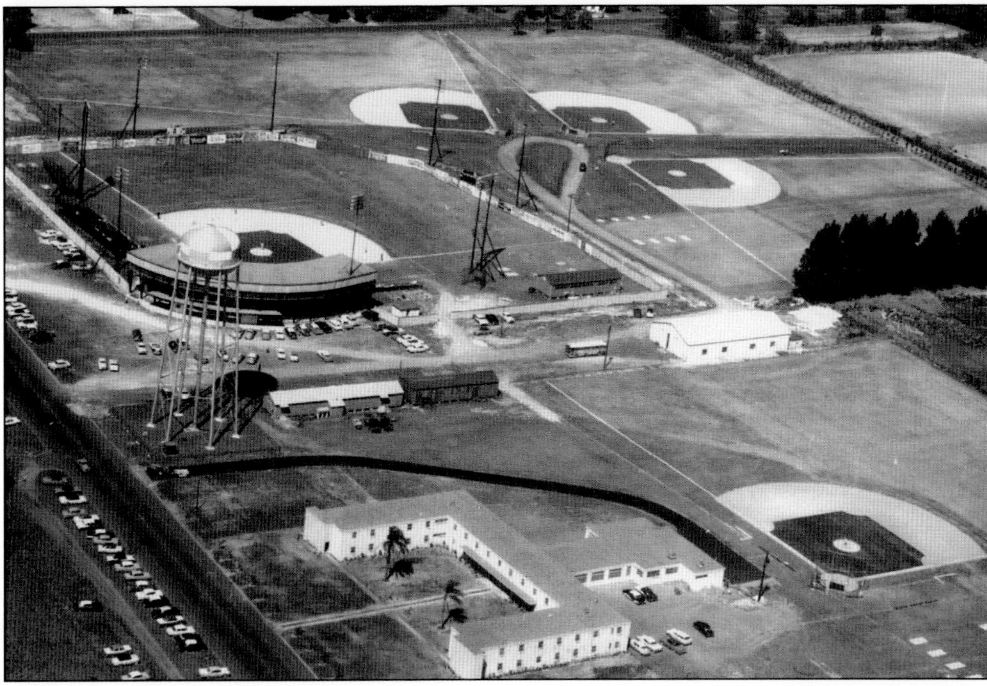

In March 1957, the New York Giants farm system spring training headquarters included a stadium and fields built by the city and a dormitory built by the Giants at a cost of $250,000 to accommodate the 300 players for six weeks.

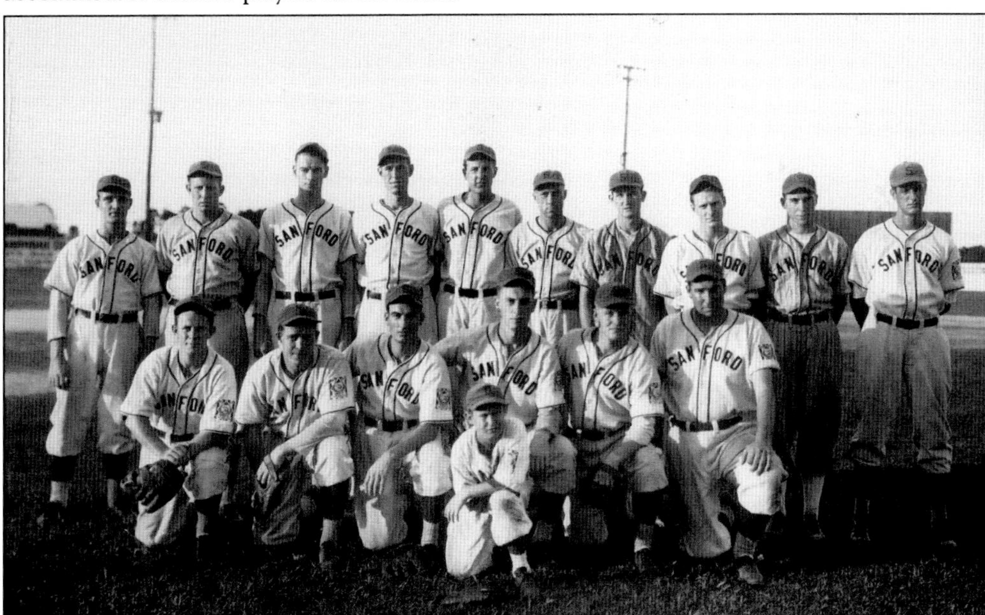

The Sanford Lookouts won the Florida State League pennant in 1939. From left to right are (back row) Joe Pender, Red Lane, Sid Hudson, Walter Carroll, James Harry Dean, Cleo Jeter, Al Nixon, Roy Marion, Hillis Lane, and Frank Hudson; (front row) Weasel Barnett, Rick Gillispie, Wee Willie Skeen, Mayo Langston, Whitey Campbell, Dale Alexander, and batboy Al McMillan.

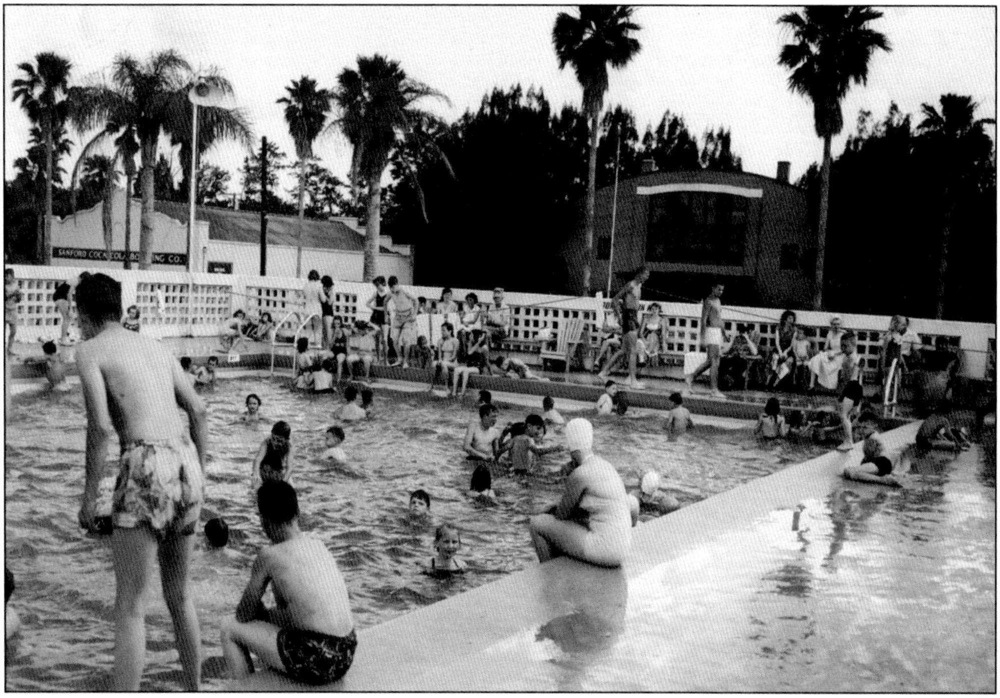

In the 1950s, facilities at Fort Mellon Park on the lakefront included a municipal swimming pool.

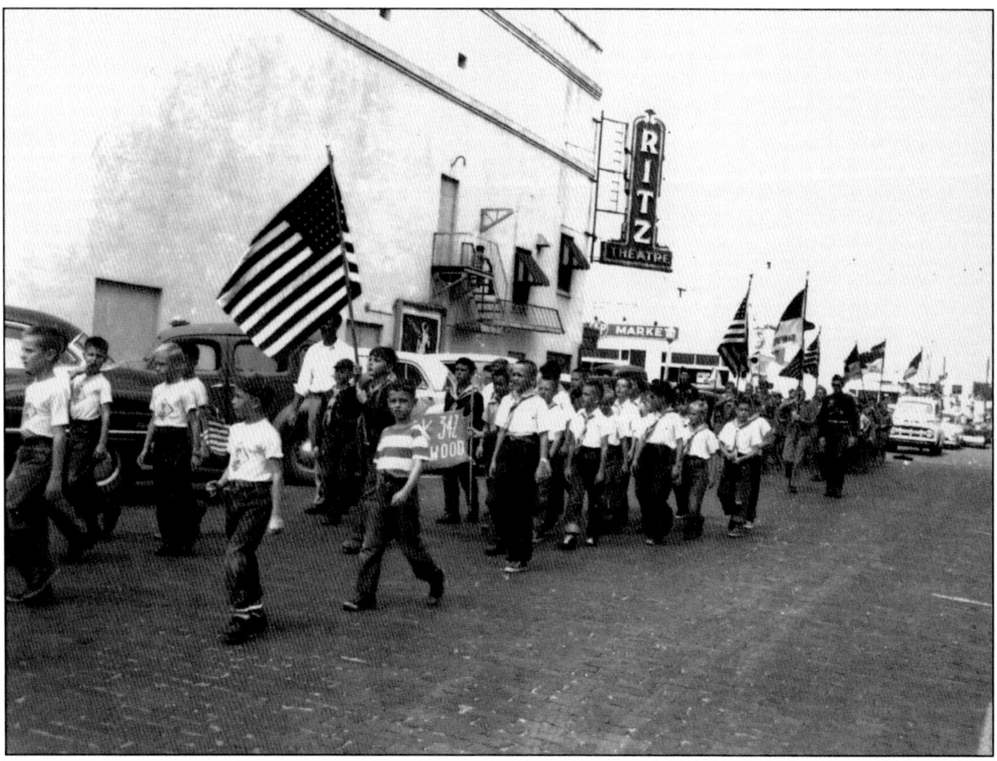

In this 1950s photograph, a Boy Scout parade passes the Ritz Theater on Second Street.

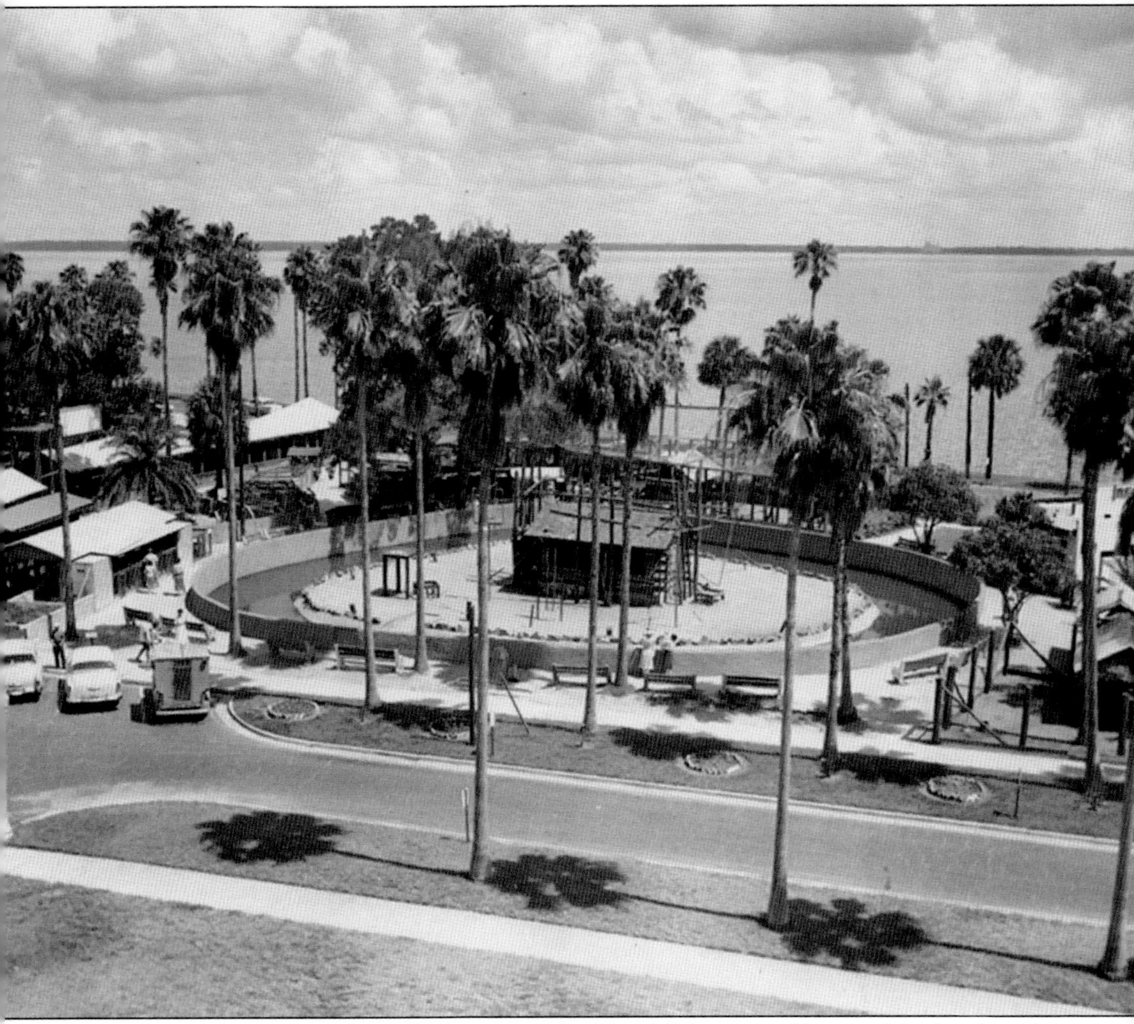

By 1950, Sanford's Municipal Zoo had grown to be Florida's largest public zoo. Monkey Island was the zoo's most popular attraction and, on many occasions, monkeys escaped their island and ended up running through city hall and through the streets of Sanford. For many years the zoo was cared for by inmates from the city jail. Famed zoologist and TV personality Jack Hanna began his career as director of this zoo. In 1971, county funds were used to purchase 104 acres to the west of Sanford and the present Central Florida Zoological Park was built.

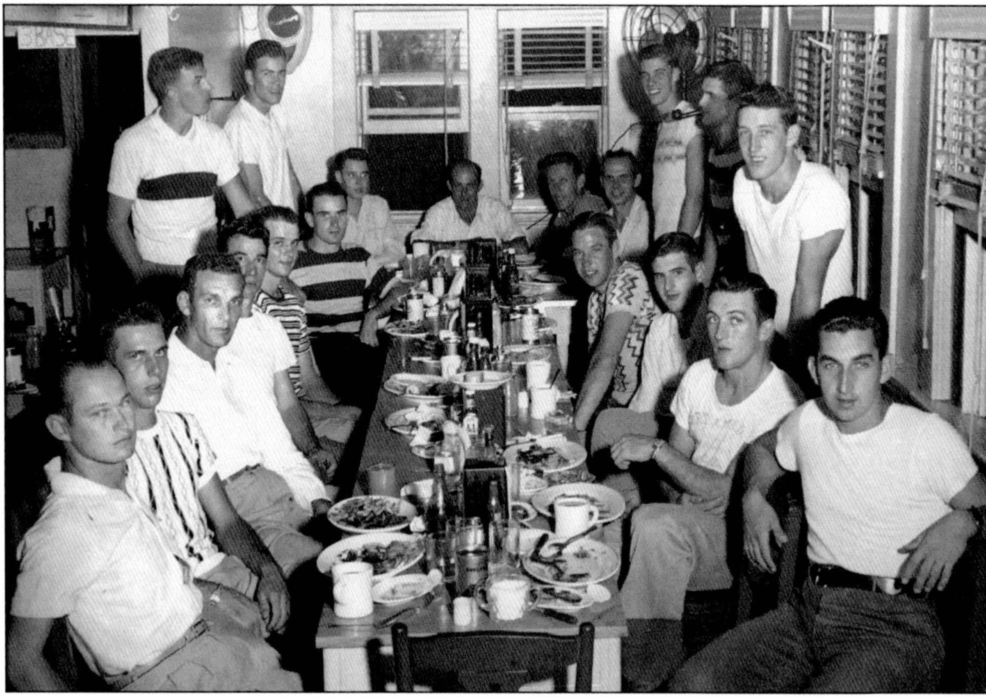

The 1949 Sanford Giants, a Florida State League team, enjoyed meals at Angel's Eat Shack. Buddy Lake is in the back on the right. Al McMillan is in the front on the left.

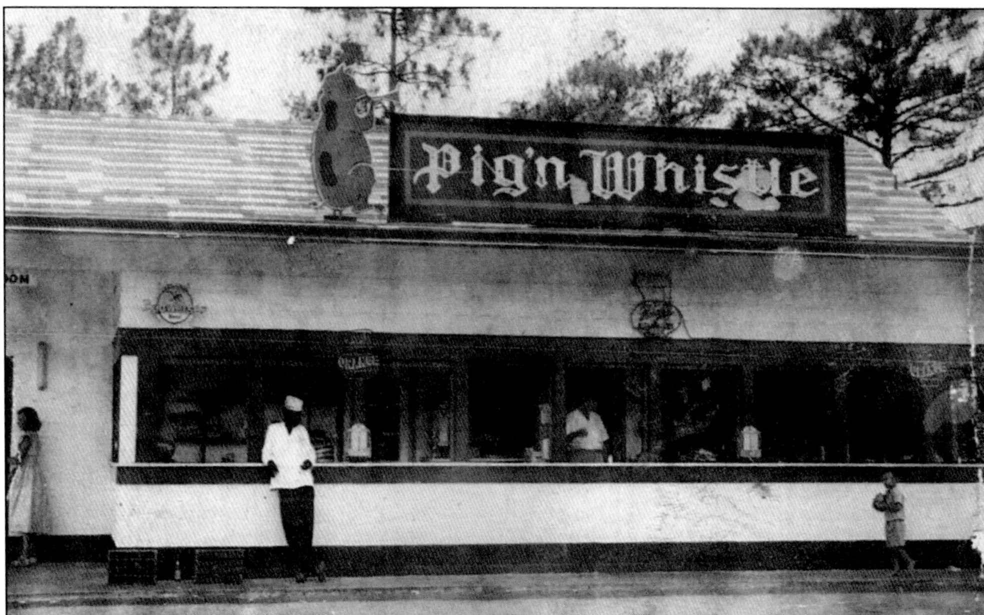

The Pig n' Whistle was a popular stop for local teenagers and Navy personnel in the 1950s. This barbeque restaurant was started in Macon, Georgia by Jim Bryan who came to Sanford in the 1920s. He sold the business to John Ivey and Harry Took in the early 1950s. Other well remembered establishments are Angel's Eat Shack, the Big Dip, and McReynolds Drugstore. (Courtesy of Billy Robinson.)

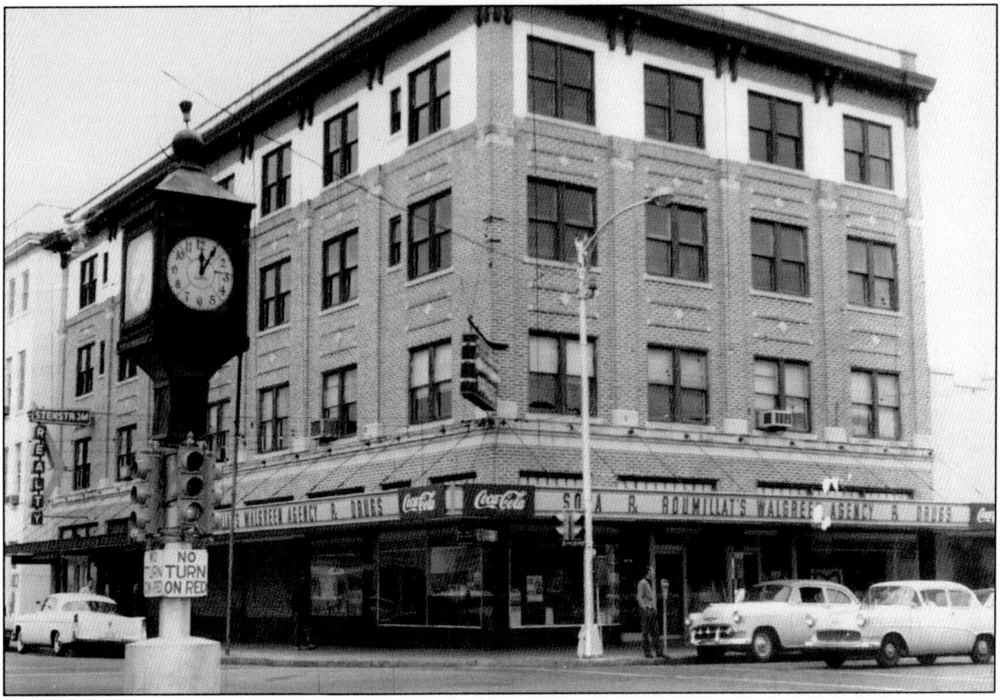

For many years the employees of Roumillat and Anderson's Drugstore were entrusted with regulating the town clock. The store was in the Brumley-Puleston Building, built in 1922 for L.A. Brumley and Dr. Samuel Puleston. It was constructed by George A. Fuller, builder of the Flatiron building in New York City.

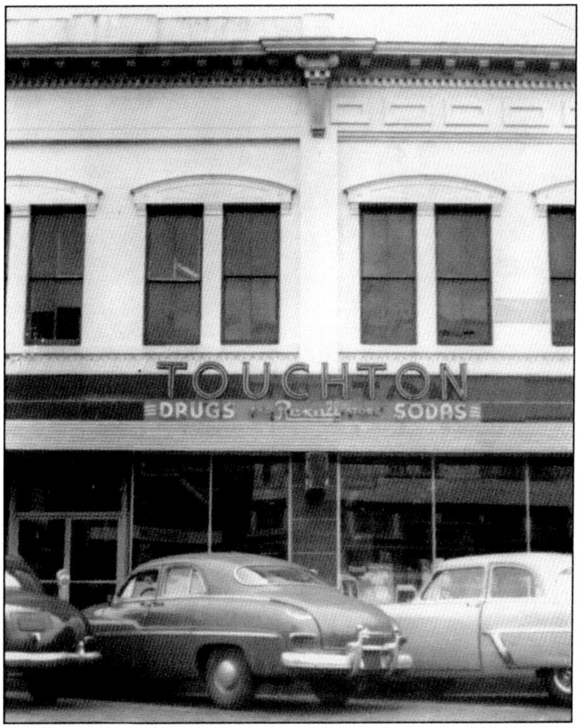

Dr. W.C. Touchton bought the Seminole Bank building at the corner of Magnolia and First Street in 1933 for $15,000. Touchton's Drugstore remained at this location until 1994 when the business was closed. Touchton's was popular in the 1950s with students at Seminole High School who enjoyed afternoons at the soda fountain.

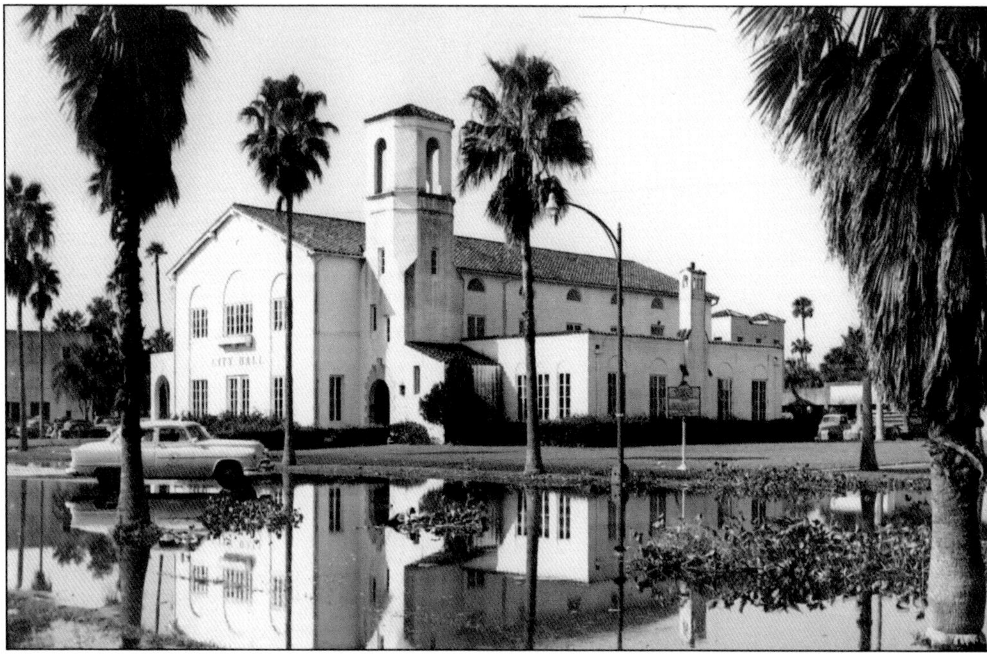

This is Sanford's old city hall at 300 Park Avenue after a season of heavy rains and Hurricane Florence on September 24, 1953. Portions of the 17-92 roadway west of Sanford were washed away to the centerline by high water and strong winds. Seminole Boulevard and Park Avenue flooded.

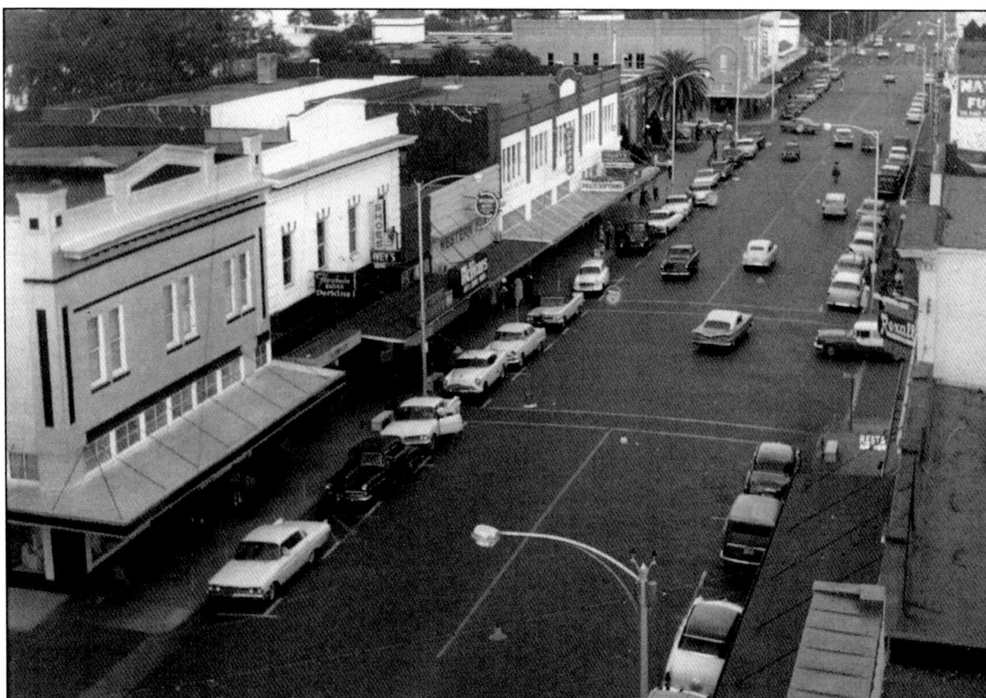

This photograph looking northeast on First Street was taken from the First National Bank building.

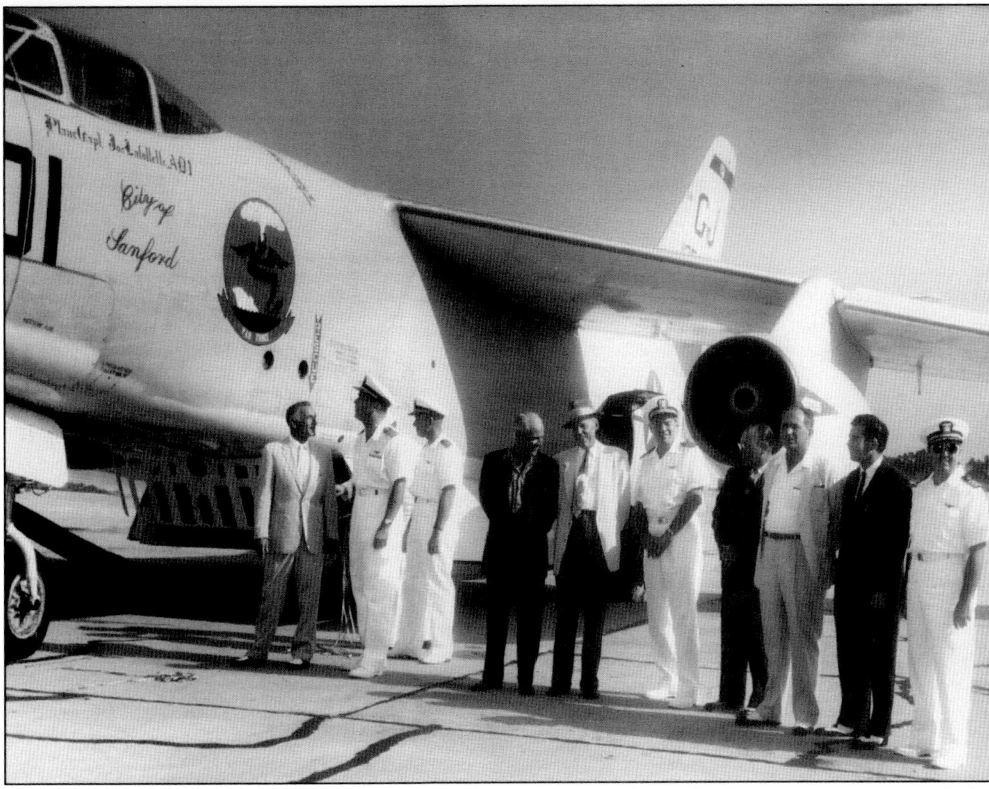

In 1960 this *A3D Skywarrior* was named the "City of Sanford" in recognition of the city's positive relationship with the Navy. It was flown as part of the VAH-3 at Naval Air Station Sanford.

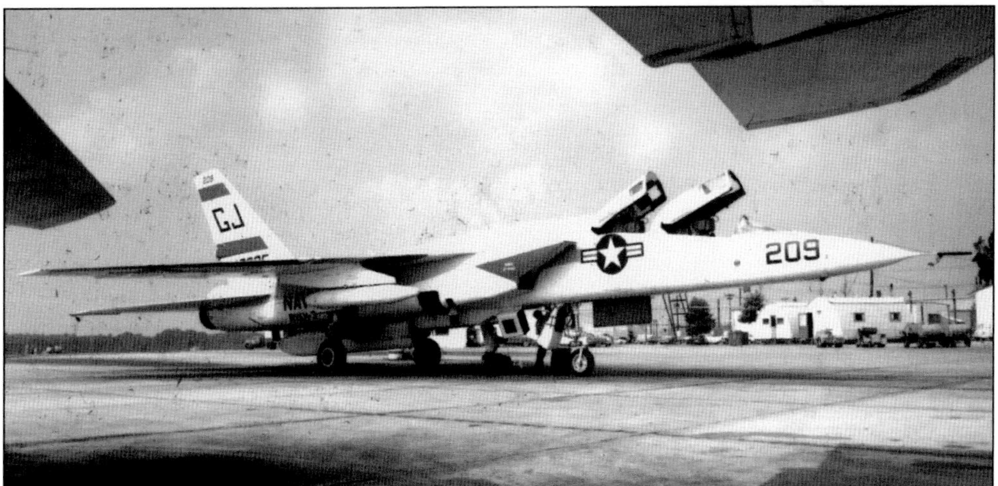

The *A3J Vigilante* arrived in Sanford in 1960. Originally designed as a bomber, this plane flew reconnaissance over North Vietnam.

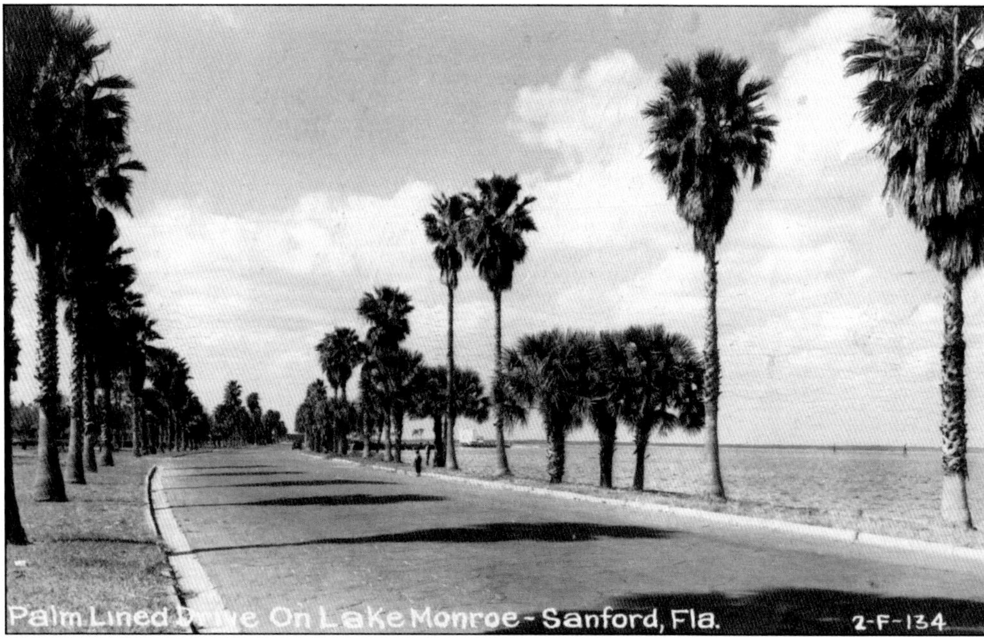

This postcard view shows Seminoles Boulevard in the 1940s.

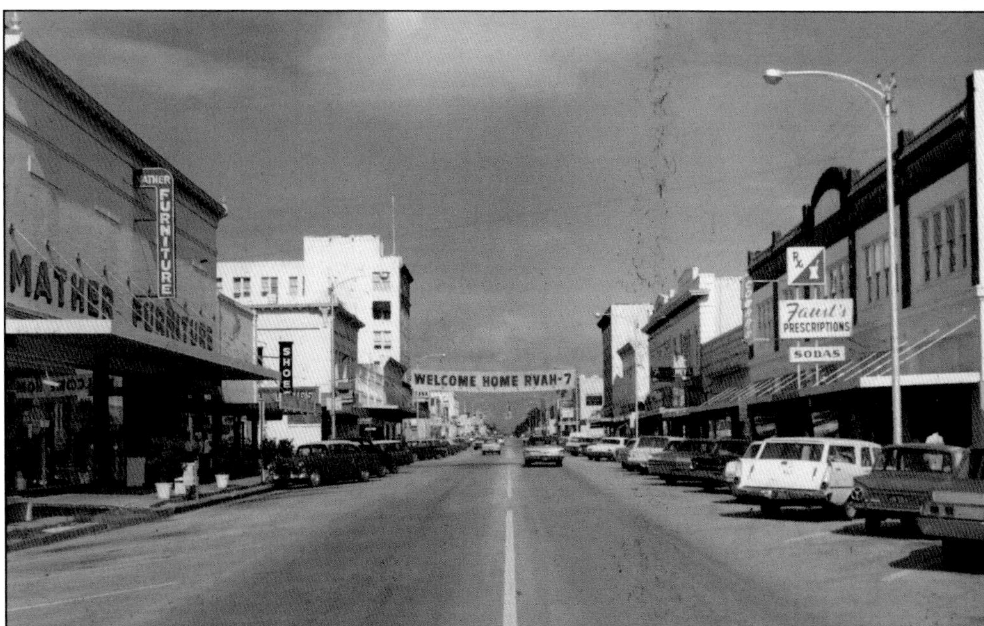

The banner in this 1966 view of First Street shows the city's support for the Sanford Naval Air Station.

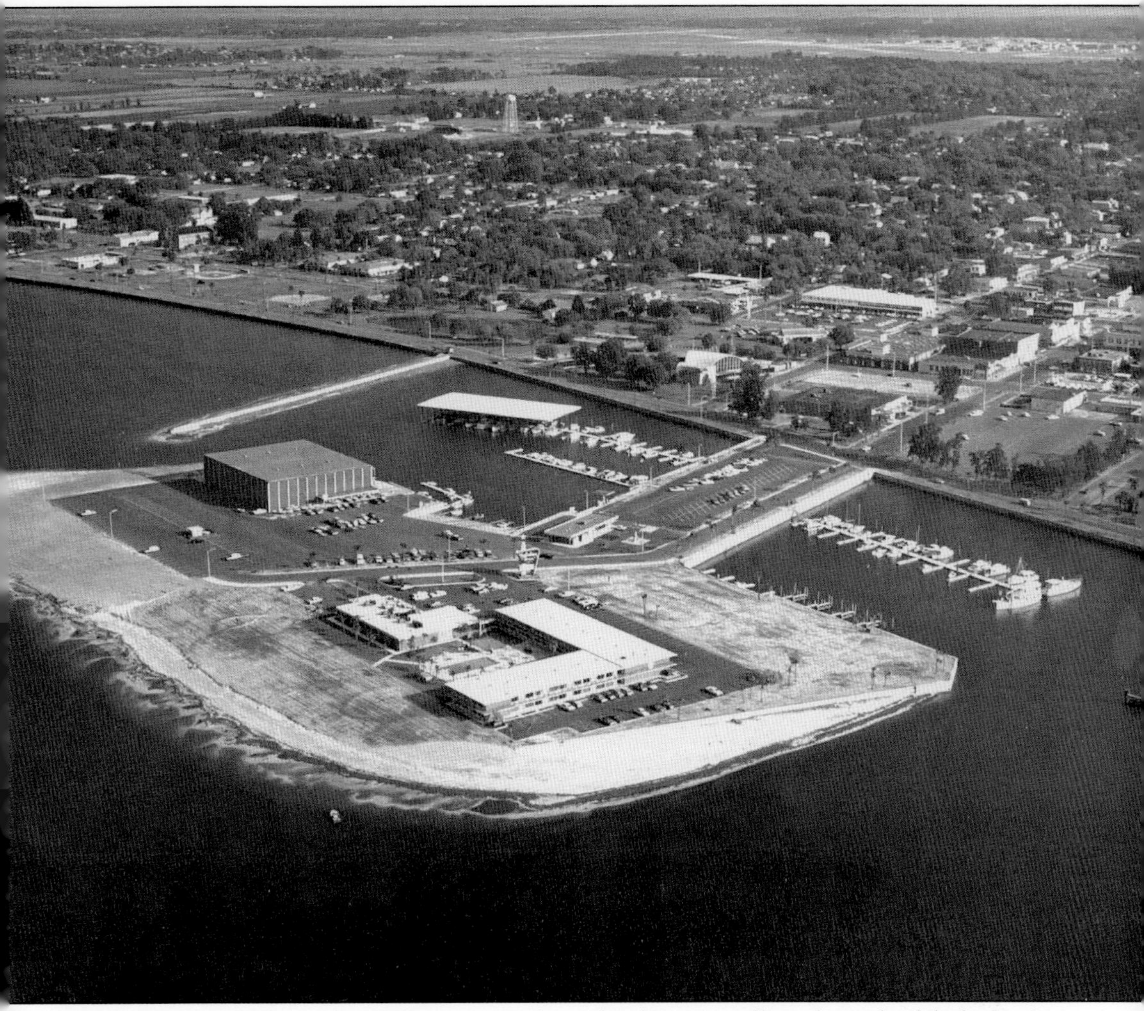

Marina Isle was built in the 1970s as part of a redevelopment effort along the lakefront. A marina and hotel were constructed on an extended Palmetto Avenue. Today, Marina Isle is undergoing another phase of development as part of Sanford's Riverwalk project.

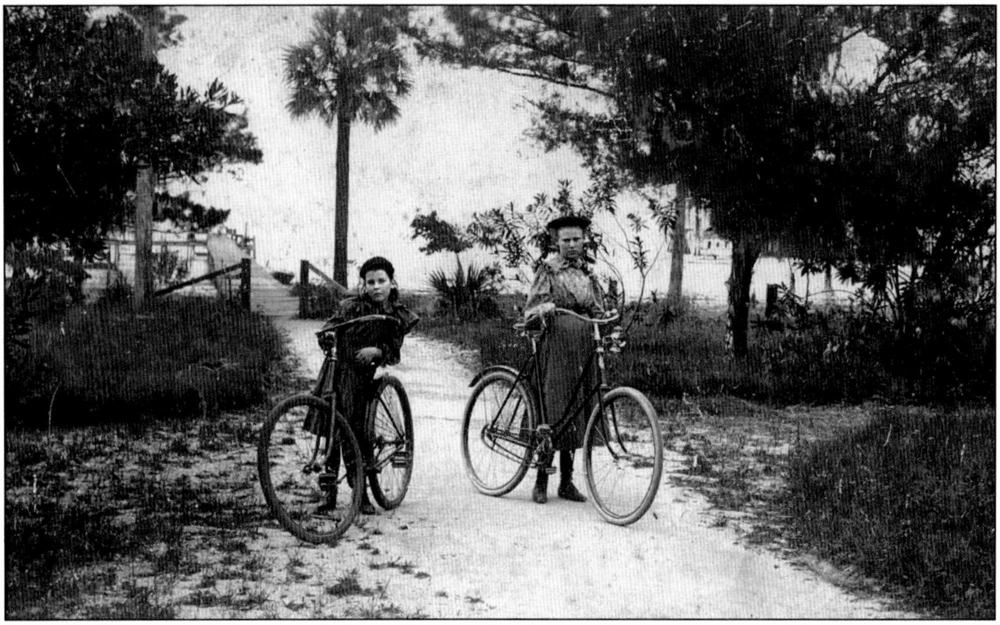

EPILOGUE

Beginning with ancient native tribes living around Lake Monroe, Sanford's history has been a story of people. From Swedish immigrants and African-American laborers to homesteaders from many states, from Cuban cigar makers and Bulgarian farmers to present-day newcomers, Sanford's foundation is one of ethnic diversity. Through their toil, ingenuity, and perseverance, each group has contributed significantly to making Sanford what it is today.

Sanford sits in the midst of Central Florida's high speed progress, yet maintains its historic charm. In recent years two National Register historic districts have been created downtown. The parkland that Henry Sanford created is still there and has been expanded. Sanford has such a large canopy of old trees that the city has been designated an official "Tree City."

Today, Sanford's once wild shoreline of palmetto and cypress trees is being redeveloped as the "Riverwalk" with a new bulkhead, bike paths, parks, homes, hotels, and shops. To the west visitors arrive on the Autotrain. To the south, on the old military road, the planes arriving at Orlando-Sanford International Airport bring newcomers every day to what is now "The Gate City of Central Florida."